THE

BIBLE

AND

The New York Times

THE
BIBLE
AND
The New York Times

Fleming Rutledge

WILLIAM B. EERDMANS PUBLISHING COMPANY
GRAND RAPIDS, MICHIGAN / CAMBRIDGE, U.K.

© 1998 Wm. B. Eerdmans Publishing Co.
255 Jefferson Ave. S.E., Grand Rapids, Michigan 49503 /
P.O. Box 163, Cambridge CB3 9PU U.K.

Printed in the United States of America

03 02 01 00 99   7 6 5 4 3 2

Library of Congress Cataloging-in-Publication Data

Rutledge, Fleming.
The Bible and The New York Times / Fleming Rutledge.
p.   cm.
ISBN 0-8028-3778-6 (alk. paper)
1. Church year sermons.   2. Sermons, American.   I. Title.
BV4253.R85   1988
252'.6 — dc21   98-28237
CIP

For Dick

beloved companion in the way of Christ

because these sermons are

as much his as mine

An introductory note to liturgically-minded readers

You will notice that the arrangement here is unusual, since the church calendar properly begins with Advent. It has been widely noted in recent years, however, that the lectionary readings from the Bible begin to pick up speed as All Saints Day (November 1) approaches. Toward the end of the "long green season" after Pentecost, apocalyptic themes predominate in the Scripture lessons, including those from the Hebrew prophets. A number of commentators have therefore observed that there is a sort of "pre-Advent" season leading up to the Feast of Christ the King, the last Sunday of the church year. The momentum of these "last days" is unmistakable to those who have learned to look for it. The Feast of St. Michael and All Angels (Michaelmas) on September 29, with its emphasis on the Last Days and the victory of God over evil, seems like a suitable place to begin a series of sermons arising out of the Biblical drama. The Scripture readings appointed to be read on the Sundays between All Saints Day and Christ the King set the stage for the apocalyptic announcements of Advent I and the appearance of John the Baptist. Just as that strange figure emerging out of the wilderness is incomprehensible apart from the context of Hebrew prophecy, so also the coming of the Messiah is best understood in the sequence of lessons appointed for the Sundays immediately preceding Advent.

Contents

Contents

Last Epiphany

Ash Wednesday

Lent I

Lent II

Lent III

Lent IV

Lent V

Palm Sunday

Contents

Contents

Foreword:
Between News and Good News

Somewhere between the land of the Bible and the world of *The New York Times*, we preachers make our home. The preacher works that sometimes tensive, sometimes near, usually quite expansive gap between then and today, between the *Times's* world of news, high fashion, money, political gossip, and carnage and the Bible's world of Good News, politics, money, carnage, and Easter.

There are sermons when we grope for connections, similes, some illustrative bridge to link these two disparate worlds. The difficulty of finding something to say which will communicate between here and there is often our greatest homiletical challenge. So we hope by means of some engaging metaphor, some undeniably relevant linkage thereby to connect what the Bible says with what our congregations today may be able to hear. We so want, we preachers, to be heard.

Did not our Lord himself, in so many a sermon, begin with, "Now the kingdom of God is like . . ."? Might Jesus' own grope for metaphor indicate that he is able to sympathize with us preachers in our contemporary efforts to bridge by rhetorical device that great expanse between the Bible and *The New York Times?*

At one time, I thought so. We've got this big problem with the old, culturally conditioned, sexist, violent, Jewish, premodern Bible and its distance from our fresh, modern, enlightened world where we get our news from the pages of the *Times,* not angels. It is typical of modernity to conceive of itself as standing upon the pinnacle of human development.

If the gap between us and Scripture were mainly one of time, history, that gaping abyss (as Lessing called it) between our age and that of Jesus, then why did Jesus seem so ardent a maker of metaphor too? What was all that parabolizing and search for simile ("The Kingdom of God may be compared to a woman who . . .") if Jesus the preacher had no gap of history or time between him and his hearers?

I think there was trouble for Jesus the preacher because the preacher was Jesus. The Kingdom of God was hard to render into speech, not because it was old, primitive, prescientific, but because it was not the kingdom of *The New York Times.* The hermeneutical gap was not between modern and premodern but between truth and lies, between God's Messiah and Moloch. The world would like to believe that it can't understand what Jesus is talking about because he's dated, Jewish, male, unmarried — or because of any of the other worldly labels by which economically controlled media like the *Times* attempt to keep the Risen Christ at bay. No. The reason why it's tough speaking of Jesus is much the same reason why they kicked him out after his first sermon at Nazareth — Jesus spoke of and enacted a Good News which assaulted our settled definitions of news.

The Reverend Fleming Rutledge works well that same conflicted, risky ground between us and the gospel. Her sermons are vivid demonstration that, all reports to the contrary, faithful biblical preaching is alive and well, interesting, engaging, demanding, and residing, of all places, in the Episcopal Church. Each of her sermons here takes seriously our contemporary congregational difficulty in hearing the gospel. Yet they are chiefly remarkable because her sermons take even more seriously the peculiar word to our time which is called Good News. That is, although she often begins by quoting the *Times,* very quickly in her sermons we realize that she is allowing the Bible to confront, unmask, and defeat the *Times* and everything it believes to be news.

Even her arrangement of these sermons, in good Episcopal

fashion, keyed to the movement of the church year, is a clue to her homiletical intent. She does not want just to speak to our world; she wants to change it. She wants to reorder our time, to reconfigure our year into the church's year of grace. Not taking the world of *The New York Times* too seriously seems an important task for a faithful preacher. With playfulness, wit, a thorough acquaintance with what's going on today, she loosens the authoritarian grip of the now, in order to bring to speech what God in Jesus Christ wants us to be tomorrow.

Is this preacher conservative? feminist? evangelical? liturgical? Fleming Rutledge challenges our conventional labels. I believe the word for which we're groping to describe her is *Biblical.* In no dry or heavy-handed way, she keeps reconfiguring our ways of construing the world into a new world. She may begin a sermon by quoting the *Times,* but she never ends a sermon until she has let the Bible have the final word.

That word, as these sermons demonstrate so well, is word unto life, and that abundantly.

Duke University Chapel   WILLIAM H. WILLIMON
Pentecost, 1998

The New Form of Speech

ST. JOHN'S CHURCH, SALISBURY, CONNECTICUT

So faith comes from what is heard, and what is heard comes by the preaching of Christ.

Romans 10:17

A good deal of attention is being given nowadays to the language of the Presidential campaign. It's generally agreed that Mr. Dole has a problem with language. His lack of eloquence is such a handicap that novelist Mark Helprin was brought in to write some of his speeches. The President and Mr. Kemp, on the other hand, need to be put on a word diet.[1]

In this age of images, with our children and grandchildren certain to be more familiar with cyberspace than with books, we need to find new ways to convey the power of language in human affairs. We have all heard the saying, "The pen is mightier than the sword,"[2] but in another twenty years there will be no one left alive who personally remembers what it was like when Winston Churchill "mobilized the English language and sent it off into battle."[3] Two years ago during the 50th anniversary of D-Day, many of us older heads were shocked to realize how little our own children knew of the titanic struggle that gripped the globe for seven years. It will not therefore be amiss if we call to mind some of Churchill's words as they fortified not only the British, standing alone against the

Nazis, but also the waiting, watching, listening Americans half a world away:

> We shall not flag or fail. We shall go on to the end. We shall fight in France, we shall fight on the seas and oceans, we shall fight with growing confidence and growing strength in the air, we shall defend our island, whatever the cost may be, we shall fight on the beaches, we shall fight on the landing grounds, we shall fight in the fields and in the streets, we shall fight in the hills; we shall never surrender.

(Speech in the House of Commons, June 4, 1940)

There is a Scottish proverb, "Fine words butter no parsnips." We know what is meant by this, but we also know that in certain times and seasons words can make all the difference. Andrew Young has recently told us a detail about the March on Washington in 1963 that we did not know. The older veterans of the civil rights movement scheduled their own speeches early and Martin Luther King's speech late, because they thought the TV cameras would be gone by then.[4] There is delicious irony in that; *the last shall be first and the first last,* as our Lord said. The world was transformed forever as a result of those "last words" that day.

One of the unique features of the Judeo-Christian tradition is its primary emphasis on the power of speech. The agent of the creation itself is the Word of God. The Psalmist says, "By the word of the Lord the heavens were made. . . . For he spoke, and it came to be; he commanded, and it stood forth" (Psalm 33:6, 9). His mere word is enough: "God said, 'Let there be light'; and there was light" (Genesis 1:3). God's Word makes things happen. In the language of the apostle Paul, "God calls into existence the things that do not exist" (Romans 4:17). This is completely different from religion in general. Not even Islam, which is considered one of the three "religions of the book," has anything comparable to the Biblical concept of revelation through the Word of God. We cannot understand even the most basic things about the Christian faith if we do not grasp this fundamental Biblical assertion: "In the beginning was the Word" (John 1:1). God does not exist in unbroken silence. He has communicated. He has gone out from himself in self-expression. But this expression is not through *vision;* it is through *audition.* As Martin Luther wrote, the Christian experience of God is *acoustical.* God has *spoken.* His speech, his communication, is his Word. In all the Bible there is not a single example of God appearing without saying anything. If there is a vision without audition, it is not God. As the prophet Habakkuk said, "*Write* the vision" (2:2). Only through God's *speaking* can we know anything about him.

This is poorly understood in the mainline churches today. I remember an encounter when I was a young seminarian, very excited about my preaching classes. A fashionably skeptical Episcopal clergyman said to me, "I don't preach any more. I never even go into the pulpit any more. I just talk with my congregation. How can human beings presume to know the Word of God?" Looking back, I am amused to remember his own arrogance; he was openly relishing the opportunity of taking a young enthusiast down a few pegs. I was duly dashed for a while but not for too long, I'm thankful to say; I had professors who understood the doctrine of revelation and who believed it.

You may be shocked to think of this clergyman who never preached, but I assure you that he was one of many. Disbelief was all the rage among the clergy in the 60s and 70s, and we have not recovered by any means. There is a real crisis of confidence about preaching in the church. Many churchgoers no longer have any idea what preaching is, and since they do not know, they no longer expect to hear it.

The dictionary gives us a definition of preaching that has nothing to do with the real thing. My favorite dictionary definition is this one: "To give religious or moral instruction, especially in a tedious, didactic, tiresome, or unwelcome manner." That's what Madonna had in mind in her song, "Papa, don't preach." Popular culture being as pervasive it is, it is a daunting prospect to try to correct this misapprehension. It may be that God has called forth the great black preachers of America to keep vital Biblical preaching alive in our time.

In the tenth chapter of the Epistle to the Romans (v. 17), the apostle Paul writes, "So faith comes from what is heard, and what is heard comes by the preaching of Christ." That is how the gospel spread. The Christian faith swept through the Mediterranean world because God gave the early Christians a new language in which to preach Christ. The best book I know about this new language was written by Amos Wilder, the brother of the playwright Thornton Wilder. The first Christians, he writes, were convinced that the promises of the Old Testament had come true; God had given them new tongues, a new song, a new speech.[5] That speech had a power behind it that was, and remains, unique.

When the Word of God is read and expounded in common worship, it has the character of an *event*. That's why Christian preaching is different from any other kind of public address. A lot of people don't realize that; we hear of rabbis and imams "preaching sermons," but with all due respect, that is not what they are doing. (To be honest, many Christian ministers are not preaching sermons either. They may be giving instruction, exhortation, or inspiration, but they are not preaching.) There were a lot of speeches at the original March on Washington in 1963, but there was only one sermon.[6] There is all the difference in the world between speaking and preaching. When preaching is going on, you feel the dynamism. You know something is happening. Wilder and others call it *a speech-event*.

Preaching is a human activity, but it is derived from God. It has nothing to do with the religious accomplishment or perfected piety or spiritual achievement of the preacher. It is an *impossible* activity; in that respect, my skeptical clergy friend was quite right. It is not possible for mere mortals to know the Word of the Lord. If it depended on us, we would remain in silence and in ignorance. This is the basic premise of the Bible. Speaking of God is only possible because God has spoken to us. To use the words of our liturgy, God opens our lips so that our mouths can show forth his praise. Incredible and foolish though it may seem, God has turned his message over to us. That's why we are called an "apostolic" church; we are founded upon this "impossible possibility";[7] God has summoned human beings, flawed and sinful, to be his apostles, to

be his mouthpieces. "This is the scandal . . . of the gospel; there is
no Word of God without the word of the human herald."[8]

Perhaps, as you hear me saying these things, you can imagine
the risk and the danger of preaching. It's scary to undertake preaching. The pulpit at Grace Church in New York where I was for 14
years had a high pulpit with a number of steps going up. I never
climbed them without remembering Donald Coggan, former Archbishop of Canterbury, who said that if your knees did not tremble
as you ascended the pulpit stairs you were not fit to preach. For
twenty years I have had a prayer of Martin Luther in my office; I
always hang it where it is the last thing I see as I open the door
to go into the church to preach the gospel. It begins, "O Lord, I
am not worthy." No preacher is worthy. That is just the point. Only
God is worthy. Only God is great. Only God can make his Word
live. When preaching is working the way it is supposed to, the
Word of God causes the preacher to disappear into the message.
The Word escapes from the preacher altogether and becomes a
transforming event in the lives of the hearers. Only God can make
that happen. No amount of eloquence on the part of the preacher
can make it happen. In fact, too much eloquence can work against
the Word, because it draws attention to the preacher instead of the
message. As St. Paul says in a key passage: "When I came to you,
brothers and sisters, I did not come proclaiming to you the testimony of God in lofty words of wisdom. For I was determined to
know nothing among you except Jesus Christ and him crucified.
And I was with you in weakness and in much fear and trembling;
and my speech and my message were not in plausible words of
wisdom, but in demonstration of the Spirit and of power, that your
faith might not rest in the wisdom of men but in the power of
God" (I Corinthians 2:1-5).

*So faith comes from what is heard, and what is heard comes by the
preaching of Christ.* That phrase, *the preaching of Christ,* is an odd one.
If we think about it, it will unlock the secret of preaching for us.
We wouldn't say that a Buddhist "preached Buddha." We wouldn't
say that a rabbi "preached Moses." We wouldn't say that an imam
"preached Mohammed." Only in Christianity do we have this odd

expression, "to preach Christ." Christian preaching is like nothing else in all the world of language. Here is the reason. In the preaching of the Word of God, the risen, reigning, living Jesus Christ has promised to be present in power. He is present in the Word, because *he is himself the Word.* God's speech, God's self-expression, *is Jesus himself.* The famous prologue of John's Gospel tells us: "In the beginning was the Word, and the Word was with God, and the Word was God. He was in the beginning with God; all things were made through him. . . . And *the Word became flesh and dwelt among us,* full of grace and truth" (John 1:1-2, 14).

As our American culture drifts farther and farther away from its Christian moorings, a movement that is probably unstoppable, it is going to become more and more important for those of us who are Christians to be, not just remnants of a denomination, but committed disciples of a living Lord. Week by week, in the preaching of the Word, we will encounter Jesus of Nazareth, not as the so-called "historical Jesus," but as the risen Christ. When the Christian preacher ascends the pulpit steps, he does not go to lay down human words from on high. The only person who is on high is the reigning Christ. I, like you, am one who despite my sin will be encountering him in his love for me, his love for you. He comes to meet us, preacher and congregation alike, in his Word. The preacher is in the same place as those who hear, for the preacher is only a channel, a vessel. She is like John the Baptist, who said, "He must increase, but I must decrease" (John 3:30).

"Faith comes from what is heard, and what is heard comes by the preaching of Christ." There is no greater purpose this morning than that you should come to a deeper trust in our Lord through what we together have heard. May we open our lives to the Word of life this very day and receive from him the love from which we shall never be separated, for this life and for the life to come.

Fides ex auditu. Amen.

What the Angel Said

ST. JOHN'S CHURCH, SALISBURY, CONNECTICUT

And it came to pass, when Joshua was by Jericho, that he lifted up his eyes and looked, and, behold, there stood a man over against him with his sword drawn in his hand: and Joshua . . . said unto him, "Art thou for us, or for our adversaries?" And he said, "No; but as captain of the host of the Lord am I now come."

Joshua 5:13-15

And the angel said unto them, Fear not. . . .

Luke 2:9-10

Here is the front cover of *Time*, December 27, 1993: "The New Age of Angels," it announces; "69% of Americans believe they exist. What in heaven is going on?" Three years later I don't see any slackening of commercial and quasi-religious interest in angels. Angel sightings are reported on the Internet. Angel "experts" show up on Oprah and Geraldo. In fact, somebody is making a lot of money out of this current enthusiasm. In addition to the ubiquitous Christmas ornaments, you can buy angel note paper, angel address books, angel calendars, angel key chains, and a whole shelf full of books including one called *Touched By Angels: True Cases of Close*

Encounters of the Celestial Kind, which as far as I can tell is a glossy, expensive version of the supermarket tabloid stories about extraterrestrials and aliens. A more recent book by the same author was a selection of the Literary Guild. It offers "practical advice for making angelic contact and tapping into angelic resources." In other words, America is in the throes of angel worship. To many observers, there is a manifest link between angels and the self-help craze: "Get in touch with your inner angel," we are advised. "Simply be the angel that you are."

Most Christian theologians take a dim view of this therapeutic, New Age angle on angels. I have always loved angels myself — I decorate my house with them at Christmas just like everybody else — but I'm beginning to think it's time to call a halt. The Bible has stern warnings against cults of angels. The whole first chapter of the Epistle to the Hebrews is explicitly directed against angel worship. I used to think this chapter from Hebrews was arcane and unteachable, but I certainly don't think so any more; it might have been written this morning. Hebrews was addressed to a congregation that saw no contradiction between the worship of angels and the worship of the one true God. That was precisely the problem. In the Bible, angels are of no interest in themselves. They exist only to direct our attention to God. Indeed, in the Old Testament, they have no separate existence. They are pure, unmitigated divine presence. Thus, when Abraham entertains angels, when Jacob wrestles with an angel, when Gideon is stunned by the appearance of an angel, we soon learn that the almighty, transcendent God himself is present in the encounter. The Biblical angel is at the furthest possible remove from the guardian angel lapel pins available at the checkout counters.

In order to understand what angels are, we need to understand what they are not. Consider the pictures of angels that we see on greeting cards and in catalogs, especially at this time of year. These so-called angels are invariably adorable, pretty, feminine, sweet, or cute. They are blown in glass, carved in wood, draped in tinsel, painted with gilt, tinted with rouge, and coiffed with hairspray. They wouldn't hurt a Lyme tick. These domesticated commercial angels are the last gasp of a trend begun in the Renaissance when angels began to be depicted as less remote, more human.[1] We have to go back to Byzantine, Romanesque, and medieval art to find the best representations.[2] These austere images have an iconic, hieratic look that hints at unearthly reality. They stare down the viewer. An art critic writes, "Nowhere in Scripture is an angel cute. Isaiah's seraphim have six wings and their cry fills the [temple] with smoke. Ezekiel's cherubim have four wings, also four faces . . . their very feet sparkle like burnished brass."[3] The angels of the Bible and of the best Christian art are not Barbie dolls with wings; they have a quality of strangeness, as though they were representatives of another order of reality — which indeed they are. When angels appear, it means the divine world has broken through into this one. For this reason, angelic appearances in the Bible always cause dread. Samson's mother received a visitation, and we are told that the stranger's countenance was "like the countenance of an angel of God, very terrible" (Judges 13:3).

If there were to be any doubt about this, look at the various Biblical references to angels. They don't flutter about carrying songbooks and playing harps. They bring fire out of rock, smite the Egyptian firstborn, wake the dead with trumpets, swing the apocalyptic scythe over the earth in the Last Judgment. As Lord Byron wrote,

> For the Angel of Death spread his wings on the blast,
> And breathed in the face of the foe as he pass'd . . .
> And the widows of Ashur are loud in their wail,
> And the idols are broke in the temple of Baal,
> And the might of the Gentile, unsmote by the sword,
> Hath melted like snow in the glance of the Lord![4]

Angels are not household pets; angels are not decorations; angels are not magical talismans to help us get parking places and protect us from getting stuck in the snow. Angels do not draw attention to themselves, but to the pure holiness of God, both in his mercy and in his judgment. In the *Time* magazine article, a Catholic theologian is quoted as saying acerbically, "If people want to get in touch with their angels, they'd be a lot better off working at a soup kitchen." That's very apt, and very Biblical. Angels don't appear at the beck and call of books instructing us to "tap into angelic sources." Angels appear at the pure will of God and for no other cause. If there are any "Angels in America" right now they are less likely to appear with magic wands and showers of gold than bearing God's judgment on us for abandoning America's traditional compassion toward the defenseless and unfortunate. Christian people need to be a lot less focused on angel sightings and a lot more focused on the 15 percent cut in the Social Services Block Grant that until recently helped a lot of truly needy people, including the "widows and orphans" who, in the Old Testament, represent those for whom God has special concern.[5]

You see, God has a case against us. That is why his presence causes dread. That is why Rainer Maria Rilke wrote, *Ein jeder Engel ist schrecklich* (Each and every angel is terrible). That is why the first words of angels to human beings have to be "Fear not." In the book of Judges, we read that during the Midianite raids on the Israelites, a strange man appeared to Gideon: "When Gideon perceived that he was an angel of the Lord, Gideon said, 'Alas, O Lord God! for I have seen an angel of the Lord face to face.' And the Lord said unto him, "Peace be unto thee; *fear not*: thou shalt not die" (Judges 6:22-23). God's judgment is encased in his mercy. The proper reaction to a seraphic appearance is one of fear, but the Lord protects his children from his judgment with his own compassion. He does this throughout the Bible. As we read in the prophet Isaiah, "In all their affliction he was afflicted, and the angel of his presence saved them; in his love and in his pity he redeemed them" (Isaiah 63:9). When the prophet Elijah is at the end of his tether and starving to death, God's angel comes to feed and restore him (I Kings 19:4-8). When Daniel is thrown into the lion's den, an angel appears to shut the mouths of the beasts (Daniel 6:21). When Shadrach, Meshach, and Abednego are thrown into the fiery furnace, "King Nebuchadnezzar was astonished and rose up in haste. He said to his counselors, 'Did we not cast three men bound into the fire?' They answered the king, 'True, O king.' He answered, 'But I see four men loose, walking in the midst of the fire, and they are not hurt; and the appearance of the fourth is like a son of the gods'" (Daniel 3:24-25).

There is something quite wonderful here. In the history of Biblical interpretation, this fourth figure in the fire is sometimes described as an angel, and sometimes, with the boldness of faith, identified as a pre-incarnation appearance of the Lord Jesus himself. Both of these interpretations have worked powerfully in the church. For in the last analysis, the true test of an angelic appearance is quite simple: *Does it glorify Christ?* If it does, then it's an angel; if not, it is just one more religious fantasy.

In this Biblically illiterate age, very few Biblical stories are known. I suppose Noah's Ark is chief among them. Another is the battle of Jericho, where "the walls come a-tumblin' down."[6] Less well known is the fact that the narrative of the battle of Jericho contains one of the most remarkable of all the angel appearances in the Bible.

You will recall that Moses was forbidden to enter the promised land; he died, and the privilege of leading the people over the Jordan passed to the young and vigorous Joshua. On the night before the assault on Jericho, Joshua was encamped with the people of Israel. We read, "When Joshua was by Jericho, he lifted up his eyes and looked, and behold, a man stood before him with his drawn sword in his hand; and Joshua went to him and said to him, 'Are you for us, or for our adversaries?' And he said, 'No; but as commander of the army of the Lord am I now come'" (Joshua 5:13). The angel in the book of Joshua has been variously identified. The rabbis of early centuries thought he was Michael the archangel, the commander of the heavenly host. One of the most breathtaking sermons I know identifies Joshua's angel, like the angel of the fiery furnace, as the Lord Christ himself.[7] Again, that is as it should be, for in the end the angels exist only to manifest the divine presence and purpose. We need not concern ourselves with the name of the angel; but rather with what he says. Joshua quite naturally inquires of the strange man with the drawn sword, "'Art thou for us, or for our adversaries?' And he said, 'No; but as captain of the host of the LORD am I now come.'"[8]

The irruption of the presence of God in the midst of our world upsets all our accustomed categories. We ask, "Why do God's people behave so badly?" "Why doesn't God answer my prayer?" "Why did this happen?" We ask, "Are angels male or female?" "Is God a Republican or a Democrat?" "Is the Lord on the Palestinian side or the Israeli side?" The startlingly irrelevant answer is neither one or the other, but simply *"No."* God is not to be captured in any of our concepts. He escapes all of our categories. He cannot be imprisoned in any of our questions. But . . . *but!* . . . "as commander of the Lord's host am I now come." I think that should give us goosebumps at the very least. Whoever this angel is, he is the one who embodies the conclusive and final victory of God over all evil as the walls come a-tumblin' down. "War arose in heaven," writes St. John; "Michael and his angels fighting against the dragon. . . . And that great dragon was thrown down" (Revelation 12:7).

The French philosopher Simone Weil once said that the only suitable question to ask another human being was, "What are you going through?" I know all about that. Someone very dear to me is going through a terrible ordeal right this minute. The readers of our lessons and other members of this congregation are going through various fiery furnaces. Many times it seems that the only answer that we get from God is "No." But the message of St. Michael and All Angels is this. As St. Paul writes, "The Son of God, Jesus Christ . . . was not Yes and No; but in him it is always *Yes*. For all the promises of God find their *Yes* in him" (II Corinthians 1:19-20). He has passed through to the other side. He has overcome the world. The future belongs to him, and we belong to him. He is with us in the flame. Satan is no match for the commander of the Lord's army. The angel of death is no match for the resurrection of the dead. "And the Lord said unto Gideon, "Peace be unto thee; *fear not:* thou shalt not die."

And so now "unto him that loves us, and washed us from our sins in his own blood, and hath made us kings and priests unto God and his Father; to him be glory and dominion for ever and ever" (Revelation 1:5-6).

Amen.

Apocryphal or Real?

ST. JOHN'S CHURCH, ESSEX, CONNECTICUT

Essex, Connecticut really is the best small town in America as far as I can tell.[1] I gather that Essex has a delightful Halloween celebration. I heard on public radio a few days ago that the politically correct police aren't going to let us call it Halloween any more. They want us to call it Spook Night, or something like that, because Halloween is a Christian word and therefore not sufficiently inclusive for a multicultural society.[2] Well, it is indeed a Christian word; as I'm sure all of you know, Hallowe'en is short for All Hallows Eve, which means that yesterday was All Saints Day. Halloween is good for children and I'm glad we have it, but we Christians have a job of work to do to get All Saints Day back into its proper place of prominence in the Church calendar. The multiculturalists can call Halloween whatever they like, but what is really important for Christian folk is that we understand and appreciate All Saints Day, one of the greatest feast days in the entire church year.

All Saints Day raises the question: What is our ultimate standing? Who are we? Is there any permanent place for us in the universe, or is it as Macbeth feared?

And all our yesterdays have lighted fools
The way to dusty death. Out, out, brief candle!
Life's but a walking shadow, a poor player,
That struts and frets his hour upon the stage,

And then is heard no more. It is a tale
Told by an idiot, full of sound and fury,
Signifying nothing. (Act V, Scene v)

This famous passage has had a powerful hold on readers' imaginations for several centuries. It is very important for Christian people to think long and hard about the possibility that Macbeth might be right.

I have a little quiz for you this morning. I'm going to read two short passages, and you figure out which one is in the Bible. The first one is a continuation of this morning's first reading:

Their posterity will continue for ever, and their glory will not be blotted out. Their bodies were buried in peace, and their names live to all generations. (Ecclesiasticus/Sirach 44:13-14)

And here is the second one:

The dead know nothing, and they have no more reward; and the memory of them is lost. (Ecclesiastes 9:5)

I guess you can tell I have set you up. Yep, that's right, the first passage is from the Apocrypha and the second is from the real Bible. I am going to suggest this morning that the second text would make a more interesting reading for All Saints Day than the first. The book of Ecclesiastes is in the canonical Scripture for a very good reason. It takes quite the opposite view from that of today's appointed reading from Ecclesias*ticus,* in the Apocrypha (also called Sirach, chapter 44). The canonical Biblical view of the human condition is that if we were left to ourselves, our lives would end in emptiness and our names would be nothing but dust.[3] You have a beautiful cemetery here in Essex, and I have walked in it many times. Sometimes I think how people will some day walk past my own grave, and they will neither know nor care who I was.

There is a world of difference between the Apocrypha and the canonical Scripture. The "let us now praise famous men" passage, though it has undeniable literary grandeur, sounds like wishful thinking to me. That's why it's not in the Bible. I don't see how we can assert that the names of obscure people are going to "live to all generations." I have never forgotten something that a friend of mine told me once. His mother had died and he was going through all her things, trying to decide what to keep and what to dispose of. He said to me, "My mother kept all these clippings and mementos that obviously meant a great deal to her. But they mean nothing to me. I don't even know why she kept them." I thought that was unutterably sad. I suppose I was thinking about myself and how some day my own children would be saying the same thing about all the stuff I leave behind. And if that is true with a separation of only one generation, it is not difficult to imagine how little of us there will be left after three or four generations have passed.

You can understand that it isn't so easy to preach to a congregation you don't know. The visiting preacher always worries that she might not hit quite the right notes. But on the other hand I am quite certain, after 22 years of parish ministry, that all of us, whoever and wherever we are, want to know the answers to certain ultimate questions: Is "dusty death" all there is? Does our tale signify anything? Will we simply be obliterated "as though we had never been born" (Ecclesiasticus)? Are we going to die damaged, unfinished, and bent out of shape? And are we going to be separated forever from those whose love has meant the whole world to us? One of the main reasons that Ecclesiastes is in the Bible is that we need to meditate very deeply on the fact that human nature in and of itself does not suggest positive answers to these questions. Here once again is Ecclesiastes on the subject:

> For the fate of the sons of men and the fate of beasts is the same; as one dies, so dies the other. . . . Man has no advantage over the beasts; for all is vanity. All go to one place; all are from the dust, and all turn to dust again. (Ecclesiastes 3:19-20)

You think that's bad? Listen to this:

> One fate comes to all, to the righteous and the wicked, to
> the good and the evil, to the clean and the unclean. . . . As
> is the good man, so is the sinner. . . . This is the evil in all
> that is done under the sun, that one fate comes to all. . . .
> The hearts of men are full of evil, and madness is in their
> hearts while they live, and after that they go to the dead.
> (9:2-3)

Every Christian should read Ecclesiastes from beginning to end
at least once a year. You have to watch out, though, because it's such
a beautifully written work of art that it almost fools you. You can
hear Judy Collins singing in the background: "To every season, turn,
turn. . . ." But that's not the idea at all. In fact, Ecclesiastes has a
sharp edge. It is the ultimate in pessimism. It gives us the lowdown
on the human condition. It makes sentimental happy endings impossible. "The hearts of men are full of evil, and madness is in their
hearts while they live, and after that they go to the dead."

Now, from this perspective, which I have deliberately drawn
as gloomily as possible, let us listen again to the second lesson for
All Saints Day from the book of Revelation:

> These are they who have come out of the great tribulation;
> they have washed their robes and made them white in the
> blood of the Lamb. Therefore are they before the throne of
> God, and serve him day and night within his temple. . . .
> They shall hunger no more, neither thirst any more. . . . For
> the Lamb in the midst of the throne will be their shepherd,
> and he will guide them to springs of living water; and God
> will wipe away every tear from their eyes. (Revelation 7:14-
> 17)

I hope that strikes you as powerfully on second reading as it
does me. When we hear these verses read ceremonially at a funeral,
or even in a Sunday morning service, they may very well go in one

ear and straight out the other. The true force of these promises can only be felt when we have truly considered the alternatives.

What lies behind these great words from Revelation? How are we to know that they are not just wishful thinking? Just yesterday, in its new feature called "Think Tank," *The New York Times* quoted an august professor of philosophy and humanities at Princeton, no less, who said that the whole idea of eternal life was grossly overrated and should be jettisoned forthwith.[4] Is he right? Hasn't humanity developed past the point of relying on these fantasies? Isn't it really more courageous, more realistic, more *evolved* to acknowledge that heaven is nothing more than a projection of human longing? Isn't Ecclesiastes, in fact, a more honest book than Revelation?

It all depends on where Revelation came from. If this vision of the eternal life of God's people arose out of a mere human religious sensibility, then it is worth no more than the picture of a sunrise on an inspirational greeting card. But if, on the other hand, these words are actually promises from the living God, then that is a different matter.

The book of Revelation has taken a bad rap. Once you get the hang of it, it really isn't all that difficult. It shouldn't be left to the David Koreshes of the world. Almost all reputable interpreters today recognize that Revelation is poetry and liturgy. It is not a Rand-McNally map of heaven. It is not a timetable for the end of the world. It is not a "Bible Code." It is by no means as weird as we have been led to believe. It is full of encouragement, hope, and comfort, especially for oppressed people. When Archbishop Desmond Tutu of South Africa was fighting the good fight against apartheid all those decades, he used to say, "Don't give up! Don't get discouraged! I've read the end of the book! We win!" The celestial vision arises out of the Revelation of Jesus Christ himself, the Son of God who reigns in heaven and who has drawn back the curtain just for a moment to allow us a glimpse of God's future.

I have some photographs of three generations of my family, taken 12 years ago on my father's 90th birthday. I look at those pictures now and I wonder who that family is. In the picture, my father is still alive, my mother still looks young, no one is suffering from depression, our daughter has not yet had her brain tumor. Twelve years have wrought a huge change. I cherish the pictures, but they always make me think of the pain and disappointment of life. You've all read biographies and seen pictures of the families of their subjects; have you ever noticed how often the caption says that the picture was taken "in happier days"? There comes a point in everyone's life, I think, when we realize that the happier days are behind us; they are not going to come again; we are going to have to struggle; we are going to live with disappointment. That is the message of Ecclesiastes. Life is like this, and no amount of wishful thinking will make it different. The only power that can make it different is the power of God himself.

That is what Revelation is about. It is about the power of God to create a completely new future:

> Then I saw a new heaven and a new earth; for the first heaven and the first earth had passed away. . . . And I saw the holy city, new Jerusalem, coming down out of heaven from God . . . and I heard a loud voice from the throne saying, "Behold, the dwelling of God is with humanity. . . . They shall be his people, and God himself will be with them; he will wipe away every tear from their eyes, and death shall be no more, neither shall there be mourning nor crying nor pain any more, for the former things have passed away." And he who sat upon the throne said, "Behold, I make all things new." (21:1-5)

I hope that gives you goose bumps. But goose bumps don't last very long. In this world, we have to live in the tension between the resplendent assurance of Revelation and the tough-minded skepticism of Ecclesiastes. That tension between the two will not go away in this life. Thinking people of faith will continue to be challenged not only by Ivy League professors but also, more acutely, by the unnerving things that happen to us. I do not think anyone can ask any more searching questions about the visions of the Bible than I have asked myself. I have not put my trust in God's coming kingdom because I have avoided the tough issues of life. Bishop Tutu does not believe in God's radiant future because of an infantile need to believe in happy endings. He believes it, I believe it, you may believe it because the God who raised his Son Jesus Christ from the dead is a God who is able to keep his promises.

So if this visiting preacher this morning has anything to say at all, it is this: Even in the best small town in the U.S.A., life is difficult. Suffering is inevitable. Failures and disappointments are more likely to come to us than not. Separation and abandonment are part of life. Many questions cannot be answered in this world. Death is real. But on this feast of All Saints, as I read you the last two verses of the hymn, "For all the saints," remember that these thrilling words rest, not on mere human wishes, but on the eternal word of God himself; on the testimony of Jesus Christ our Lord.

> But lo! there breaks a yet more glorious day;
> The saints triumphant rise in bright array;
> The King of glory passes on his way.

> From earth's wide bounds, from ocean's farthest coast,
> Through gates of pearl streams in the countless host,
> Singing to Father, Son, and Holy Ghost, Alleluia, alleluia!

Amen.

SERMON FOR AN INTERFAITH SERVICE ON
THANKSGIVING DAY 1996

The Thankful Life

TRINITY CHURCH, LIME ROCK, CONNECTICUT

We thy people, the flock of thy pasture,
will give thanks to thee for ever;
from generation to generation we will recount thy praise.

Psalm 79:13

The famous Dr. Samuel Johnson, author of the first major English dictionary, renowned conversationalist, wit, and man about town, was also a man of deep Biblical faith. When after heroic labors the Great Lexicographer finally finished his Dictionary, he sent the last sheet of manuscript round to the publisher, Andrew Millar. Mr. Millar exclaimed to the messenger, "Thank God I have done with him!" When this was reported to Dr. Johnson, he smiled and said, "I am glad that he thanks God for anything."[1]

Being thankful is to some extent an art form. A Jewish friend gave me an example of Jewish thanksgiving: If the head of the household dies in a sudden and untimely fashion, the response is, "Well, at least we can be thankful he has sons to say Kaddish for him." Or, if there are no sons, "Well, at least his daughters might marry well and the widow won't have to want for anything." Or if there are no children at all, "Well, we can be thankful there are no children for the poor widow to support." In the aftermath of a pogrom in Russia, as a Jewish baker saw his business going up in flames, he said, "So, at least they burned out my competitor, too." Finding something to be thankful for in the midst of disaster is an enduring gift. Wresting humor and ongoing life out of suffering is our best way of being human. And above all, the Bible teaches that the life of thankfulness is the proper way for human beings to be related to God. He is the giver, and we are the recipients. The most important thanksgiving of all, the one that transcends all human contingencies, is thanking and praising God for being God.

I went into a shop last week to buy Thanksgiving cards. I chose this particular shop because it had a large selection. I went through them all and bought a few, but I came away essentially dissatisfied with their messages. They were all totally generic. All references to God had been excised. For example, one of them had these words from the well-known hymn of Henry Alford: "Come ye thankful people, come, / Raise the song of harvest home, / All is safely gathered in ere the winter storms begin." Period. The next line is missing: "God our Maker doth provide / For our wants to be supplied." The center of the hymn is absent. Here is part of another message: "That flowers have blossomed by the paths / That thread our working days, / That love has filled us with delight, / We offer heartfelt praise." Full stop. It sounds as if that praise were going off into the ether somewhere; there isn't a hint of whom it might be directed to. Such are the commercial imperatives of a religiously diverse society.

As I look out over this congregation today, I have no way of knowing what brought you out at ten o'clock on a morning when you could be sleeping late or roasting your turkey, but I suspect most of you have made the extra effort to be here because you want God to be in the equation. You are here because Thanksgiving without God seems somehow a contradiction in terms. You know that "heartfelt praise" isn't supposed to dissipate into thin air; it is supposed to rise to the throne of the Lord. I don't think you are gathered here today simply to say thank you in some vague and nonspecific sense. Rather, in the words of the hymn, "We gather together to ask *the Lord's* blessing."

The Psalms teach us the purpose and goal of praise. One of the loveliest expressions in all of Scripture is in Psalm 22, verse 3: — "Thou art holy, *enthroned on the praises of Israel.*" Our praise and thanksgiving is actually envisioned as the throne of God. "He who brings thanksgiving as his sacrifice honors me" (Psalm 50:23). It is wonderful to remember this. The simple human action, "Thank you, Lord," is a royal tribute, part of the array of his glory. His throne is fashioned, not of ebony or pearl or emerald or gold, but of our thanksgivings.

Nowhere is the motif of thanksgiving and praise to God more conspicuous than in the Psalms. Indeed, it could be said that it predominates more than any other theme. "Know that the LORD is God! It is he that hath made us, and we are his. . . . Enter into his gates with thanksgiving, and into his courts with praise! O give thanks unto him and bless his name! For the LORD is good; his steadfast love endureth for ever, and his faithfulness to all generations" (Psalm 100:3-5). The theme of gratitude is the *cantus firmus,* the constant undergirding melody of the Biblical song. The giving of thanks is not just an activity to be taken up at certain times and set aside at other times. It is a whole way of life. It is the foundation of our relation to the God whose steadfast love and faithfulness are celebrated in the Hebrew Bible from beginning to end.

Giving thanks is an art form because it requires not only discipline and practice, but also imagination and soul. We begin with the basic exercise of saying thank you to God at meals. Moving on from there, we find it relatively easy to thank him for our families, for our homes, for prosperity, for the beauty of creation. Beyond that, I have noticed, it becomes more difficult. People have a much easier time articulating their petitions than their thanksgivings. When prayer lists are made up, the lists of requests are generally longer than the list of thanksgivings. This is exactly the opposite of what it ought to be. The Bible reveals that gratitude is the foundation for all other prayers; it is the basis of a godly, righteous, and holy life.

The life of thankfulness — Biblically speaking — is lived in view of the hard things of existence. As the life of thanksgiving deepens, we discover that the more mature prayers of thanksgiving are not those offered for the obvious blessings, but those spoken in gratitude for obstacles overcome, for insights gained, for lessons learned, for increased humility, for help received in time of need, for strength to persevere, for opportunities to serve others. Some of the most heartfelt prayers in my own life have come to me at moments when God enabled me to be of assistance to someone else, or to endure some hardship to his glory. Learning that all these things are gifts from God, and not our own achievement, is the foundation of all life lived in the sight of God. I once had a friend who, when congratulated for her wonderful attitude in the face of adversity, said, "I thank God every day for my cheerful disposition." This is a model of Biblical faith. She did not turn away the compliment; she redirected it toward the Lord. She acknowledged the gift, but she made a powerful witness by turning the attention away from herself toward the creator.

A few years ago one of my most beloved seminary professors died. Since he and his wife had lost their only child, it fell to me to be in charge of the care of his elderly widow. I knew I was supposed to do this — it was my duty — but I rather dreaded it at first. I was very busy with many things, and it took a lot of time. I had never known her very well, because when her husband was alive she had remained somewhat in the background. During the remaining years of her life I visited her and took care of many arrangements. To my surprise it became a pleasure and a joy, for this reason: she was incredibly grateful. Instead of complaining that I did not come often enough, she thanked me profusely for coming at all. She appreciated the little insignificant favors that I did for her as though they had been lavish gifts. When I dropped in for a few moments in between other commitments, you would have thought I was paying her a state visit. I have been thinking about this ever since. Her thankfulness *created a new situation.* Obeying the commandment became something I *wanted* to do, not something I *had* to do. Gratitude is soul-enlarging. Gratitude is liberating. Gratitude calls forth a response of loving reciprocity. Gratitude really does create new conditions. Instead of coercion, there is freedom. Instead of constriction, there is amplitude. Instead of duty, there is delight. Surely this is what the Psalms teach us about our covenant relationship to God.

Thanksgiving is the proper part that the covenant people play. The best motivation for keeping the commandments is thankfulness. We do not keep them out of a dogged sense of duty, but out of gratitude. The Psalms present thanksgiving as a call to faith, to recognize what God has done, to meditate upon his wonderful works, to build a faithful life upon the recognition of his acts of deliverance. Gratitude is the only proper human response to God's great work of salvation. "We thy people, the flock of thy pasture, will give thanks to thee for ever; from generation to generation we will recount thy praise" (Psalm 79:13).

The motif of gratitude in the Psalms teaches us of the very nature of God. The most important thanksgiving of all, the one that transcends all human contingencies, is thanking God for being God. He is *enthroned on the praises of Israel*. The Psalms recount his acts of salvation and evoke acts of adoration in return. His faithfulness in spite of our unfaithfulness is told and retold: "Many times [God] delivered [his people], but they were rebellious in their purposes, and were brought low through their iniquity. Nevertheless he regarded their distress, when he heard their cry. He remembered for their sake his covenant, and relented according to the abundance of his steadfast love. . . . Save us, O LORD our God, and gather us from among the nations, that we may give thanks to thy holy name and glory in thy praise" (Psalm 106:43-47). The purpose of salvation is that we might give him thanks. The effects of thanksgiving are freedom and joy. The commandments are written on our hearts that we might keep them with gladness and with a song. The meaning of life is grounded in the praise of God. "Save us, O LORD our God . . . that we may give thanks to thy holy name and glory in thy praise. Blessed be the LORD, the God of Israel, from everlasting to everlasting!

        "Let all the people say, 'Amen!'
        Praise the LORD!" (106:47-48)

Advent Begins in the Dark

ST. JOHN'S CHURCH, SALISBURY, CONNECTICUT

*In our sins we have been a long time, and shall we be saved?
We have all become like one who is unclean, and all our
righteous deeds are like a polluted garment . . . thou hast hid
thy face from us, and hast delivered us into the hand of our
iniquities.*

Isaiah 64:5, 7

Every year, Advent begins in the dark. Today's reading from the
prophet Isaiah sets the stage. "In our sins we have been a long
time, and shall we be saved? We have all become like one who is
unclean, and all our righteous deeds are like a polluted garment. . . .
Thou hast hid thy face from us, and hast delivered us into the hand
of our iniquities. . . . Be not exceedingly angry, O Lord, and remember not our iniquity for ever" (Isaiah 64:5-9). Today's Psalm repeats
the theme: "O Lord God of hosts, how long will you be angered?
You have fed your people with the bread of tears" (Psalm 80:4-5).

In any given Episcopal congregation at this time of year, there
will be two groups of people. One group, seeing the purple hangings
and hearing the lessons about sin, judgment, and the Wrath of God
will say, "Oh, good, it's Advent." The other group will say, "Where
are the Christmas decorations? Why aren't we singing Christmas
carols?" It takes some practice to get used to Advent. Once you do,

though, you will never want it any other way. The more the world outside lights its trees, the more sparkle and glitter it throws about, the more it sings "Have yourself a merry little Christmas," the more you will want to immerse yourself in the special mood of Advent. No other denomination does Advent as conscientiously as we do. It is one of the most important, most cherished contributions that the Episcopal Church has made to Christian worship. Advent teaches us to delay Christmas in order to experience it truly when it finally comes. Advent is designed to show that the meaning of Christmas is diminished to the vanishing point if we are not willing to take a fearless inventory of the darkness.

Now, don't get me wrong. Episcopalians have long since learned to lead a double life during December. Outside these doors, I carry on about Christmas as much as anybody. I become positively intoxicated by the seasonal offerings. I can't get enough wreaths, lights, ribbons, carols, holly, panettone. But at the same time, even as the season outside gets more exuberantly festive, those who observe Advent within the Christian community are convicted more and more each year by the truth of what is going on inside — inside the Church as she refuses cheap comfort and sentimental good cheer. Advent begins in the dark.

Isaiah depicts the silence and absence of God in today's reading: "Thou hast hid thy face from us." W. H. Auden, in his classic work *For the Time Being: A Christmas Oratorio,* writes about Advent this way:

> . . . we are afraid
> Of pain but more afraid of silence; for no nightmare
> Of hostile objects could be as terrible as this void.
> This is the Abomination. This is the Wrath of God.

I collect Advent texts. The Biblical readings are set for us, but they are filled out each year by contemporary voices that add their own notes. Here is an example from the news. A few months ago, a funeral was held in Belgium for one of the little girls who was slowly and systematically starved to death in a dungeon by a man so perverted that he was disowned by his own mother. At the Roman Catholic funeral, the priest's hand trembled violently as he recalled the passionate prayers said for the children all over Belgium. In a voice of intense anger he said, "Is the good Lord deaf?"[1] That is an Advent question. Here is another Advent text from the *Times:* A woman told of praying for her husband's safety the night before he took off on Pan Am Flight 103 over Lockerbie. After his death in the explosion, she said her view of God had changed. "I don't dislike him," she said. "I'm not mad at him. I'm afraid of him." That idea, too, belongs to Advent. It is the season of the Wrath of God.

Many people do not like to hear these things during the Christmas season. That is understandable. As T. S. Eliot famously said, "Human kind cannot bear very much reality."[2] We would rather build fantasy castles around ourselves, decked out with angels and candles. Indeed, I read yesterday that Americans now spend several hundred million dollars a year on scented candles, frequently marketed as "spiritual" aids. This is precisely the sort of illusion about spiritual health that the church, in Advent, refuses to promote. This season is not for the faint of heart. During the trial of Susan Smith, who drowned her little boys, many commentators wrote that our fascination with the case had to do with our displacement of our own dark impulses onto this unfortunate young woman, upon whom we could then lock the door. It requires courage to look into the heart of darkness, especially when we are afraid we might see ourselves there. Isaiah says that even our best selves are distorted and unclean: "Even our righteous deeds are like filthy rags" (Isaiah 64:6). Advent begins here, in the dark.

About twenty-five years ago Dick and I received a Christmas card (during Advent) that to this day we still think is the best Christmas card we ever got. Its first page was a brilliant orange-red with these words from the Christmas story in the Gospel of St. Luke printed on it: "The day will dawn on us from on high." Then you opened it and received a shock. On the inside, printed in somber black and white, was a photograph of a wretched slum dwelling. In the shadow of the wall sat a small black child in tattered clothing, staring into space with enormous starved eyes. The inscription on the inside, completing the verse begun on the orange cover, was this: ". . . to give light to those that sit in darkness and in the shadow of death" (Luke 1:79).

Some who received this card were outraged by it. We do not want to see anything unpleasant at Christmas, they said. They wanted something pretty, something happy. But I still think that it was a true Christmas message in a way that the glittery cards can never be. The authentically hopeful Christmas spirit has not looked away from the darkness, but straight into it. The true and victorious Christmas spirit does not look away from death, but directly at it. Otherwise, the message is cheap and false. Instead of pointing to someone else's sin, we confess our own. "In our sins we have been a long time." Advent begins in the dark.

Last Sunday in our Bible class, the question was asked: If God has truly come in Jesus Christ, why do things remain as they are? Why do so many terrible things happen? Where is God? These are the Advent questions. The Church has been asking them from the beginning, all the way back in the first century AD when the Gospel of Mark was being put together. The early Christians were facing a crisis. Voices within and without the community were saying, "Where is the King? Show us some evidence! He said he would return, but there is no sign of him. The world has not improved. Where is God?" And in its perplexity, the young Church told and retold a story to herself, a story once told by Jesus of Nazareth — the parable of the doorkeeper: "It is like a man going on a journey. When he leaves home he puts his servants in charge, each with his work, and commands the doorkeeper to be on the watch. Watch therefore — for you do not know when the master of the house will come, in the evening, or at midnight, or at cockcrow, or in the morning — lest he come suddenly and find you asleep. And what I say to you I say to all: Watch" (Mark 13:33-37).

We can still feel the tension in the atmosphere of the parable. Were it not for the master, the household would have no reason for existing; yet he is away. The expectation of his return is the driving force behind all the household activity, yet often it seems that he will never come. Everybody has been told to be in a state of perpetual readiness, yet sometimes it seem as though it has all been a colossal mistake. Strangely, however, in spite of all this, the Christian believer will experience the urgency and stress in the text as a sign of its continuing truth. The heartbeat of the parable remains strong, even accelerated, just as the drama of salvation accelerates in Advent. The atmosphere of crisis is the story of the life of the Christian community in The Time Between for two thousand years.

If you were to say to me that I have not answered the Advent questions, I would have to say you are right. We do not know why God delays so long. We do not know why he so often hides his face. We do not know why so many have to suffer so much with so little apparent meaning. All we know is that there is this rumor, this hope, this expectation, that the Master of the house is coming back. The first Sunday of Advent, as you can tell from the hymns, is not about the first coming of Jesus, *incognito* in the stable at Bethlehem. It is about the Second Coming, "in glory, to judge the quick and the dead." It is about the final breaking in of God upon our darkness. It is about the promise that, against all the evidence, there is a God who cares. Where is God? Until he comes again, he is hidden among us, "the wounded surgeon,"[3] the bleeding Victim, the One who hung on the tree, accursed for our sake. It is this *hiddenness* that gives Advent its special character. The church's life in Advent is hidden with Christ until he comes again, which explains why so much of what we do in this night appears to be failure, just as his life appeared to end in failure. If Jesus is the Son of God, he is also the One who identifies himself with "the least, the last, and the lost,"[4] who takes their part, who is born into the world as a member of the lowest class on the social ladder and does not cease to identify himself with our human fate until he is given up to die the death of a slave.

This is not the end of the story. It is the beginning of the end. As many theologians have pointed out, the church lives in Advent, The Time Between, *The Time Being* as Auden calls it. In a very deep sense, the entire Christian life in this world is lived in Advent, between the first and second comings of the Lord, in the midst of the tension between things the way they are and things the way they ought to be. "I don't dislike God. I'm not mad at him. I'm afraid of him." Like many other Pan Am 103 families, the woman who fears God and lost her husband has given herself in service to others who have lost their loved ones in air crashes. She has not clutched at the scented candles, but has chosen to go out among others who suffer. In the words of the Advent collect, "now in the time of this mortal life" she has "cast away the works of darkness and put [on] the armor of light."

I asked my mother to tell me why, in our family when I was growing up, we did not decorate our house until Christmas Eve. She said, "I think Christmas should come in a burst." That's it exactly. The human race cannot expect to receive any lasting comfort from this world. It must come from somewhere else — in a burst of transcendent power breaking in upon us from beyond our sphere altogether. Last night in the Bach concert, the thrilling voice of the Evangelist sang, "And suddenly . . . !" *(Und alsobald)*. That's why we are singing, today, "Sleepers, wake! A voice *astounds* us!" The news of God's entrance into the world ruled by sin and death is nothing less than astounding. After a long and agonizing silence that seems never to end, the voice at last is heard in the wilderness: "Comfort ye, comfort ye, my people, saith your God" (Isaiah 40:1). To each and all on this first Sunday of Advent, we bring this announcement: God will come, and his justice will prevail, and he will destroy evil and pain in all its forms, once and for ever. To be a Christian is, yes, to live in solidarity every day of our lives with those who sit in darkness and in the shadow of death, but also to live most truly in the unshakeable hope of those who expect the dawn.

"I don't dislike God. I'm not mad at him. I'm afraid of him." *And the angel said unto them, Fear not.*

Amen.

A People Prepared

ST. JOHN'S CHURCH, ESSEX, CONNECTICUT

*Zechariah was troubled when he saw {the angel Gabriel},
and fear fell upon him. But the angel said to him, "Do not
be afraid, Zechariah, for your prayer is heard, and your wife
Elizabeth will bear you a son, and you shall call his name
John . . . he will turn many of the sons of Israel to the Lord
their God, and he will go before him in the spirit and power
of Elijah, to . . . make ready for the Lord a people prepared.*

Luke 1:12-13, 16-17

This is the second Sunday of Advent, so here is an Advent story. Wei Jingsheng, the Chinese dissident recently released from 18 years' imprisonment, tells of a journey he took when he was a young man. As his train pulled into a station, it was besieged by throngs of dirty, hungry children in rags. Mr. Wei began to pass biscuits out the window to them. His fellow passengers strenuously objected, saying that they were the children of class enemies. Mr. Wei ignored the protests and continued to pass out the bread. Soon he noticed that passengers at other windows began to do the same. This little incident taught Wei Jingsheng of the power of one individual example. Since that time he has not ceased to be what Graham Greene called "a piece of grit in the state machinery." A journalist comments,

"In a culture that strongly discourages individuality and that demands submission to authority, Mr. Wei is an extremely unusual figure, stubborn, patient, and humorous."[1]

Wei Jingsheng is an Advent person. He doesn't know that, but God often uses people without their knowing it. Wherever people overcome fear to speak a word of truth to power, there is the Advent spirit. Wherever there are voices in the darkness speaking out for light, there is the Advent hope. Wherever there are people willing to face personal danger for the sake of freedom, there is the Advent frontier. The work of God is located there.

This sermon is about the Advent life. It is about being *a people prepared.* Not every congregation wants to be a people prepared. Many want to be a people lulled into self-satisfaction. If you are in that category, the second and third Sundays of Advent are not safe days to be in church. On these Sundays, every year, in churches around the globe that use the common lectionary, John the Baptist blazes forth out of the desert to shock us out of our complacency. He addresses us as he addressed the religious seekers of his own day: "You brood of vipers! Who warned you to flee from the wrath to come?"[2]

But first, to understand John, we need to go back in the Scripture a bit. My text for today is from the story in the first chapter of Luke where the angel Gabriel comes to Zechariah in the temple to announce the conception and birth of his son John. Everybody knows the nativity story from Luke, but not very many know the complete story as it unfolds. The first two chapters of Luke in their entirety are among the greatest treasures of the New Testament, incomparably rich and evocative in their imagery. Here is part of what Gabriel says to John's father Zechariah: "Do not be afraid, Zechariah, for your prayer is heard, and your wife Elizabeth will bear you a son, and you shall call his name John. . . . he will be filled with the Holy Spirit, even from his mother's womb. And . . . he will go before [the Lord] in the spirit and power of Elijah . . . to make ready for the Lord *a people prepared.*"

The Advent message is about being a people prepared for the coming of the Lord. In a world largely given over either to repressive brutality, as in China, or to self-indulgent pleasures as in our own country, John the Baptist is here to show us where to stand. If we understand our position, we will understand Advent, and if we understand Advent, we will understand what it means to be *a people prepared*.

If you love Advent, you are blessed. Most serious Episcopalians love Advent because it tells us the truth about the human situation. It makes us realize that being Christian is not some kind of religious warm bath. Like John the Baptist, Advent is out of phase with our time. It encroaches uncomfortably upon us, making us feel some degree of dissonance, with its stubborn resistance to the usual round of shopping and wrapping and baking and partying. I have never seen a picture of John the Baptist on any Advent calendar, yet he is the foremost figure of Advent.

All four New Testament evangelists agree: there is no good news, no gospel of Jesus Christ without John the Baptist. John's whole life was lived with but one purpose; he was born, a man of destiny, to declare the imminent arrival of the coming Messiah. This voice crying in the wilderness is extraordinary in many ways, but most of all for the single-mindedness with which he pursued his mission even to death, for John the Baptist feared no man, not even Herod the king, and no woman either, not even Herod's wife, who in the end arranged to have his head cut off. But let us take note: this firebrand who recognized no superior was utterly submissive before the One whose coming he lived and died to illuminate. "John said to the people, 'One is coming who is mightier than I, and I am not fit to untie the thong of his sandal'" (Luke 3:15-16). To be the witness, to point away from himself to Jesus Christ — this is the destiny of John, and in these things he is a model for every Christian preacher.

There is very little in John's character or his history to appeal to the modern sensibility. If people today think of him at all, it is usually as a head on a platter.[3] I have preached about him during Advent for twenty-two years, yet I find him each year to be more uncanny and intractable than ever. After two thousand years, he still stands there, irreducibly strange, gaunt and unruly, utterly out of synch with his age or our age or any age. Compared to John, even Elijah is warm and fuzzy. John's *character*, however, was never the central focus, not even for the early church. Though his person is remarkable by any standard, it is not his person that marks him out; it is his *role* — more accurately, his *location*.

In order to locate John we need to go back into the Old Testament, to some famous words in the book of the prophet Malachi: "Surely the day is coming; it will burn like a furnace . . . says the Lord God Almighty. . . . But for you who revere my Name the sun of righteousness will rise with healing in its wings. . . . Behold, I will send my messenger, who will prepare the way before me. . . . Behold, I will send the prophet Elijah before that great and terrible day of the Lord comes" (Malachi 4:1-2, 5).

These words about Elijah are the very last words of our Old Testament. In between the time of the close of the Old Testament and the opening of the New, Jewish expectation was focused on the figure of Elijah the prophet, who had not died but been taken up to heaven in a fiery chariot. When Elijah came back, it was believed, that would be the sign that the end of the world was at hand. Luke says, "And [John] will turn many of the sons of Israel to the Lord their God, and . . . he will go before [the Lord] in the spirit and power of Elijah" (Luke 1:16-17). John the Baptist is the new Elijah, standing at the edge of the universe, at the dawn of a new world. That is his *location* as the sentinel, the premier personage of the Advent season — the season of the coming of the Messiah.

John's divinely ordained location in the world, according to the New Testament, is to stand on the frontier of the ages as God begins to turn the world away from its past of sin and bondage into a future of promise and freedom. John's function is to proclaim the coming reversal of the downward spiral of human history, to deliver the message of the arriving Son of God. It is not an easy message to hear. "You brood of vipers! Who warned you to flee from the wrath to come? Bear fruits that befit repentance. . . . Even now the axe is laid to the root of the trees; every tree therefore that does not bear good fruit is cut down and thrown into the fire" (Luke 3:7, 10). The appearance of John on the banks of the Jordan River means that "the hour of the kingdom of God has struck."[4] The wickedness of this world is truly doomed; the Lord of the universe is about to step on the stage of world history to reverse its course. When Elijah comes back, *the next person to appear will be God, and it will be the first day of the Age to Come.*

All four evangelists tell us that the arrival of the Messiah is immediately preceded by the work of John the Baptist, whose single-minded life and horrendous death at the hands of the powers and principalities[5] is a preview of Jesus' own death. What a strange story we Christians have to tell! It is in the suffering and death of God's servants at the hands of despots and tyrants that God's new rule is made manifest. As we are beginning to be aware, all over the world Christians are being persecuted for their faith in horrendous ways that you and I can scarcely imagine. These Christians know they stand with John the Baptist. They are paying the price for holding their positions on the frontier where the goodness of God's coming Age opposes the rulers of "this present evil age" (Galatians 1:4). They stay in their appointed location in order to bear witness to the One whose coming John the Baptist lived to illuminate.

Now it is for you and me to reflect, this Advent season, on our own positions. What does it mean to be *a people prepared?* Where are you and I located along that frontier where John stood? Where do we stand on the great divide between this age of despotism, disease, and death, and God's coming Kingdom of truth, liberty, and life? Our lives are not very dramatic compared to those of Christians in China and Sudan and other countries where they face imprisonment, torture, and death. No one is asking us to confront totalitarian governments or gunmen with machetes. But being *a people prepared* means understanding that the Christian life means participating in the struggle where the forces of evil are confronted by the power of God. The New Testament repeatedly describes the Christian life as a battle. It is full of tension — the tension between the values of this world and those of the world to come. This warfare is conducted on many fronts. For instance, I think of a businessman who refuses to go along with corrupt company policies even though it would benefit him financially; he is holding his position on the Advent frontier. I think of a woman I spoke with a few weeks ago; she has renounced the opportunity to run off with a new man and has recommitted herself to her marriage. I think of social workers and teachers who remain content with their salaries, parents who insist on limits even when it makes their children intensely angry, writers and accountants and builders and researchers who stand for excellence in an age of declining standards — these are Advent people, holding their positions in spite of personal losses.

What does it mean to be *a people prepared?* What does it mean for you who are here this morning? Each one of you individually and all of you together as a congregation are given opportunities every day to reconsider what it means to be *a people prepared* for the coming of the Lord. Who is getting ready for Christmas? You may have noticed that the counsel John gives to those who come to him is almost 100 percent economic: *Be content with your wages; give to the needy.* I saw a television story about the retail season. A woman was interviewed standing in the aisles of F. A. O. Schwarz with her children. She said, "We're going to be able to spend about $1500 more this year." Is that the way to get ready for Christmas? I think of a couple I know, in fact several couples I know, who this very week are sitting down together to plan the year-end gifts they will send to social service agencies. Who is getting ready for Christmas, the woman in the store with her budget for luxuries, or the couples with their lists of charities? To all of us John says, "Bear fruits that befit repentance."

And so to all of us who are here today, getting ready for our worldly Christmas, let us at the same time observe Advent. Let us make a place in our hearts for that strange, lonely sentinel on the frontier of the ages, still pointing away from himself to the One Who Is To Come,[6] identifying for us the place we are to stand. Whenever we do the right thing in spite of its cost, we are doing what Christian soldiers do; we are standing firm on the battlefield between the powers of this world and the powers of the Age to Come, one foot in the territory of the enemy, and the other, the decisive foot, firmly planted in the Kingdom of God. What is your piece of territory? It may not be a very big piece of ground, but it is the one God has given you to hold, and it will be part of God's new world in the Great Liberation. Let the news go forth: God is on the move. He is creating a new humanity. You and I belong to it. Let us honor the Master by holding on to our piece of territory, passing out our bread to those who need it, rejoicing to be *a people prepared* until he comes again.

Amen.

The Master and the Best Man

GRACE CHURCH, NEW YORK CITY

> John {the Baptist} said, "I am not the Christ, but I have been
> sent before him. . . . The friend of the bridegroom, who stands
> and hears him, rejoices greatly at the bridegroom's voice; there-
> fore this joy of mine is now full. He must increase, but I must
> decrease." .
>
> John 3:27-30

Last week's *New York Times Magazine* contained an interview with the Dalai Lama. I found myself pleasantly surprised by it. The person speaking was not uttering the solipsistic banalities that one dreads hearing these days from typical purveyors of spiritual goods in the religious marketplace. In fact, what he had to say was refreshingly *un*spiritual; it was humorous, savvy, down-to-earth. The most obvious point of difference between his views and those of Christianity is his optimism about human nature. Still, one comes away with the impression that this a person with whom one can have a real conversation.[1]

The part of the interview that struck me most, however, was the Dalai Lama's response to the question: Was he ever angry? Perhaps to encourage him, the interviewer suggested that "even Jesus" became angry. And the Dalai Lama replied, apparently with some asperity, "Don't compare me with Jesus. He is a great master, a great master. . . ."

[38]

In the Fourth Gospel we find these words of John the Baptist: "I am not the Christ, but I have been sent before him. . . . The friend of the bridegroom, who stands and hears him, rejoices greatly at the bridegroom's voice; therefore this joy of mine is now full. He must increase, but I must decrease."

"Don't compare me with Jesus." One must love the Dalai Lama for that. For just a moment it seemed as if he stepped into the role of John the Baptist, the one who points away from himself to Christ.

Let us think for a moment, though, about those words, "a great master." This is not the way that Christians describe Jesus. The words "great master" in a Buddhist, Hindu, or even New Age context mean something quite different from what Christian faith affirms about Jesus of Nazareth. In Christianity, there are no "spiritual masters." There are only sinners in need of a Savior. Jesus is not *a* great master; he is *the* great Master. Nor is he a master in the sense of a teacher who simply leads his disciples along the same path that he himself treads. As our Lord says, he *himself* is "the Way, and the Truth, and the Life" (John 14:6). If those words were spoken by any other guru or spiritual leader, including the Dalai Lama, we would judge him to have gone off the deep end.

John the Baptist is the central personage of the Advent season. Last Sunday and this Sunday are his days. His divinely ordained role in the world is to do one thing: to be a voice calling, "Prepare ye the way of the Lord." It is not "a great master" that he proclaims, but *the Lord.* We preachers have a hard task every Advent, having to preach about John the Baptist two Sundays in a row, but believe me, we learn to love him. The preacher feels deep gratitude to John, who said, "He must increase, but I must decrease." John has set the example for us all. He says in effect, don't look at me; look at Jesus. John rejoices because the bridegroom is coming. He is not jealous that he is not the bridegroom; he is thankful to be the best man. His joy is full. Years of preaching have taught me how wonderfully comforting that thought is.

Christian faith is completely different from that of other religions. Though it contains teaching, it is not built on teaching. Though it speaks of Truth, it is not built on truths. Though it describes spiritual experiences, it is not built on spiritual experiences. Alone among the religions of the world, Christian faith is built on a person: not on what he *taught,* but on *who he was:* Jesus *himself* — not his teaching or his example or his deeds, but his *person.* Of course we are not saying that his teaching and example and deeds are of no importance, but they are subordinate to *who he was.*

But now we must acknowledge that the matter of who he was is not so well understood, even in the churches. Ordinarily I am skeptical about polls, but a recent Gallup poll about Jesus sounded to me as if it was on the right track. Two out of three Americans were willing to say that Jesus was divine in some form, but when they were asked if he were God in the form of a man they were less willing to commit themselves. Nine out of ten expressed admiration of him as an ethical teacher, but far fewer thought faith in him was necessary. On the other hand, three-fourths agreed with the idea that Jesus was alive in heaven, but nearly three-fifths did not know that he delivered the Sermon on the Mount. My own observation would be that, as the Gallup survey concluded, "America's image of Jesus Christ is to some extent murky." Indeed.

The Advent season, coming as it does just before Christmas, is a time for clarifying who Jesus is. John the Baptist, the herald out of the wilderness, hails him in all four gospels in unmistakable terms as the unique Messiah of God, the one in whose person the Kingdom of God has arrived. The image of the bridegroom is clearly intended to convey this message, for it is essentially the same metaphor familiar to Israel from the Sinai desert, where she became the bride of Yahweh. John's function in all four gospels is to leave no doubt about Jesus' identity.

Yet still, even in the churches, the argument about who he was goes on. Christmas, the commemoration of Christ's birth, has been co-opted to a great extent by those who regard the holiday as a semi-pagan winter solstice festival or, worse, as an opportunity for sentimental reflections about the "miracle of childbirth" and the consolations of vaguely religious wishes for peace and good will. Here, perhaps, the Dalai Lama is on weakest ground. In the *Times* interview he states that he believes the twenty-first century, unlike the twentieth, will be one of peace and justice. To that, the Christian will say (and with all due respect the evidence is all on our side on this one), *not likely.* I was thinking that this week as I read the *Times.* Just one day after the massacre on the Long Island Railroad, a kind and generous immigrant shopkeeper in Yonkers, a husband and father of three small children, was shot dead minding his store. Speaking for myself, it was the smaller incident coming right after the larger one that hammered the truth home once again: the human race is in a desperate fix. The human race does not need any more spiritual masters; it needs a Savior. The proclamation of John the Baptist is that *the one and only* Lord of lasting peace and justice is on his way.

A German theologian [Baumstark] once wrote that Christmas is not so much the festival of Christ's birth as it is "the feast of Nicene dogma." That's a heavy phrase, but it has a wondrous message in it. When the Christian church was young, it was necessary for the church leaders to get together and agree on what the fundamentals of the faith were. The most important question that had to be hammered out was the Christological one. *Who was Jesus?* Was he a man who became very spiritual? Was he a reincarnation of someone or other? Was he a person who achieved a high degree of moral superiority? The basic issue boiled down to this: was Jesus really God, or was he just *like* God? You know the answer if you know the Nicene Creed: "I believe in one Lord Jesus Christ, the only-begotten Son of God, begotten of his father before all worlds, God of God, Light of Light, very God of very God, begotten, not made, being *of one substance* with the Father."

The new issue of *Vanity Fair* features a long story about Richard Gere, the movie star. He has been a Buddhist for twenty years. The article goes into some detail about how much Buddhist practices have helped him. It is not my purpose to argue with that. I mention it just to draw the distinction. There is a good deal of discussion of practices and observances and religious techniques in the *Vanity Fair* article, but there is no mention of any saving person. (Unless, of course, you count Cindy Crawford.) In contrast, the Christian gospel proclaims a person, a person in whom all the people of the world will find their true salvation, a person to whom all religious masters will ultimately bow the knee.

When I was a child in Franklin, Virginia, my aunt, Mary Virginia, lived nearby. There is very little to tell about her in worldly terms. Unlike my father (her brother) she left very little trace in the history of our town. She did not leave me any money or silver or jewelry. This is what she left me: she left me Jesus. That was her legacy, which explains why I love her memory so much. It gladdens me this morning to remember how she used to call Jesus "the Master" as she told me stories about him. I always associate the term with her. It is nice to think how clear she was about what it meant. For her, and for the little girl at her knee half a century ago, there could be no doubt: Jesus was not *a* master; he was *the* Master.

On Christmas Eve at Grace Church, when the candles are lit and the organ begins to play "O Come, All Ye Faithful," the choir will start down the south aisle. For many years now, as the procession makes the turn at the back and starts up the center aisle with the cross going ahead of us, the choir and congregation begins the second verse.

> God from God, Light from light eternal,
> Lo! he abhors not the Virgin's womb.
> *Only begotten Son of the Father,*
> O come let us adore him.

The preacher today, like John the Baptist, has nothing to give you but Jesus. That is all; and that is everything. It is God himself. "He must increase and I must decrease." He is "the Way, and the Truth, and the Life."

"O Master, let us walk with thee."

Amen.

The Bisecting Messenger

GRACE CHURCH, NEW YORK CITY

*The Word of the Lord came to Nathan the prophet, saying
. . . "Go and tell my servant David . . . 'The Lord declares
to you that the Lord himself will build a house for you . . .
and your house and your kingdom will endure forever.'"*

II Samuel 7:4, 11, 16

*In the sixth month God sent the angel Gabriel to a virgin
named Mary. The angel went to Mary and said, "You will
give birth to a son and you will call his name Jesus. . . . The
Lord God will give him the throne of his father David, and
. . . his kingdom will have no end."*

Luke 1:26-17, 31-33

If I were to name my favorite Old Testament hero, I guess it would
have to be David. The Biblical narratives make him come alive
for us as few other people of ancient times. Here is a real man's man,
and a woman's man too — handsome, sexy, magnificent in statecraft,
a lion on the battlefield, a brilliantly gifted poet and musician, a
flamboyantly physical presence yet deeply introspective and prayer-

ful, a man of action and a man of contemplation, gigantic in his faults as in his virtues, but deeply repentant for those faults as many powerful men never are.

However, the deathbed scene of King David is as pathetic as his life is titanic. He has become so feeble that he cannot leave his room, and he shivers with cold constantly, pathologically. His servants and family pile covers on him to no avail. Finally, they resort to a stratagem suitable for an oriental potentate — they put a young woman in bed with him to keep him warm. This may sound titillating, but since the king has become impotent, it is not even the last flickering of a once-bright flame, but a pitiful dying away into ashes — the kind of humiliating decline that we all pray to escape.

Now we shift from the tenth century BC to the twentieth century AD. John Updike has paid a five-day visit to Finland and tells us about it in *The New Yorker*.[1] Now as we all know, Updike is that rare writer who has achieved the kind of success that most writers can only envy from a great distance. He is famous all over the globe and has accumulated a lot of money. Far from suffering from writer's block, he turns out a novel every couple of years and a superhuman number of essays. He gives the impression of a man intimately familiar with sex and power.

However, when John Updike goes to Finland for five days, he goes alone, with what he refers to as "a deeper, less comfortable self." It is August, but raining constantly and so cold that even the hardy Finns are wearing caps and gloves. He finds the language utterly mysterious and is treated rudely by a saleswoman in a candy store. He tries to sleep in his sterile hotel room, but lies awake for hours, jet-lagged and struggling with a nameless dread. He goes out on his rainy balcony in the middle of the night and looks at the sleepy town; "Nothing moved," he writes, "not even the clouds moved — yellow layers of nimbus that seemed the hellish underside of some other realm. I had never before been . . . this far north on the planet and the arrangement of reservations and obligations whereby I would make my way home seemed impossibly rickety and precarious. The precariousness of being alive and human was no longer hidden from me by familiar surroundings and the rhythm of habit. I was fifty-five, ignorant, dying, and filling this bit of Finland with the smell of my stale sweat and insomniac fury."[2]

Now you and I know that John Updike is neither ignorant nor dying. He is in the prime of his life, at the peak of his powers and the pinnacle of his fame. Yet even a celebrity has to be alone with himself at three o'clock in the morning, even as you and I.

Sometimes when I read the papers I have the distinct feeling that there is a dull yellow cloud over the world that gives the whole landscape an infernal aspect. Where is there any movement? Civil war in Algeria, Mozambique, Sri Lanka for years on end; Brazil's once-vibrant economy coming apart, the hopes of Haiti dashed once again, poverty as bad or worse in India than in the forties, Northern Ireland no closer to peace . . . and even a diehard Anglophile like myself must wonder whether, with the Prince and Princess of Wales not speaking to each other, there will always be an England after all.

As Advent draws to its close, the special nature of the season summons us to somber reflections on the "precariousness of being alive and human." You will notice that the Episcopal Church does not decorate for Christmas during Advent. For four weeks, we are invited to live with our "deeper, less comfortable selves" — that self that is necessarily alone at three o'clock in the morning, even if someone else is sleeping alongside — sometimes, *especially* if someone is sleeping alongside, someone from whom we feel helplessly estranged. W. H. Auden wrote,

> Lay your sleeping head, my love,
> Human on my faithless arm. . . .

All our arrangements and obligations are "rickety and precarious," and in the last analysis all our human arms are faithless; "the arm of flesh will fail you; ye dare not trust your own."[3] I myself am younger than Updike, I am in excellent health and feel as if I have great deeds ahead of me, but at three o'clock in the morning I know that I am ignorant and I am dying.

In King David's palmy days he made plans to build a great

temple. The prophet Nathan said to the King, "The Word of the Lord came to me saying, 'Go and tell my servant David, "Are you the one to build *me* a house?" The Lord declares to you that the Lord himself will build a house for *you.*'" God will not permit himself to be housed. The house of David will be built by God, not the other way around. Nathan announces, "The Lord will build a house for you . . . he will raise up your offspring to succeed you . . . your house and your kingdom will endure forever."

Well, as you know, in spite of this prophecy, the house of David collapsed into ashes, as David's own life had done. David's great achievement, the United Monarchy, was divided and conquered, first by the Assyrians, then by the Babylonians. The children of Israel were humiliated and carried off to foreign lands where they did not speak the language, where the salespeople mocked them, where nothing moved and the yellow underside of the clouds cast a hellish glow over the world.

How odd, then, that Nathan's prophecy should be kept and treasured. In 1947 AD, a scrap found in the cave of the Dead Sea Scrolls was found to contain a reference to this very prophecy. Why had the Essenes preserved these words, why did the Hebrew historians and scribes cherish them and pass them along when the promises had turned to ashes? Had not the splendid temple of David's son Solomon been reduced to rubble? There had been no progress toward an everlasting kingdom. Nothing had moved.

Yet Israel continued to hold on to the promise. Why did they do that when it was so palpably crazy to continue to believe it? They did it for one reason and one reason only; the message was said to be, not from man, but from God. It was said that *the Lord had spoken* to the prophet Nathan. God stated that he was not in the least dependent on rickety human arrangements. In Nathan's words, we see God wresting the initiative away from David with sovereign ease; "You aren't going to build a house for *me,* I'm going to build a house for *you.*" Independently of anything David has said or done, God has made a decision to be merciful to his people *through the line of David.* The focus has shifted away from human arrangements and obligations to the initiative of God. The fourth Sunday of Advent is the right day to remember the meaning of the term *Annunciation*. Annunciation means that God is saying, "Stand back and see what I am about to do!"[4]

Now hear the Gospel for today: "In the sixth month God sent the angel Gabriel to . . . a virgin named Mary. The angel went to her and said, 'You will give birth to a son and you will call his name Jesus. . . . The Lord God will give him the throne of his father David, and . . . of his kingdom there will be no end.'" What is an angel? They are great mysteries to us, and the Bible permits us only a very few glimpses. This much, however, we can say for certain: "angel" means "messenger," and specifically, *God's* messenger, a being who arrives in our midst directly from the presence of undiluted power. Angels descend from the seat of cosmic majesty into the dust and ashes of our dying world. They bring their news from another place, another sphere altogether. They come into the kingdoms of this world from the kingdom of our Lord. An angel, to use a phrase of Emily Dickinson's, is a "bisecting messenger."[5]

At some point in the middle of the night between Friday and Saturday, I woke up in the dark — my husband will testify that this is true — and I had dreamed that our two daughters had been murdered and we would never again have any children or any grand-children. I simply cannot describe to you the horror of that night-mare. Yet this sort of thing is no nightmare, but fact, for many people, many mothers, throughout the world — Rachels, "weeping for their children because they are no more" (Matthew 2:18, cf. Jeremiah 31:15). There cannot be any ultimate good news for me, any waking up from the nightmare, until there is ultimate good news for them. Good news for the U.S.A. is not good news unless it is good news also for Afghanistan and Siberia and Ethiopia and Haiti. Good news for the young and healthy is not ultimate good news unless it is also good news for the infirm, the impotent, and the dying.

Where is our everlasting kingdom to come from? Not from our faithless arms, that's for sure. The Queen of England cannot guarantee a kingdom; Mr. Gorbachev cannot guarantee a kingdom; Cory Aquino, may God be with her, cannot guarantee a kingdom.

History appears to be going round and round on itself. At three o'clock in the morning, with the doomsday clock ticking away, it is not at all certain that there will be any grandchildren.

But something has happened. This is the message of the Annunciation. *God has moved.* The angel Gabriel has bisected the ghastly yellow clouds. Heaven has come to earth — real heaven, not Shirley MacLaine's New Age heaven, but the heaven of the God of Abraham, Isaac, and Jacob, the God and Father of our Lord Jesus Christ. "The Lord God will give him the throne of his father David, and of his kingdom there will be no end." I am going to build you a house, says the Lord. Jesus is the house. The Word was made flesh and dwelt among us. God, in Jesus of Nazareth, has entered the world of the ignorant and dying — *Emmanuel,* God with us — and his throne will be established forever, by the only power in heaven and earth that is able to do such a thing. This is the meaning of the Virgin Birth: *God* has moved. God has moved, not we to him in our impotence, but he to us. The vicious circle of our existence has been bisected by the Son of the Most High. He has reached down into my deepest and most uncomfortable self — and yours — and he has established himself there as the everlasting Father. The promise made to David is fulfilled in Christ; his throne will be secure for all time. When we are alone at three o'clock in the morning, the one who is beside us is the promised Son of David, and his arm is faith*ful,* now and forever. Rejoice! Rejoice! Emmanuel shall come to thee, O Israel!

Amen.

The Magical Kingdom

CHRIST'S CHURCH, RYE, NEW YORK

Of his kingdom there will be no end.

Luke 1:33

Christmas Eve! How magical it is! No matter how old or jaded we may be, it never fails to work its enchantment. How disappointed we would all be if there were not more people than usual here tonight to share in the romance of the "midnight service." You know, I'm sure, that it has long been customary in churches to complain about the Christmas Eve crowd. "Who are these people?" "Where are they the rest of the year?" "They've had too much to drink!" "They don't put anything into the offering!" "They take up all the best seats!" I will confess to you that I used to say these things myself. No more. I feel truly sorry for people who are not in church tonight. How sad not to be seeing the candles, not hearing the organ, not singing the carols, and *above all how sad not to be hearing the story of salvation.* So to each and every one of you, but especially to those who have not been to Christian worship for a long time, welcome, welcome, and welcome again. The preacher tonight has you especially in mind, and I have prayed that, during this hour and a half that you will spend with us, the Lord Jesus Christ whose birth we celebrate will touch your heart in some ineffable and unforgettable way.

[49]

Why are you here tonight? Some of you were raised in this parish and wouldn't dream of not coming, but others have no feeling about Christ's Church, Rye, one way or the other. Some of you have come alone tonight; others are with large families. Some of you made plans to be here and some of you decided to come on a last-minute impulse. Some of you have had arguments with other family members about coming to church tonight. Some of you have been dragged here against your will, out of loyalty or guilt or simple resignation to seasonal inevitability. Some of you are mourning the loss of loved ones whose names are on the memorial list, and others — many, *many* of whom I myself remember well and miss, very much, tonight. Those of you who are young tonight are full of hope and anticipation; most of your Christmases are still in front of you. Those who are older are filled with memories of the Christmases past that will never come again. Some of you look forward to going home to hearth and presents and tree; others dread going home. Whoever you are, and whatever condition you are in, I offer you a joyful welcome to the worship of our Lord and Savior tonight.

According to an article on the front page of today's *New York Times,* the Christmas Eve sermon is supposed to be the most difficult to write. I'm not so sure about that. On this night, we are all very much the same. Underneath our glossy suburban surface, underneath the blazers and fur coats, back of the ho-ho-hos, behind the lingering taste of the eggnog and the buzz of the wassail, there is a human soul — your own — yearning to hear a message of new beginnings, restored relationships, a hopeful future. Whoever you are, the preacher is here tonight in solidarity with you, a person who, like you, has known both the joy and the pain, the light and the shadow, the exuberant thrills and the bitter disappointments of this mortal life.

The day after tomorrow, I am taking my seven-year-old granddaughter to see *The Nutcracker* at Lincoln Center for the first time. Am I doing this for her? Not really. I am doing it for me. I want to reconnect with the magic. I want to see my favorite moment again. Much as I love the Christmas tree that grows and the snowflakes that dance, that's not the part that really gets to me. The scene that makes grown men and women choke up is the part where, after the scary mice are conclusively defeated, the little boy and the little girl, holding hands, begin their magical journey through the enchanted forest together, unafraid, the phantoms and monsters banished, the danger over and past, led and protected by a luminous star into a kingdom of radiant delight where men treat women like precious jewels, every child has a fairy godmother, and princesses never die — that is what we all want, an enchanted realm of happiness where no disappointment can never enter again.

Magic is what we want. What is Las Vegas, the "all-American city," but the illusion of magic? The illusion of magic puts millions of dollars in motion every December, as we give permission to the advertisers and the retailers and the entertainers to let us pretend for a few weeks that there really is such a thing as magic, even though we know, *we know* there isn't. One episode is all it takes to shatter the illusion: one year ago today, JonBenet Ramsay was murdered. One image is all it takes to dispel the enchantment; on the top of the front page of today's *Times* there is a searing photograph of a small, sobbing Mexican boy, his little body naked and bandaged, his mother massacred.[1] Where is the magic? We can send Christmas cards about peace on earth as often as we like, but that won't make peace happen. The human race is utterly incapable of turning itself around under its own steam. The children who go to see *The Nutcracker* will grow up to be victims of disappointment just like all the rest of us. There is no magical kingdom anywhere.

In another time and another place, in a world no better and no worse than this one, where men and women struggled against chaos and violence and darkness just as we do, St. Luke the Evangelist wrote a bewitching story. "In the sixth month the angel Gabriel was sent from God to a city of Galilee named Nazareth, to a virgin betrothed to a man whose name was Joseph, of the house of David; and the virgin's name was Mary. And . . . the angel said to her, 'Fear not, Mary, for you have found favor with God. And behold, you will conceive in your womb and bear a son, and you shall call his name Jesus. He will be . . . called the Son of the Most High; and the Lord God will give to him the throne of his father David, and he will reign over the house of Jacob for ever; *and of his kingdom there will be no end.'"*

You will notice that this is not a cutie-pie angel like that Raphael cherub that appears on coasters and shopping bags. It's not a fluffy, marcelled Victorian angel either. Angels in the Bible are always frightening. That's why the angel always says "Fear not." If it isn't frightening, it isn't an angel. The angel is scary because he[2] comes directly from the presence of God to earth. The angel of God brings news that God is breaking into this world order with power from another sphere altogether. Ultimately, everything we do tonight depends on that. If the angelic messenger is not telling the truth about the kingdom that has no end, then you have come out from your warm homes tonight to a folk festival, nothing more.

This service is not a mere celebration of a mother and her newborn child, either. Before long, virginal conceptions, by cloning or other means, may be commonplace events. This is not that sort of "miracle." This is the unique story of God incarnate. The proclamation of the angel is not from within this sphere at all. It is an announcement of an inbreaking event from somewhere else, *from the kingdom without end.* The infant in the manger is not us and we are not him. He is the Other. He has come from the "realms of glory." If the enchanted atmosphere of this night means anything at all, it means that something wonderful has broken through to us *from beyond ourselves.*

The baby is not a clone of any of us. If he were, he could do nothing to help us, because the human race has proven itself unable to turn itself around. We must be rescued from another dimension. So Jesus is not a creation either of God or of man; he is himself our Creator. If Jesus were not the only-begotten son of God, then this enchanted evening, however lovely, would be no more lasting or significant than a magician's illusion, and you and I are fools for imagining that it could be otherwise. And yet — and this is the mystery of Christmas — Jesus is the incarnation of the Creator God himself, but at the same time, though he is entirely Other than us, he has become *one of* us. Nothing less than God himself has become *Emmanu-el,* God with us. And more: he has come to share our life in a way that simply staggers imagination. He has not simply held out a bouquet to us. He has entered mortal existence in all its dimensions of regret, failure, heartbreak, disgrace, and death. The secret of Jesus, revealed in the Incarnation, is that he and he alone is fully present in *both* the human realm and the divine. In him, and in him alone we see God come to abide with us.

You have probably heard about the new Martin Scorsese movie about the Dalai Lama, *Kundun.* I have been intensely interested in Tibet and the Dalai Lama (who is my age) since I was fourteen years old and read *Seven Years in Tibet.* I still read everything about Tibet that I can get my hands on, and I will go to the movie next week. But it is very important to understand that when Tibetan Buddhists say that the Dalai Lama is an incarnation, they do not mean the same thing that we mean when we say the Nicene Creed. "God of God, Light of light, very God of very God. . . ." Jesus is not the umpteenth reappearance of an enlightened human being. Jesus is the only-begotten Son of God, *"of one substance* with [God] the Father."

I have thought and prayed long and hard about what I wanted to bring you tonight. God has brought me back to this pulpit after an absence of seventeen years. I am not the same person I was. I am a lot older and a lot wiser. I have seen many things, in my own family and among my parishioners, that I could only dimly imagine when I was in my thirties — many severe illnesses, much despondency, many misdeeds and failures, much death. So have most of you. We are all in this together. And so, on this holy night, what message do I bring?

Like all the rest of you, I am nothing more than what we used to call ourselves in the old Prayer Book a "miserable offender." One of my many sins is that I care a lot about being in fashion. But there is one way in which I have been strengthened to go against the current intellectual fashion. I am not embarrassed to stand here and tell you that I believe Jesus to be the unique Son of God, my Savior and my King. In and of myself I bring you nothing that will last any longer than these candle flames. But I do not bring just myself. For you whose ears are anointed by the Holy Spirit tonight, I bring *the gift of faith.* In an America where orthodox Christian belief is under pressure from every direction, I bring my deepest conviction, tested in the flame, that the ancient Christian message is the truth, yesterday, today, and forever.

And so, as a minister of the gospel among you on this blessed night, I declare to you that the baby in the manger is the Son of God. The message of the angel is that the course of human history has been reversed by the only One who has the power to reverse it. It is God himself who enters history on Christmas Eve, with the promise that in the kingdom that has no end, sadness will be turned into joy, sin will be vanquished by righteousness, and death will be overcome by resurrection. "For behold, I bring you good tidings of great joy, which shall be to all people, for unto you is born this day in the city of David a Savior who is Christ the Lord"; and "of his kingdom there shall be no end."

Amen.

Monsters at the Manger

GRACE CHURCH, NEW YORK CITY

A voice was heard in Ramah, wailing and loud lamentation,
Rachel weeping for her children, refusing to be comforted,
because they were no more.

Matthew 2:18

Every year at Christmastime I am amazed anew at the powerful hold on people's imaginations that the nativity story has. Everybody seems to like it. An acquaintance of mine who is stubbornly agnostic says that he reads it to himself every Christmas, but he does it in the bathroom where his atheist wife won't see him.

For most people in post-Christian America, the pulling power of the narrative is probably sentimental and nostalgic. People's attachment to the King James Version reinforces this probability. It is therefore more important than ever for those who take Christian faith seriously to be aware of the deep and far-reaching claims the story actually makes.

Can a mature, educated citizen of New York City in this day and age believe that Matthew and Luke were telling us some form of the truth? How are we going to tell the story to the next generation of children? Do the crèche figures really mean anything, or are they just decorations like nutcrackers and snowmen? Maybe you have heard about the "Reindeer Ruling," which was handed down by a court in

Pennsylvania a few years ago. The judges said it was all right to have a crèche on public property provided that Rudolphs and Santas were combined with the nativity scene. Amusing as this may be, it is also a good thing because it forces us churchgoers to think seriously about what sorts of distinctions we need to make, and why.

Today is the tenth day of the Twelve Days of Christmas. The fourth day is Holy Innocents Day, and the appointed reading for this Sunday is the story of Herod and his plan to get rid of the infant Jesus before he can grow up to become a threat. The Holy Family is wonderfully preserved by God, who sends them down to Egypt, but there is a wholesale massacre of baby boys back in Judea. This gruesome story is set right into the drama of the nativity by St. Matthew, and the Church from time immemorial has insisted on it as part of the Christmas celebration.

Most people don't know this, though. For various reasons, Christianity became very sentimental in the nineteenth century and has remained so ever since. To see the plain evidence of this, all you have to do is look at the words of the Christmas carols. The ones written before the Victorian era are full of references to Satan, sin, evil, death, and judgment. "The Holly and the Ivy" even has the blood of Jesus in it. The most unremitting of these older, more astringent carols is the sixteenth-century Coventry Carol. Don't let its gorgeous harmonies lull you into thinking it tells a pretty story. It doesn't. In fact, the Coventry Carol is quite a stark rendition of the story of the Slaughter of the Innocents.

> Herod the King in his raging
> Chargèd he hath this day
> His men of might, in his own sight
> All young children to slay.[1]

The key verse in Matthew's telling of this event is a quotation from the Old Testament: "What was said through the prophet Jeremiah is fulfilled: 'A voice is heard in Ramah, wailing and loud lamentation, Rachel weeping for her children, refusing to be comforted, because they are no more.'"

What does that make you think of? It makes me think of a remarkable speech by Geoffrey Canada, who heads an agency that serves poor children. The speech was reprinted on the op-ed page of the *Times* just before Christmas. The title of the article is "Monsters." Here is just one paragraph:

> Our children face monsters who kill in the night and the day, monsters who lurk in the dark. They see monsters on their way to school, in the park, in the hallways at night — monsters who leave traces of their brutal work, staining floors and walls, the vestiges of which tell of horrors unspeakable to such young minds. Our children know that we cannot see the monsters, not really, because if we saw them we would certainly protect them. What group of men and women would sacrifice their children to monsters?

As you can see, my sermon this morning is not for children. Today, Christmas is for adults. This is the time for looking at monsters and naming them. This is the time to entertain seriously the arguments against believing the Christmas story. Ivan Karama-zov in Dostoevsky's novel said that belief in God was not worth the suffering of even one child. We must listen to this objection again and again.

I took my mother to church on Christmas morning and we sang the familiar carols. My mother is a remarkable person, not afraid to ask the hard questions. As we were driving home after the service, suddenly she said, "'Joy to the world, the Savior reigns.' What on earth does that mean? The Savior doesn't reign. Just look at all the horrible things that are going on." That's an observation made to order for the tenth day of Christmas. In our reading today, we come up against the fact that, in the Christmas story as in today's world, the angels and the monsters coexist.

How can any reader of newspapers believe in angels? Did you have the feeling that I did on December 29 when two of the most evil stories about child abuse ever to be seen in the *Times* appeared on the front page? I try to maintain an Ivan-Karamazov-like sense of unblinking outrage about life, but I confess that those stories took me further into the sufferings of children than I wanted to go on the fifth day of Christmas. The details are much too ghastly to discuss here. Suffice it to say that the thought of a four-year-old boy being abducted, assaulted, and tortured for two whole days (imagine it!) and then hanged in a closet is a radical challenge to my faith. Where was that little boy's Savior during his indescribable ordeal? The mind reels, and we turn away.

If it were not for the Rachel passage, I believe the claims of the Christmas story would be unendurable. In that case, Baby Jesus and the angels and shepherds would have no more significance than Frosty the Snowman. This Christmas and every Christmas, the Rachel passage says to us that we can't run away from the suffering of the world. The suffering of the world is part of the story.

Everybody knows Handel's *Messiah,* and a goodly portion of the Manhattan population goes to hear it every Christmas. I wish that more people had an opportunity to hear Hector Berlioz' *L'Enfance du Christ.* It tells the story of the Slaughter of the Innocents and the Flight into Egypt. Among its many wonders is its tender, wrenching, deeply moving description of the Holy Family as they undergo terrifying hardships as refugees. Think of it — Jesus was a refugee, like the Somalians, the Haitians, the Kurds! Berlioz shows them fleeing from the tyranny of Herod, meeting with contempt along the way because they are Jews, almost starving to death, taken in at last by a family of compassionate heathen Ishmaelites.

It is the paranoia of King Herod that drives the Holy Family into exile. In a memorable portion of Berlioz' oratorio we hear Herod working himself up into a homicidal frenzy. Like many a tyrant, he is pathologically insecure, only too ready to undertake mass murder to shore up his own position. Like Pontius Pilate some thirty-two or three years later, he senses his own overthrow in the presence of Jesus. Like Pilate, like every tyrant, Herod knew better than God's own people that the reign of a Savior meant the end of his own.

According to a recent news article, most churches in besieged Sarajevo gave up having worship services months ago. However, a Christmas Eve service was held a few days ago in St. Anthony's

Roman Catholic Church in the heavily damaged city center. For safety, it was conducted underground, in a basement. Astonishingly, the standing-room-only crowd contained Muslims and Jews as well as Catholics. One young Jewish woman, a literature student, was asked by a reporter why she had come. "We [the people of Sarajevo] have shared everything else," she said. "I just wanted to be here with all the others to share this."

The parish priest, Father Lucic, stood before a makeshift altar laid out on top of a desk and said, "How can we speak of a happy Christmas as we stand here in the heart of this besieged city, ruined by artillery fire, with cemeteries filled with those who have died, with those of us who remain having to survive without electricity, heat, water, or . . . food? What is there left in life for us to celebrate when we have lost fathers, mothers, brothers, sons, and even our children? Why should we lift our hearts when . . . we must worry whether we will be raped, or slaughtered with a knife, or simply beaten to death?"

The priest then began to speak of Jesus' suffering and death, especially the sense of abandonment he felt at the time of the Crucifixion.[2] This, the reporter says in a telling phrase, was "the comfort Father Lucic offered from the Christian Gospels." The priest's final words were, "Jesus teaches us that human judgments are not the last judgments, that human justice is not the last justice, and that the power that humans exercise over one another is not the final power."

How can we believe this? How can we go on singing "Joy to the world, the Savior reigns," in view of the fact that the monsters continue to devour the children with undiminished ferocity?

The Christmas story is anchored to our lives and to the wickedness of this world by the grief of Rachel, "weeping for her children, refusing to be comforted, because they are no more."[3] The authors of Scripture did not turn away from the unimaginable suffering of children. God the Father did not turn away. Jesus did not turn away. We see in his death on the Cross and in his Resurrection from the dead the source of our conviction that "human judgments are not the last judgments, that human justice is not the last justice, and that the power that humans exercise over one another is not the final power." But we must keep Ivan Karamazov's protest in our minds every day. The nativity story might as well be about reindeer and snowmen for sure, if it has nothing to say about the small victims. I believe that, by putting Rachel's lament at the heart of the Christmas story, Matthew has shown us how to hold on to faith and hope until the Second Coming. Only as we share in the prayers and the laments of bereaved families, not looking away, can we continue to believe that the Savior reigns even now in the faith and tenacity of Father Lucic and all those who continue to stand for humanity in the face of barbarity. Only by attending to the horrors of this world can we continue to sing the words of that great eighteenth-century hymn-writer Isaac Watts:

> He comes to make his blessings known
> Far as the curse is found.
>
> (Hymn, "Joy to the World")

For only a faith forged out of suffering can say with conviction that the angels and monsters will not coexist forever, that Muslims and agnostics and Christians and Jews will be drawn together in ways that we cannot yet imagine, that the agonies of the victims will some day be rectified, and that the unconditional love of God in Jesus Christ will be the Last Word.

Amen.

Who Are Those Magi?

ST. JOHN'S CHURCH, SALISBURY, CONNECTICUT

*And I saw no temple in the city, for its temple is the Lord
God the Almighty and the Lamb. And the city has no need
of sun or moon to shine upon it, for the glory of God is its
light, and its lamp is the Lamb. By its light shall the nations
walk; and the kings of the earth shall bring their glory into
it . . . and its gates shall never be shut by day — and there
shall be no night there; they shall bring into it the glory and
the honor of the nations.*

Revelation 21:22-26

The famous story of the Wise Men, or Magi, is the centerpiece
of the Feast of the Epiphany. The tale is known, in a vague sort
of way, even to people who are almost completely ignorant of Scripture. I learned the other day that a pair of faithful parishioners who
were trying to find out the names of the three Wise Men looked in
vain. They were looking in the wrong Gospel, for one thing; the
story is not found in Luke, but in Matthew. Furthermore, their names
are not found in Scripture at all. The New Testament does not even
tell us how many Wise Men there were; it just says, "Behold, wise
men from the East came to Jerusalem." The names and the number
three come from much later tradition, as does the far-fetched claim
that their bones are buried in the cathedral at Cologne.

The Wise Men, whether three or thirty-three, have always been favorites. The Old Masters specialized in painting their exotic features; costume designers have had a field day with velvet and fur and gold lamé; wood carvers have painted their crèche figures with silver gilt, and the illustrators of Christmas cards return again and again to those stately camels, those swaying palm trees and that resplendent star gleaming in the night air of the Arabian desert. If the desert is covered with snow, that's all right too. As is so often the case, the original Bible story has been decorated with so many fanciful details that it is hard to recover the simplicity and restraint of the original narrative.

When Matthew put the story of the Magi in writing, he was not telling a tale just for the fun of it, certainly not for the benefit of painters, sculptors, and pageant directors. Least of all did he write in order to inspire the faithful to make pilgrimages to tombs in cathedrals. If we look at the Biblical story with all our preconceptions set aside, something quite different emerges.

Each of the four evangelists — Matthew, Mark, Luke, and John — has a different angle on the story of the Messiah. It's important to know something about each one. Matthew begins his story with the simple statement that the Virgin Mary "gave birth to a son and . . . gave him the name Jesus." Matthew doesn't tell us anything about shepherds or mangers. Everything he wants us to know is in the story of the Magi. "After Jesus was born in Bethlehem of Judea, during the time of Herod the King, Magi from the East came to Jerusalem."

Who were these Magi? Matthew doesn't explain, because his contemporaries were familiar with the term. Originally they were a caste of Zoroastrian priests, but by Jesus' time the term Magi had a broader application. It referred to a respected class of scholars who devoted themselves to the study of natural sciences, medicine, mathematics, astronomy, and astrology. Where in "the East" did they come from? They could have been from modern Iran or Iraq, Arabia or even India — we simply don't know. For Matthew, they represent the very best of the pagan world. These travellers from the mysterious East have no Scripture, no salvation history, no covenant, no special revelation — they do not even know the name of the God whose manifestation they seek — but they have nevertheless undertaken a journey which (we can rightly assume) was of great length and hardship.[1] They are led by an astral phenomenon, by their own studies, and by what they have heard concerning a "King of the Jews."

It is clear that in Matthew's eyes the Magi are noble and enlightened figures. However, they were not kings. Where did the idea come from that they were kings? Here's how it happened. Not very long after the New Testament became Scripture, Christians began to notice some verses in the Old Testament that sounded a lot like Matthew's account of the Magi. The first of these is from Psalm 72:10-11: "The Kings of Tarshish and the Isles shall offer presents. The Kings of the Arabians and of Sheba shall bring gifts. Yea, all kings shall fall down before him: all nations shall serve him." The second is from the prophet Isaiah: "Kings shall come to the brightness of thy rising . . . herds of camels will cover your land . . . and all from Sheba will come, bringing gold and frankincense" (Isaiah 60:3, 6). That's where the camels in the Christmas crèche come from — not from the Christmas story at all, but from the Old Testament. Early Christian Biblical interpretation attached the prophetic passages to Matthew's story. This is a very different matter from giving the Magi names and personal histories and burial places totally unrelated to the Biblical record. On the important principle of allowing Scripture to interpret Scripture, we may follow the lead of the early interpreters and think of the Magi as representative, not only of pagan learning and wisdom, but also of the power and wealth of heathen nations who come to bow down before the King of Israel. The point is that they were Gentiles, outside the covenant of promise.

There is a passage in the book of Revelation which I have taken as my text today. St. John describes the city of God, the New Jerusalem: "I saw no temple in the city, for its temple is the Lord God the Almighty and the Lamb. And the city has no need of sun or moon to shine upon it, for the glory of God is its light, and its lamp is the Lamb. By its light shall the nations walk; and *the kings of the earth shall bring their glory into it* . . . and its gates shall never be shut by day — and there shall be no night there; they shall bring into it the glory and the honor of the nations."

Here, I believe, is a way for us to understand something of what Matthew wants us to see. In the Age to Come, the whole world will bring its treasures into the celestial city. Everything that is honorable, beautiful, and good will be taken up into the kingdom of Christ, the Lamb of God. Everything that is glorious and effulgent will be offered as a tribute to the One whose Name is "King of kings and Lord of lords." Great art, music, poetry, science, mathematics, whether overtly Christian in origin or not, will become part of the pageantry of heaven glorifying the crucified, risen, and reigning Messiah, Jesus Christ. This is the way I read the passage from Revelation; it makes a wonderful combination not only with Matthew's story of the Magi, but also with many passages from Isaiah like the one which Handel, God bless him, set so memorably to music in *Messiah:* "Arise, shine; for thy light is come, and the glory of the LORD is risen upon thee. . . . And the Gentiles shall come to thy light, and kings to the brightness of thy rising" (Isaiah 60:1-3).

These are very bold claims, politically incorrect in the extreme. The mood in America today is hostile to the vision of Isaiah and Matthew. Christians are being charged with cultural and religious imperialism. It is widely believed nowadays — in what used to be Christian America — that, for those who insist on being religious, one religion is as good as another, and that the missionary zeal of Christianity is an embarrassment. I don't really see any way out of this dilemma. Christians believe in the unique divinity of Christ and his Lordship over the entire cosmos. The God who created the stars and, as Isaiah says, called them all by name, has not set up a separate system of spiritual discernment apart from Christ.

I had to put my car in the shop last Thursday in Litchfield and I had plenty of time to walk around. Right on the village green, opposite the stunning white Congregational Church, in that most classic of all New England towns, there was a shop advertising horoscopes, crystals, Tarot cards, and other occult paraphernalia. Is this just harmless fantasy, or commercial opportunity, or is it a question of "whatever works for you"? Is it all just part of the new religious smorgasbord? When confronted by religious phenomena, the Christian will ask a simple question: *Does this point to Christ?* The Wise Men grasped the message of the star, not as a guide to personal good fortune or spiritual enlightenment, but as a sign of the Messiah, not only for the "religious" people (the Jews), but for the heathen Gentiles (that's us) as well. The thing about the Magi is that they recognized Jesus Christ as the one to whom they owed their ultimate allegiance. Their astrology led them, not to messages about romance and good fortune, but to the Messiah of Israel. Matthew is telling us that the homage paid to the Christ child by the Magi prefigures the time when the whole world will recognize and bow before Jesus Christ, as St. Paul says: "Every knee shall bend, in heaven and on earth and under the earth, and every tongue confess that Jesus Christ is Lord, to the glory of God the Father" (Philippians 2:10-11).

As you know, I have spent most of my ministry in New York City. A significant number of my good friends are secular, un-churched people. Many of them have deep scorn for Christianity. I believe this is a fact of American life that, more and more, we believers are going to have to face. It is going to take more intellectual and moral courage to be a confessing, practicing Christian than it used to. We are all going to have to take our stand before Herod. The Magi should be a great comfort to us. They brought all that they had to the Lord, not just their expensive presents, but their very lives. We, too, have our own journeys — you and I. We must come through our own deserts and across our own mountains. We must follow whatever star is given to us. But, dear people of God, let us be sure that our stars point to Christ. There are many false Messiahs in the world. There are many gods that are not the God and Father of our Lord and Savior. Let us not be led off into trackless paths leading to this or that religious novelty. The only God of the religious and the irreligious alike is the God whom we find revealed in his Word — the Holy Scriptures of the Church.

Now, please note one more thing. Across the path of the Magi falls the shadow of the Cross:

Myrrh is mine, its bitter perfume
Breathes a life of gathering gloom;
Sorrowing, sighing, bleeding, dying,
Sealed in the stone-cold tomb.

(Hymn, "We Three Kings,"
by John Henry Hopkins, Jr.)

The baby sought by the Wise Men was born to save, not just the good religious people, but even more, those who are *not* the chosen, *not* the beloved, *not* the initiated, *not* the deserving. This baby was born to live and die, as the apostle Paul says, "for the *un*godly" (Romans 5:6). But not just to die. His death would have passed forgotten had he not been God incarnate. That is the rock-bottom truth on which everything about our faith is founded. When the parade is over, when the costumes are put back into the closet, when the New England winter seems to go on forever and there is nothing but Ash Wednesday to look forward to, when the sophisticated scoff and the despots rage, then it is that we most truly gather around the central proclamation of our faith:

Glorious now behold him arise,
King, and God, and sacrifice.
Prayer and praising, all men raising,
Worship him, God most high.

Amen.

The Bottomless Glass

ST. JOHN'S CHURCH, WASHINGTON, CONNECTICUT

On the third day there was a marriage at Cana in Galilee, and the mother of Jesus was there; Jesus also was invited to the marriage, with his disciples. When the wine failed, the mother of Jesus said to him, "They have no wine." And Jesus said to her, "O woman, what have you to do with me? My hour has not yet come." His mother said to the servants, "Do whatever he tells you." Now six stone jars were standing there, for the Jewish rites of purification, each holding twenty or thirty gallons. Jesus said to them, "Fill the jars with water." And they filled them up to the brim. He said to them, "Now draw some out, and take it to the steward of the feast." So they took it. When the steward of the feast tasted the water now become wine, and did not know where it came from (though the servants who had drawn the water knew), the steward of the feast called the bridegroom and said to him, "Every man serves the good wine first; and when men have drunk freely, then the poor wine; but you have kept the good wine until now." This, the first of his signs, Jesus did at Cana in Galilee, and manifested his glory; and his disciples believed in him.

John 2:1-11

Not long ago I attended a memorial event in a secular setting. The tributes and reminiscences went on for about an hour and a quarter. Most of them were very well done, but during the more self-indulgent ones I found my attention drifting. I began wondering what trivial anecdotes people would tell about me some day as though they revealed the inmost depths of my character. I wondered how many of the other people present were thinking the same thing. After the various speakers had finished, there was a luncheon. Those of us at my table talked about how, as we grow older, much of our lives consist of going to funerals. T. S. Eliot's line from *The Waste Land* came to mind: "I had not thought death had undone so many."

The conversation turned to the subject of *regret*. The great French cabaret singer Edith Piaf was known for her song *"Non, je ne regrette rien"* (No, I regret nothing). Could this be true? I wondered aloud; isn't regret a part of life? We all agreed that it was. We agreed ruefully that as we look back, we have a sense of opportunities lost, time wasted, careers derailed, relationships spoiled, youth fled.

I often read the personal ads in magazines. Nowhere will you find a more comprehensive index of human longing. The wittiest and most literary ones are, predictably, in *The New York Review of Books*. They are almost Shakespearean in their range and variety, depicting human foibles in the most elegant disguises. Here is my all-time favorite:

> REFLECTING OVER THE PAST, it seems at mid-life that there's not much more time to search for dreams. Married man of means and mien looks for a woman who feels that there should have been more to it all. Age and marital status unimportant. Discretion assured.

That's an exceptionally poignant and candid summary of the regret at the heart of human life. Note this man's description of himself: "means and mien." He's got money and he's distinguished-looking. "There is not much more time to search for dreams. . . . There should have been more to it all." If you are too young to know this feeling, don't worry, you'll get there sooner or later.

The wording of this married man's ad grabs me. Most personals have a bogus, pasted-on veneer of confidence, but not this one. This man is letting his guts show. Obviously disappointed in his marriage, he seeks a fling to restore his hopes, his youth, his future. He has the "means" to pay for the fine wines, the tailored suits, the cruises and the opera tickets, but there is a wistful sense of deprivation in what he has written. Doesn't this illustrate the paradox of affluent America today? — amidst our obsessive piling up of possessions and seeking after status, we suffer from a sense that we are still hungry, still thirsty. Instead of singing defiantly with Piaf that we regret nothing, there are times when we are more likely to be asking with Miss Peggy Lee, "Is that all there is?"

"There's not much more time to search for dreams." I do not believe there is any one within earshot today, however well defended, who does not recognize the creeping chill of that feeling — "there should have been more to it all." And when this feeling assails us, when this sense of having been deprived gnaws at us, we take refuge in all sorts of escapes; we buy something and charge it, we drink, we pop a pill, we grab for sexual adventure, we throw a lavish party, we read the latest self-help book or go to the guru of the moment. Some even climb Mount Everest, only to discover that, in the words of one who did, "I wondered if I had not come a long way only to find that what I really sought was something I had left behind."[1] And so at the very center of life we learn that even in moments of apparent victory there lies close under the surface the ceaseless craving of the human heart.

In today's reading from John's Gospel, we discover Jesus at a wedding where the wine has run out. We can imagine the dismayed host saying, "Is that all there is?"

The marriage ceremony in Cana of Galilee in Biblical times was not at all like an Episcopal wedding. A wedding party in small-town Palestine would have been, hands down, the event of the year for most of the participants. People looked forward to a marriage celebration for months. The partying went on for seven days.[2] Rabbis abandoned their fasts and students their studies. Everyone brought presents, and in return, the host was expected to keep his guests well supplied with food, drink, music, and merrymaking. It was therefore more than a minor disappointment to have the wine run out. It was a catastrophe.

So Jesus was at this wedding, and his mother came to him and reported, "They have no wine."

Now this story of Jesus' first miracle at Cana is not so easy to explain. There are a lot of things going on at a lot of different levels, and there are some discrepancies and distractions, too. One of the most obvious distractions is Jesus' reply to his mother, "Woman, what have you to do with me?" Some people are so undone by Jesus' supposed rudeness to his mother that they never get past that to the center of the story. The fact is that Jesus is doing, here, what he does at several other points in the Gospels; he is declaring his independence of the usual human ties and obligations.[3] He is not rude to his mother, but in his refusal to call her "mother," he sets a distance between her and himself. (If you see the new movie *Kundun*, about the Dalai Lama, you will see a similar formality between the boy ruler and his mother.) Jesus lives, not according to human arrangements, but according to God's will. He must listen to another voice. The time of his mother's authority is over.

Notice Mary's response. If her feelings are hurt, she does not let that get in the way. She is, as always, the model of the true believer. She relinquishes her special relationship. She insists on nothing. She suggests nothing. She demands nothing. She understands that something more than human motherhood is here. But Mary is not passive. Notice how she responds. Even though she has no idea what Jesus might do, she makes a space for him to act. She speaks to the servants, saying, "Whatever he tells you, do it."

Now let's focus for a moment on the wedding party itself. On the surface, no doubt, everything looked fabulous. Jewish families of Jesus' time, like families of every time, would have spared no expense. I'm reminded of the most lavish wedding I ever went to. It was obvious to everyone who attended that hundreds of thousands had been spent. However — and as Dave Barry says, I am not making this up — they ran out of food. As I approached the head of the line, the last slice of the filet mignon was being served. It almost seemed farcical. To complete the picture, I should tell you that the bride and groom are now divorced. "There should have been more to it all."

There's something else wrong at the wedding at Cana in Galilee. There are those water-pots standing by. Do you know why they were there? They were there for the Jewish rite of purification. They are "a reminder that all is not well and that there is a need greater than that of a further supply of wine."[4] Water from them is used for the washing away of sin. It is used, but it doesn't work. It doesn't improve the situation. It is tasteless and colorless and joyless and it doesn't take away sin. The Epistle to the Hebrews tells us that religious rituals "can never make perfect those who draw near. . . . In these sacrifices [these purifications] there is a reminder of sin, year after year" (Hebrews 10:1-3). The water in the story represents all our human attempts, and especially our religious attempts, to make things right.[5] We may chase after women, or men, or four-star restaurants, or the perfectly buffed body, or the ultimate religious experience, but there is no one of us who does not know the fear of the news that comes at last — "There isn't any more." Even Sir Isaiah Berlin, that great man who perhaps had less reason for regret than most of us, noted shortly before his recent death that he did not at all like the idea of life coming to an end.[6]

Now back to the story. "Do whatever he tells you," says Mary to the servants. Jesus says, "Fill the jars with water." This is a big order. Each jar held 15 to 25 gallons, and there were six jars. At a minimum then, we are talking about 90 gallons (most scholars suggest at least 120 gallons). If there are 4 quarts to a gallon and each quart yields six glasses, that's a minimum total of two thousand, one hundred and sixty glasses.[7] The servants, trusting Jesus, haul this huge amount of water and fill the jars. Jesus says, "Now draw some out, and take it to the steward of the feast."

The evangelist John is a great storyteller. He doesn't bore us by saying anything so pedestrian as, "The steward tasted the water and discovered that it had turned into wine." Instead, the next thing we hear is the steward's exuberant shout to the host, congratulating him: "Everybody else I know puts the good wine out first and then when people's taste buds are shot, they bring out the cheap stuff. But you have kept back your good wine until now!"

I want you to feel this in your inmost being. What has Jesus done? Twenty-one hundred glasses of the finest vintage for one little wedding party in a backwater village! What does this mean?

It is the Gospel of John that gives us Jesus' words, "I am come that they might have life, and that they might have it more abundantly" (10:10). The wine so freely given represents Jesus' gift of himself. He is the "bread of life," the "light of the world," the "true vine," the "good shepherd," the "resurrection and the life" (John, chapters 6, 9, 15, 10, and 11). Every Jew in Jesus' time knew that the wedding feast, throughout the Hebrew Bible, was the primary image of salvation, the banquet of redemption in the Kingdom of God. And so when Jesus, *at a wedding,* poured out more good wine than anyone had ever seen, those who had eyes to see and ears to hear recognized that the future blessings of the heavenly kingdom had become present in the miracle of Jesus. "This," John writes, "the first of his signs, Jesus did at Cana in Galilee, and manifested his glory; and his disciples believed in him."

This is my first visit to your parish. For the first time in my twenty-two years of ministry I find myself nowadays preaching, more often than not, to congregations I do not know. It is much easier to preach to the same people every week; if you miss the target one Sunday, you get another chance the next. This may be the only chance I get with you. I take this responsibility very seriously. As I prepared this sermon, I asked the Lord in prayer to give me his Spirit and his Word this morning so that my visit will be a visit not from myself, but from him.

Jesus of Nazareth steps on the scene. He sees our predicament. He hears our news — *the wine has run out,* and we are still in our sins. He sees us, he sees our whole society, he sees the whole world full of disease and violence and cruelty and death, afflicted with conditions that religious rituals have never been able to improve. He sees us, he loves us, and he has come to pour out his life for us. The message of Christmas was that the Son of God is born among us. The message of Epiphany is that the Son of God is powerful to save. Whenever you find yourself asking, "Is that all there is?" remember: *no, it is not all.* There is the promise of God through faith in Jesus Christ, and that is everything. And please understand this: the promise of Jesus does not refer only to some far-off future day. He gives his life to us now, not a life of partying and drinking and conspicuous consumption ending in emptiness, but a life of service to others and to God's suffering world, a life that is built not on chasing dreams and fantasies, but being built by the Holy Spirit into a fellowship of love that gathers even now at the Lord's table. He, the only-begotten, the Messiah of Israel, is the One, the only One who is able to give purification, the only One who is able to wipe away regret forever, the only One in whose name we find ourselves redeemed and restored and brought into an eternal future where there will be no need to search for dreams, because the dream of all humanity is summed up in the Cross and in the Resurrection of our Lord Jesus Christ. He goes to prepare a place for us at his own unending banquet. May he confirm this truth in your hearts, today and for ever.

Amen.

The Meeting of the Lord[1]

ST. JOHN'S CHURCH, SALISBURY, CONNECTICUT

{Simeon} took {the baby Jesus} up in his arms and blessed God and said, "Lord, now lettest thou thy servant depart in peace, according to thy word; for mine eyes have seen thy salvation which thou hast prepared in the presence of all peoples, a light for revelation to the Gentiles, and to be the glory of thy people Israel."

Luke 2:28-32

The Feast of the Presentation of our Lord in the Temple at Jerusalem comes on Sunday only once in seven years, so this is a rare opportunity. The purpose of this special celebration today, however, is not to warm your heart with a lovely service but for one thing only: to draw your attention to the story of the recognition of Jesus by Simeon and Anna.

Many Episcopalians know the Song of Simeon, or, as it is called, the *Nunc Dimittis,* because those are the words in Latin for the first phrase of the familiar poem, or canticle: "Now lettest thou thy servant depart in peace, according to thy word, for mine eyes have seen thy salvation." Those words, and the man who spoke them, Simeon, are at the center of our worship today.

Yesterday morning here in Salisbury, it looked to me as though about two thirds of our congregation was in attendance at the screening of the documentary about the 10th Mountain Division. I was amazed at the number of local men who were in that fabled unit. The film made quite an impression on me for a number of reasons, but for now I will just identify one theme — that of youth and age. The "10th Mountain men" were mostly in their very early twenties during World War II, at the peak of their physical capacities. Fifty-five years later, they are in their seventies. They are an extraordinarily fit-looking crew even today, but nevertheless, there are inevitable diminishments. Looking back on what we did when we were young and strong is certain to evoke reflection on what life has meant, what it all adds up to, what the point of it all is, and what God expects of us as we get older and can no longer engage in heroic exploits. The themes that were repeated over and over by the veterans in the film were not those of youth. They were the things that we prize more and more as we get older: friendship, brotherhood, sacrifice.

Simeon and Anna, the two characters that figure in today's story, are extremely old. However, they represent the very best that Israel stood for. They were veterans in the service, so to speak. We can compare them to those in the military who keep watch. This is not the most glamorous assignment, but it is indispensable. We are all familiar with the Navy expression, "on my watch." We don't want anything bad to happen on our watch, because if it does, our comrades will suffer from our negligence, and we will be responsible.

What sort of watch were Simeon and Anna keeping? We are told that Simeon was "looking for the consolation of Israel," and that Anna, who spent every day and evening in the Temple fasting and praying, was "looking for the redemption of Jerusalem." These are two different ways of saying that they were bending every bit of their remaining energy and strength toward the expectation, toward the hope, of God's promised Messiah. Their whole lives had been directed toward that end. In fact, "it had been revealed to [Simeon] by the Holy Spirit that he should not see death before he had seen the Lord's Christ."

What exactly was the Messiah expected to be? For the great

majority of the people, the Messiah was envisioned as a commanding, even military figure who would rescue the Jews from domination by the hated Romans and restore the nation of Israel to the glory of King David's time. In other words, most people's idea of the Messiah was thoroughly predictable; he would make them Top Nation, Number One. That's what you and I would have wanted too. Patriotism, after all, is one of the strongest human motivations.

Simeon and Anna are in a different category. They are both prophets, meaning that the Holy Spirit is directing them.[2] They do not see with ordinary human sight. They are enabled to discern the action of God in the world when it is hidden from others, because God has called them for this purpose.[3] You will notice that I did not say, "They are *able* to discern . . ." but "They are *enabled*." They do not have this capacity by nature or by human effort. It is God's doing. He is at work, not only in the infant Jesus, but in the hearts and minds of those who see him with faith. They are *enabled* by God's Spirit to recognize the Messiah's presence in this absurdly unlikely situation as the two poor and humble parents from the bottom rung of Judaean society come inconspicuously into the Temple to perform their duty according to the Law of Moses.

I am not able to visualize the scene as St. Luke describes it without reference to the painting of it by Rembrandt, even though I haven't seen it in the flesh since I was twenty years old (it is in The Hague). The first impression one gets is of the vastness of the temple interior, as though it were the largest of large cathedrals. Rembrandt had considerable knowledge of the Jewish community in Amsterdam and was friendly with many Jews. He was interested in synagogues and drew on them for inspiration in painting the Jerusalem Temple.[4] He has portrayed an extraordinarily imposing space. Crowds of people are milling about in the background, as they do in any large city house of worship. Some of them are there to pray, but many of them are there as tourists. They don't know and don't care about the little family group kneeling before the High Priest. Mary has come with her husband and baby to fulfill her obligation under the Law of Moses. We should pause to note how thoroughly Jewish it all is. There was a time when Christians scarcely realized that Jesus was Jewish. More and more today, after all that has happened, it is urgent that we remember how very Jewish he was, how he was born into and raised by a devout Jewish family. Mary and Joseph, Simeon and Anna are the epitome of faithful Jews. Luke wants us to see that Jesus is no interloper; he emerges from the very heart of Hebrew history and life. Luke is telling us that both the Law (Mary observes the Law) and the Prophets (Simeon and Anna are both prophets) are fulfilled in Jesus.

In Rembrandt's picture, a ray of light from a window high up in the dim structure falls upon the little group. Mary and Joseph are too poor to bring a lamb; they have presented their two pigeons to the High Priest, who, in his imposing regalia, is silhouetted with his back to us. All the attention is on the moment of recognition as the old man takes the baby in his arms, just as Luke describes it, and opens his mouth to say, It is he! I have been waiting all my life to see him! "Lord, now lettest thou thy servant depart in peace, according to thy word; for mine eyes have seen thy salvation, which thou hast prepared in the presence of all peoples, a light for revelation to the Gentiles, and to be the glory of thy people Israel."

Anna is not in Rembrandt's picture; she arrives a moment later, we are told: "And coming up at that very hour she gave thanks to God, and spoke of him to all who were looking for the redemption of Jerusalem."

Simeon and Anna are models for us. Simeon knows by the power of the Spirit that, at the end of life, the one thing that counts is the meeting with Christ the Lord. Now he can die in peace, according to the Lord's promise. He has fulfilled his watch. He has kept the faith. He has hailed the conqueror. Anna has never ceased throughout decades of widowhood to keep hope alive. Now that she has received her heart's desire she immediately responds by doing two things: by praising God, and by telling others.

This is the Epiphany season, a very happy time in the church year. I for one hate to see it come to an end. Lent is right around the corner. But the New Testament always gives us hints of Lent even in the midst of joy. After the beautiful *Nunc Dimittis,* Simeon has something more to say, something more disturbing. He tells

Mary: "Behold, this child is set for the fall and rising of many in Israel, and for a sign that is spoken against (and a sword will pierce through your own soul also)." Even in the overwhelmingly joyful moment of revelation the shadow of the Cross is already present. This is not Alexander the Great, this is not Napoleon, this is not Winston Churchill or General Eisenhower. This is a man who for his triumphal entry into Jerusalem thirty-three years later will come riding absurdly on a donkey. This is a man who will stand with his hands bound before the Roman procurator and will refuse even to defend himself. This is the man who will be pinned up naked by the roadside to be mocked and vilified by the passersby.

On this Feast of the Presentation, as we reflect on Simeon and Anna in the context of our own lives, we need to be thinking of the ways that the Holy Spirit is moving among us. It is not the same thing as being decorated with a Silver Star for exceptional gallantry. After the film yesterday one of the 10th Mountain men, Edward Nickerson, was introduced with a flourish as one who had won a Silver Star. He gently but firmly brushed aside the implied obeisance by saying a very generous and very wise thing: "Nobody knows who deserves what." How true that is. Only God knows what silent and unnoticed heroism is going on anonymously as unheeding crowds swirl past. It is in the watching, it is in the waiting, it is in the patience and the self-sacrifice and the trust in God's promises that the meaning of life is learned. There is comradeship and brotherhood and love to be had, not just on the battlefields of bygone days, but now, today, in the midst of the much more mundane but nevertheless still crucial battles against sin and death that we all must fight. In Jesus Christ, there is redemption and hope and the promise of transformed life — through suffering, yes, but as St. Paul wrote, "I consider that the sufferings of this present time are not worth comparing with the glory that is to be revealed in us" (Romans 8:18).

And so I repeat: the purpose of this special celebration today is not to warm your heart with a lovely service. It is for one thing only: to draw your attention to the meeting of Jesus with Simeon and Anna, that you should recognize that you too are called to meet him at this very hour. His Body and Blood are given to sustain you on all your battlefields, in all assaults of your enemies, and ultimately for the most miraculous thing of all, the transformation of your enemies into friends and brothers. For the Son of God comes not only "for the glory of his people Israel" but also for those Gentiles who did not know him and did not care; and that, we should not forget, might have meant you and me, cast off forever. Instead, he gives himself to the last breath, the last drop of blood, in the final assault by the powers of darkness. Do not fail to greet him today, and, like Simeon and Anna, to sign on in his service — the service that is perfect freedom.

Amen.

The Love Olympics
Go to Jerusalem

TRINITY CHURCH, COPLEY SQUARE, BOSTON

Love bears all things, believes all things, hopes all things, endures all things. Love never ends. . . .

I Corinthians 13:7-8

Now about eight days after these sayings Jesus took with him Peter and John and James, and went up on the mountain to pray. And as he was praying, the appearance of his countenance was altered, and his raiment became dazzling white. And behold, two men talked with him, Moses and Elijah, who appeared in glory and spoke of his departure, which he was to accomplish at Jerusalem.

Luke 9:28-31

Two weeks ago there was a very funny little article in *The New York Times* Styles section about the fact that this year, for the first time in decades, Valentine's Day fell on the Saturday of a three-day holiday weekend. How long, the writer wondered, was the romantic mood expected to continue? After the roses and the chocolates and the candlelight dinner on Saturday night, then what to do for an encore on Sunday? Must you do it all over again? The writer continued, "What about Monday? Can you get out of there by then? What is this anyway — some sort of love Olympics?"[1]

Valentine's Day inspired all sorts of musings this month. The columnist Frank Rich wrote, "After three intense weeks of the most graphic national discussion of sex in the history of the Republic, we have finally arrived at Valentine's Day. How can we reclaim romance from a culture in which love-making is now a transaction to be described by Peeping Toms, recorded on tape, collected as DNA evidence and parsed into semantic distinctions that are the legal answer to the Kama Sutra?"[2]

Even the word "love" is in trouble. According to the latest issue of *Vanity Fair,* Madonna has ended her relationship with the father of her celebrated baby. That's no surprise to anyone. The little girl, however, will continue to be referred to from time to time as a "love child." The pull-quote from the Frank Rich column seems relevant here: "What's love got to do with it?"

On the Sunday following the first revelations about the White House intern, the President and the First Lady attended the morning service at Foundry Methodist Church in Washington. The pastor, who knew they were coming, chose I Corinthians 13 as a reading. "If I speak in the tongues of men and of angels, but have not love, I am a noisy gong or a clanging cymbal. And if I have prophetic powers, and understand all mysteries and all knowledge, and if I have all faith, so as to remove mountains, but have not love, I am nothing." It's pretty likely that the members of the congregation that day in our nation's capital were hearing some static on the line as the passage continued: "When I was a child, I spoke like a child, I thought like a child, I reasoned like a child; when I became a man, I gave up childish ways."

This same chapter on love was selected recently for a famous televised occasion in England. At the funeral of Diana, Princess of Wales, Prime Minister Tony Blair read it with conviction. But as the chosen Scripture reading for that service in Westminster Abbey, what was it intended to refer to? Mr. Blair is a churchgoer himself, so very possibly he understood it in its Biblical context, but what did the two billion television viewers think? The passage is often read at weddings, but no one could possibly have understood it on that day as a reference to married love. Were St. Paul's words supposed to remind us of the love of a mother for her sons, or the love of a princess for her people, or the love of the people for her, or what? Most likely, it was heard as a sort of all-purpose tribute to a generic idea of love. But that is precisely what the passage is not.

It has often been noted that the famous Corinthian chapter on love really describes Jesus. He is the supreme model of mature love, today and forever. Jesus "is patient and kind"; Jesus "is not jealous or boastful"; Jesus "is not arrogant or rude." The capacity to postpone gratification lies at the very heart of mature love: Jesus "does not insist on his own way." The love of Jesus "never ends." It's a good bet that most wedding guests hearing I Corinthians 13 understand it sentimentally, not being aware that the passage is really about the love of Christ as it takes shape in the Christian community. In actuality Paul's words have nothing at all to do with romantic love — which, for all its fabled intensity, is a relatively short-lived phenomenon. The funny article about Valentine's Day gently mocks romance: "What about Monday? Can you get out of there by then? What is this anyway — some sort of love Olympics?"

You may not have realized it when you walked into church this morning, but this Sunday is a major turning point in the church's year. Only Palm Sunday can beat it for high drama.[3] Today, the transfigured Christ turns his blazing face toward disfigurement and certain death in Jerusalem at the hands of his enemies. This week, the church turns away from the light of Epiphany into the shadows of Lent. Listen again to St. Luke's account of the story which is always read on this day: "Now about eight days after these sayings, Jesus took with him Peter and John and James, and went up on the mountain to pray. And as he was praying, the appearance of his countenance was altered, and his raiment became dazzling white. And behold, two men talked with him, Moses and Elijah, who appeared in glory and spoke of his departure, which he was to accomplish at Jerusalem."

According to Matthew, Mark, and Luke, this event — called the Transfiguration — is the most unambiguous revelation of Jesus as

Messiah prior to the Resurrection. As Peter, James, and John watch
the dazzling scene, the voice of God himself declares Jesus to be his
Son. The appearance of Moses and Elijah ratifies the designation of
Jesus as the Chosen One of Israel, the fulfillment of the Law (Moses)
and the Prophets (Elijah). This is the original "mountaintop experience." Our old friend Peter, always the one to speak first and later to
regret it, delivers one of his biggest boners on this occasion: "'Hey,
Lord, wow, this is fantastic. Let's make three booths, one for you and
one for Moses and one for Elijah' — not knowing what he was saying."

It is part of our fallen human nature to want to build booths
and ski lodges and resort hotels on top of mountains. We don't want
to come down from the high. We want the romance to go on
indefinitely, and if it doesn't, we will try any number of artificial
aids to make the love Olympics last longer — and when that doesn't
work, we are apt to try it with a new person. Jesus, however, is the
one truly new person. He knows he cannot stay on the summit
soaking up the view. He and Moses and Elijah speak together, but
not of peak experiences. They speak of "his departure which he was
to accomplish at Jerusalem."

"And a cloud came and overshadowed them; and [the disciples]
were afraid." Peter and James and John saw two things that day on
the mountain. They saw Jesus with the veil lifted to reveal his glory;
and then they saw the clouds coming.

For you see, love cannot stay on the mountaintop. It must come
down. Love must go where it is most needed, not at the pinnacle of
youth and beauty and sexiness, but in the valley of the shadow of
death. The passage from I Corinthians is read today, not because
somebody thought it would be nice to read for Valentine's Day, but
because it is about Jesus as he sets forth to be crucified. "Love bears
all things, believes all things, hopes all things, *endures all things.*"

A few years back, I was crossing the street near my parish in
New York City. A taxi came roaring around the corner and knocked
me to the pavement. A crowd gathered, and an ambulance was called.
It took an unusually long time to arrive. It was forty minutes before
I was actually put on the gurney. In the meantime, I lay on the
asphalt. I was aware of a lot of people standing around looking down

at me. What I remember most about that long wait was the great distance between me on the concrete and the faces high above. In those minutes I very much needed someone to get down on the ground with me, to put a coat under my head, to hold my hand and *stay down* with me until help arrived.

The new book by Taylor Branch, *Pillar of Fire,* continues the story of the civil rights movement begun in his first Biblically named volume, *Parting the Waters.* The second volume comes to a climax with Martin Luther King, Jr., travelling to Oslo as the guest of the King of Sweden to receive the Nobel Peace Prize. As the undisputed leader of a movement that had captured the imagination of people around the globe, as the newly minted toast of nations, he now had access to the crowned heads of Europe and the inner circles of power in Washington. Surely he could not be faulted if he became a highly paid fixture on the lecture circuit. Who would have blamed him if he had retired from the barricades, directing future operations from the rear? Here are two sentences from the final paragraph of Taylor Branch's book: "Martin Luther King confronted furies ahead . . . [his] King's inner course was *fixed downward,* toward the sanitation workers of Memphis."[4] In Memphis, there was a bullet waiting.

Love *comes down.* "Love bears all things, believes all things, hopes all things, endures all things." Love is grateful for the experience on the mountaintop, but knows that it cannot stay there. Love persists when the glory has faded, when the romance has fled, when the curtain has been dropped on the stage set. Love never gives up. The King James Version is stronger in some ways; Love "suffereth long and is kind; love vaunteth not itself; is not puffed up, doth not behave itself unseemly, is not easily provoked . . . love never faileth." Love does not even require reciprocity; love goes to Memphis, love gets down on the pavement, love goes to Jerusalem where the enemy lies in wait.

A few months ago I clipped out a letter from a church magazine. It was written by a physician, a woman named Joanna Seibert. This is what she said:

Today I visited an 8-year-old girl dying of cancer. Her body was disfigured by her disease and its treatment. She was in almost constant pain. As I entered her room, I was overcome almost immediately by her suffering — so unjust, unfair, unreasonable. Even more overpowering [however] was the presence of her grandmother lying in bed beside her with her huge body embracing this precious, inhuman suffering.

I stood in awe, for I knew I was on holy ground. . . . The suffering of innocent children is horrifying beyond words. I will never forget the great, gentle arms and body of this grandmother. She never spoke [a word] while I was there. She was holding and participating in suffering that she could not relieve, and somehow her silent presence was relieving it. No words could express the magnitude of her love.

Love bears all things, endures all things. On this day, Jesus turns his back on his glory and begins his descent into the valley. He comes down from the mountain; he comes down from the throne of the majesty on high; he comes down from the infinite spaces of uncreated light and prepares to enter the darkness of human suffering and human pain. God is not looking down with detachment from a great distance. God did not remain majestically aloof somewhere over the rainbow. God is not a distant observer of our struggles. I had a friend, dying of cancer. He said to me, "I have never doubted the existence of God. But does God care that I'm sick?" Yes. Yes, God does care. As Jesus of Nazareth sets his face toward Jerusalem, he is about to become in his own person the embrace of God for all the misery of all the world.

And so wherever one human being reaches out for another in the midst of suffering, wherever a person in power stoops down to help, wherever the mighty bend to the lowly, there is the Lord. Whenever you do this, you are becoming Jesus' disciple.

And whoever you are and whatever your pain, this very day in the power of his Word spoken, he reaches out, he comes down, to seek *you,* to find *you,* to embrace *you.* The love Olympics have gone to Jerusalem.

Amen.

The Ash Wednesday Privilege

ST. JOHN'S CHURCH, SALISBURY, CONNECTICUT

Against you only have I sinned, and done what is evil in your sight.

Psalm 51:4

I heard on the radio this morning that Fred Goldman has made O. J. Simpson an offer. He will withdraw any and all financial claims if O. J. will sign a detailed written confession. He says that the family has never cared about the money; what they want is the confession. I believe him. I think he means it.

In South Africa, the Truth and Reconciliation Commission has been charged with eliciting confessions from all those who seek amnesty from Nelson Mandela's government. No one will receive amnesty unless they are willing to come forward and give an accounting of their crimes. In Guatemala, by way of contrast, the Truth Commission will not hold anyone accountable. They will investigate who died and who disappeared, but not who did it. The perpetrators will never have to admit anything or confess to anything.

I vividly remember a pastoral situation a few years ago. The son of a well-to-do family had gotten involved in a serious dispute with the family's maid. He was a white college graduate; she was black and only semi-educated. The level of rancor escalated and spilled over into the community. Lines were drawn. The parents of the young man took his side 100 percent. I listened to both sides, and then I told the parents, "I really believe that all she wants is an apology." I am sorry to say that there was no apology forthcoming. The white family had dug in its heels.

Confession, apology, remorse, repentance: these things are powerful. I have been preaching on Ash Wednesday for many years and I believe, now more than ever, that this is the pre-eminent day in the church year for us to come to terms with ourselves before God. More than any other day, Ash Wednesday focuses directly on the theme of self-knowledge. We will shortly read Psalm 51 on our knees. This great Psalm has always been associated with the liturgy of Ash Wednesday. Traditionally it is associated with King David at the time of his adultery with Bathsheba. The Bible is full of searingly honest confessions, but nowhere more strikingly than here.

The writer Janet Malcolm has written about people who are unable to confess:

> There are a few among us . . . who are blessed or cursed with
> a strange imperviousness to the unpleasantness of self-
> knowledge. Their lies to themselves are so convincing that
> they are never unmasked. These are the people who never
> feel in the wrong, who are always able to justify their con-
> duct, and who in the end . . . cause their fallible fellow-men
> to turn from them.

Janet Malcolm acknowledges that all of us resist self-knowledge. She writes:

> We are all perpetually smoothing and rearranging reality to
> conform to our wishes; we lie to others and ourselves con-
> stantly, unthinkingly. When occasionally — and not by dint
> of our own efforts but under the pressure of external events
> — we are forced to see things as they are, we are like naked
> people in a storm.[1]

Psalm 51, the Ash Wednesday Psalm, is the acknowledged

masterpiece of Biblical self-knowledge. "I have been wicked from my birth, a sinner from my mother's womb." Never in the history of the human race has anyone looked at himself more unflinchingly than the author of this incomparable penitential Psalm. "I know my transgressions, and my sin is ever before me." The Psalmist takes all the responsibility upon himself. Never does he say, "I was just doing my job," or "I didn't know," or, "I was just following orders." Nowhere does he say, "My mother didn't love me," or "My father beat me," or "The devil made me do it." All these things may be true, but they are not reasons for us to excuse ourselves. All these human reasons dissolve when seen in the white light of the righteousness of God. "You [Lord] are justified when you speak, and upright in your judgment." On Ash Wednesday, we come together to acknowledge that God has a case against us, and to throw ourselves on his mercy. We come together to pray Psalm 51, not just as sinful individuals, but as a community of sinners seeking to confess and seek not only amnesty, but restitution.

I believe it was the Duke of Wellington who was supposed to have said, "Never explain; never apologize." That has got to be some of the worst advice ever given. It takes maturity, wisdom, and true manliness to offer a handsome apology. And what's more, people are disarmed by a sincere apology. A woman who had been wronged by her husband said to me, "You know, I do forgive him. But I wish he would be more sorry. It is so much harder for me because he is not very repentant." A heartfelt confession of guilt and desire for forgiveness is such a great thing to do for another person. The climax of Mozart's great opera *The Marriage of Figaro* comes at the end, when the Count, unmasked, kneels at his wife's feet and sings, *"Contessa, perdono,"* and the Countess sublimely responds, "I do forgive you."

There is a strange statement in verse 4 of Psalm 51: "Against you [God] only have I sinned and done what is evil in your sight." Why does he say that he has sinned only against God? Sin hurts everybody — it hurts those who are victimized, exploited, used, damaged, scorned, neglected as a result of pride, greed, anger, lust, envy, self-will. Why does the Psalmist say he has sinned against God only?

The reason for this is of central importance. Sin, at bottom, is not an *ethical* concept at all. It is a *theological* concept. Sin is only understood to be sin when God is understood to be God. The recognition of sin comes as the Psalmist is confronted in prayer with the reality of God, the power of God, the holiness of God who has the absolute right to make demands and render judgments. "You are justified when you speak." We need to learn this; we are so accustomed to the kind of reasoning that says, "But I'm not hurting anybody," "Nobody will know," "Everybody else is doing it," "It isn't anybody's business." But in the last analysis, the Bible reveals, every sinful action, every sinful thought, is directed against God. Our concept of sin, like our concept of God, is too small until we learn to say with the Psalmist, "Against you [God] only have I sinned and done what is evil in your sight."

The genius of Psalm 51, and the source of its ageless significance, is this: in its impassioned petitions, the Psalmist demonstrated that *he has learned to see sin as God sees it.*[2] When we see that sin is an offense against the author of all goodness, then it floods in upon us that the goodness of the Lord is precisely the place where all our sin is lifted up and done away. The recognition of sin is our response to God's holiness and mercy. On Ash Wednesday, as we look into the depths, not only of our own sin but that of the whole human race, even as we consciously acknowledge the seriousness of our predicament before God, *at that same moment* we recognize God as the one who extends his mercy to us even in the midst of our condition. As Paul wrote: "While we were *still sinners,* Christ died for us" (Romans 5:8).

Look at the Psalm again. It begins,

> Have mercy on me, O God, according to your loving-
> kindness:
> in your great compassion blot out my offenses.

This is a prayer of a person who knows there is hope, who knows there is mercy, who knows that God is full of compassion. The knowledge of grace has preceded the confession of sin. The person who confesses sin in this free way, holding nothing back, making no excuses, blaming no one but himself, is the person who knows that God is truly able to do away with sin and make a completely new person out of the sinner. The author of Psalm 51 knows this. He prays,

> Create in me a clean heart, O God, and renew a right spirit within me.

So great is his confidence in God that he is able to refer to himself as a miserable offender and, at the same time, to say "make me hear of joy and gladness." The combination of uttermost penitence and unconquerable confidence lies at the very heart of the knowledge of who we are before God and what he intends for us.

This is Ash Wednesday. This is the day in the year set apart for the most searching self-inventory before God, the most honest assessment of our sinful nature that we can possibly offer him. Our temptation will be, as always, to try to squirm off the hook in some way. But, you see, all these evasions fall pitifully short of the reality and power and holiness of the living God.

> Against you only have I sinned,
>   and done what is evil in your sight. . . .
> Deliver me from death, O God,
>   and my tongue shall sing of your righteousness. . . .

In a moment, we are going to read this Psalm together, and then we are going to say the Litany of Penitence. As we reflect on the perfect love of God, we are going to confess lack of love. As we remember how Jesus came to serve us, we are going to confess our failure to serve others. As we acknowledge the faithfulness, the self-giving, the unconditional grace of the Lord, we are going to confess our unfaithfulness, our self-indulgence, our smallness of mind and heart. Our assessment of ourselves and our praise of God will merge in one great corporate act of worship as we "lift up our hearts" to God with the confidence of the Psalmist:

The sacrifice of God is a troubled spirit;
 A broken and a contrite heart, O God, thou wilt not
  despise.

Because, you see, God has shown us a great thing. We do not need to surround ourselves with defenses and barricades. We do not need to lie to ourselves and others. We do not need to live out an exhausting, lifelong charade of pretense lest someone discover that we are not what we appear to be. In the Christian community, we can let ourselves be seen as the sinners we really are, because we are not going to be left like naked people in a storm.

There is Another who has taken the sentence upon himself, and in so doing, has nullified it. Jesus, the Son of God, has voluntarily taken our place, naked in the storm. He himself hung *naked* on the cross, bearing in his own body the *storm* of the wrath of God against sin. Jesus drew into himself the hostility of Satan, and the hatred, envy, wrath, and malice of the entire human race. As St. Paul writes in the Ash Wednesday Epistle, "God made [Jesus] to be sin who knew no sin, that in him we might become the righteousness of God" (II Corinthians 5:21).

Amen.

Noah's Ark

ST. JOHN'S CHURCH, SALISBURY, CONNECTICUT

The story of Noah's ark is probably the most well-known of all
Bible stories because of its perennial appeal to children. "The
animals went in two by two, the elephant and the kangaroo." It is
therefore very difficult to persuade people to read the story on an adult
level, but that's what we're going to try to do this morning. Unless
you are very well versed in the workings of the church's lectionary (the
readings appointed for each Sunday), you may be wondering why we
are having the story of Noah on the first Sunday in Lent. What is the
connection between the ark and the temptation of Christ? What does
Noah have to do with the passion and death of Jesus?

One of the most fascinating features of the lectionary is its
sweep through the Old Testament during Lent. If you look at the
whole three-year Lenten cycle, you will see that the fifteen passages
selected from the Hebrew Bible are mountaintop passages. They are
chosen because they express the inmost depths and uttermost heights
of the faith of Israel. The Lenten texts from the Old Testament are
foundation stones of Jewish and Christian belief. If we look at them
carefully, we will have made at least a beginning toward a more
faithful understanding of the organic connection between the history
of Israel and the Passion of Jesus Christ our Lord. During the Sundays
of Lent, we will be looking at the passages in Cycle B: Noah,
Abraham's sacrifice of Isaac, the Ten Commandments, the Exile into
Babylon, and the New Covenant.

To begin, then, with the story of the Ark: The first question that many people want to ask is, "Did this really happen?" I'm not going to spend any time on that. There are many stories about universal floods in the literature of ancient peoples. Catastrophic local floods have no doubt been magnified in these stories to global proportions. The important thing for Christian believers is the meaning of the story, for the theological sophistication of the ancient Hebrew narrative is far greater than anything in the Gilgamesh Epic or elsewhere.[1] Could God do this? Would God do this? Did God do this? Those are not the deepest questions. The question for faith is whether this is or is not the right description of our relationship to God.[2]

The story begins with a divine decision to wipe out the human race. Everything from here on out depends on whether we think God has the right to do that or not. We tend to look at things from our own very constricted point of view. Things are not too bad for me personally, so why should God be mad at me? Those things we read about in the papers don't apply to me. I don't run a dope ring; I don't exploit migrant workers; I don't hack people to death with machetes; I don't rape battered women; I don't live off the stolen money of murdered Jews; I certainly don't dismember my wife or burn my baby with cigarettes. One of the big differences between the Bible and us is that we Americans are individualists, whereas the Bible thinks in terms of the whole human community. It is taken for granted in the Old Testament that sin contaminates the entire society. The whole population is accountable to God for the state of the world. If we are thinking Biblically, we know that if something bad is happening across the ocean in Rwanda or over the state line in Columbia County, that doesn't mean we here in Salisbury are excused. On Ash Wednesday we confessed to a selfish state of mind not only on behalf of ourselves, but on behalf of those who were not there. The special purpose of Lent is that we should become like the Biblical writers who *have learned to see sin as God sees it.*[3]

In the other flood stories of ancient times, it is not clear why the various gods start the flood. One of them tries to start it only to be frustrated by another god. After it began, the gods were terrified at what they had done, cowering like dogs. When it was over, they quarreled among themselves. In the Biblical story, God is majestic and purposeful. He is not threatened by other gods, for there are no other gods. He is not frightened by nature; he is Lord of nature. Nothing is outside his control. In this era of ours when the study of comparative religion throws all religious texts into one critical pot as if all were of equal merit, it is important to recognize the vast differences between the Bible and the others. The Genesis version of the flood story is "a landmark in the history of religion."[4] The concept of God that appears here is a world away from the squabbling nature deities of the Mesopotamian epics.[5] But not only is the depiction of God superior in the Bible, the view of human nature is far more coherent and challenging also. The picture of human society that we see in Genesis is ethically and morally profound.

There are a lot of different ways of looking at the world. Most people see it the way the ant sees the elephant — only that minuscule portion that's in front of one's own itty-bitty nose. The Bible demands that we see the bigger picture. Again, most people will color the world according to the mood they themselves are in, whether joyous or depressed. And most of us will construe the world based on the well-being of our own family and friends, or at the most our "fellow Americans." Rare indeed are the souls who have a lively concern for those who are far off or strange. Yet, as one of you pointed out in the Bible class last Sunday, Christian faith is supposed to make a difference in our perspective on things. The worst thing reported in *The Litchfield County Times* this week is that James Taylor may be dumping asbestos, but the news around the world is that the Hutu have started massacring the Tutsi once again in the supposedly Christian nation of Rwanda, and that children in countries all over the Third World are dying by the thousands because their parents cannot afford the few cents that it takes to boil their drinking water. Christians are not supposed to be satisfied with the world as it is.

And so in the first five chapters of Genesis prior to the Flood story, we see how the world that was "very good" when God first made it turns into a sinkhole of selfishness, corruption, violence, and killing.

The people who have been discussing Genesis on Bill Moyer's television program are mostly reading it from a literary standpoint; you could do worse (you could not read it at all), but they are missing the theological perspective that forms the heart and soul of the Old Testament. Faith understands that although God made the world beautiful, humankind ruined everything by rebelling and disobeying. From that moment on, the path leads in only one direction — downward. That is the picture we are supposed to see when the Noah story begins. We are supposed to understand and to grasp by faith that God had no reason to put up with humanity one moment longer.

However, God is already preparing his plan of salvation. I don't think a phrase like "plan of salvation" means much until we stop to think about what it involves. If a group of climbers on Mount Washington gets caught in a blizzard, it is probably their own stupid, stubborn fault; but they are going to need rescuing or they will die, so the rescue teams need a plan of salvation, so to speak. Many people, including me, would say that if people are going to climb Mount Washington in bad weather, they are going to have to take the consequences. Well, that is exactly what God could very well have said to us. A big flood was a perfect way to get rid of the whole lot of us along with all the prejudice, abuse, neglect, deceit, hatred, murder, torture, war, and all the other ills that flesh is heir to. And so the narrator tells us, "The Lord saw that the wickedness of man was great in the earth, and that every imagination of the thoughts of his heart was only evil continually. And the Lord was sorry that he had made man on the earth, and it grieved him to his heart. So the Lord said, 'I will blot out man whom I have created from the face of the ground, man and beast and creeping things and birds of the air, for I am sorry that I have made them.' . . . But Noah found favor in the eyes of the Lord."

It is important to notice that Noah does not utter a single word during the whole story, four long chapters. One commentator refers to the "unbroken silence" of Noah. It is quite a contrast to the incorrigibly chatty Noah portrayed on Broadway a couple of decades ago by Danny Kaye. The silence of Noah points up the pre-eminent role played by God throughout. It really isn't a story about Noah at all; it is a story about God. The story puts us in the place where God is so we can see how the elephant looks, not to the measly ant, but to the Creator who made the ant and the elephant in the first place. When God looks at us, he does not see the finery in which we dress ourselves, hoping to hide; he sees us captive to sin and death.

But now look. Even before God decrees the flood, he has already set a plan of salvation in motion. He has already selected Noah. God has picked him out from his birth (Genesis 5:29), which once again demonstrates that any righteousness human beings might have is derived from God's favor rather than any capacity of our own. The emphasis, again, is not on Noah's innate righteousness, but on his role as God's agent for the creation of a new beginning for humanity. I wish we had time to dwell on the details of the story — the scrupulously careful building of the ark according to God's specifications, the animals and Noah's family entering and God himself shutting the door, the description of the rising waters and the floating ark, and the lovely narration of the sending of the dove until she finds dry land. I do think that Michelangelo, great painter that he is, has done Biblical theology a disservice by painting the sufferings of the drowning people so vividly. If the narrator had wanted us to focus on that, it would have been described. The attention is, rather, on the wonder of the ark and its cargo, floating safely in the midst of the cosmic waterburst. We are meant to be struck by the providence of God in preserving Noah and the earth's creatures from God's own righteous wrath at sin.

Now we come to the climax. Imagine the scene. It is not described as though Noah and his family were the only people left after a nuclear holocaust, where "the living will envy the dead." The tone is quite different. When Noah emerges, there is a sense of spaciousness and blessing. Life begins again. As soon as they stepped out, "Noah built an altar to the Lord, and . . . offered burnt offerings on the altar. And when the Lord smelled the pleasing odor, the Lord said in his heart, 'I will never again curse the ground because of man, for the imagination of man's heart is evil from his youth [!].'" Note the paradox here. In a sense, nothing has changed; as we shall learn in the next chapter, humanity is still sinful. For the first time since the Fall, however, God performs an unambiguous act of divine grace. He reveals that his covenant with Noah and his descendants is unconditional. In spite of the evil imagination of the human heart, "While the earth remains, seedtime and harvest, cold and heat, summer and winter, day and night, shall not cease." It is the first step in God's mighty plan to redeem the earth. The next step will be God's word to Abraham.

And God said to Noah, "This is the sign of the covenant which I make between me and you and every living creature that is with you, for all future generations: I set my bow in the cloud, and it shall be a sign of the covenant between me and the earth. When I bring clouds over the earth and the bow is seen in the clouds, I will remember my covenant which is between me and you and every living creature; and the waters shall never again become a flood to destroy all flesh."

What do you think of when you see a rainbow? Pots of gold? The color spectrum? The rainbow bridge to Valhalla in Wagner's opera? Next time, think of this: it is the sign of God's promise not to destroy us. It is his guarantee of protection against the effects of our own rapacity and greed. St. Peter says (in today's Epistle) that the Flood is the image of Baptism: "In the days of Noah, during the building of the ark a few persons, were saved through water. Baptism, which corresponds to this, now saves you . . . through the resurrection of Jesus Christ . . ." (1 Peter 3:20-21).

I have no way of knowing how all this affects you, but I know how it affects me. I am deeply convicted, more so each year, of the profound sinfulness of the human race. Yet because of the Cross and Resurrection of Jesus Christ — because of that and nothing else, because of that and nothing less — I am also convicted of the truth of what the Bible tells us about God's plan of salvation. The rainbow bridge does not lead to Valhalla, where the gods quarrel so much that they destroy themselves. The rainbow bridge leads to the Cross and to the empty tomb on Easter Day.

Amen.

The Strange World of Abraham

ST. JOHN'S CHURCH, SALISBURY, CONNECTICUT

God himself will provide the lamb for a burnt offering, my son.

Genesis 22:8

Let's think for a few moments about strange countries. We all know the difference between familiar territory and strange territory. For instance, I feel more at home in New England now than I do in Virginia, and yet when I do return to the South, I can re-enter my native culture as though I had never left. On the other hand, though, if I were to go to Saudi Arabia or Nepal or some other non-European country, I would be lost. Everything would be strange — the language, the food, the customs. It would be impossible for me to negotiate being there without a guide.

I have a friend who has been to Tibet four times. I am in awe of her capacity for travelling under arduous, even dangerous, conditions and laying herself open to experiences utterly alien to our own. I wonder if some of you don't also admire people who take such risks. Well, believe it or not, you and I can undertake such an adventure when we open the Bible, especially the Old Testament. This morning I invite you to undertake this daring activity.

Of all the stories in the Bible, the one we read today is certainly one of the most foreign of all. The whole idea of Abraham being told by God to sacrifice Isaac is virtually incomprehensible to us. It seems to come to us from another world, a strange sphere that we do not understand, where a father hears God's command to kill his own son and acts as if God had every right to do such a thing. A foreign world, indeed.

In order to enter this apparently alien realm we have to begin by setting aside the questions that we would ordinarily ask, because they will invariably be the wrong questions. We are asking questions in English, but the story is, so to speak, in Tibetan. We are asking how God could do such a thing, but the narrator is not interested in that question at all. We are so desperate to get the story under control that we try to explain it away as, for instance, an explanation of how human sacrifice came to an end in Canaan. We read the story as though God were called into question by it, but the person who has learned to live in the country of the Bible comes to know that we, not God, are the ones who are called into question.

In order to enter this foreign country, we should see the story of Abraham's journey to Mount Moriah first of all in its context. The story of Abraham begins in Genesis 12; its climax occurs with our story ten chapters and 40-odd years later. The beginning parallels the ending; the first thing that happens is that God says to Abraham, "Leave your country, your people, and your father's house, and go to the land I will show you" (12:1). This was no small thing to ask in the ancient world, where a man's whole identity was with his people. Abraham, in obeying this command of God, was becoming a lifelong exile from everything that was safe and knowable. He was setting out for a strange new world with nothing to trust except the promise of God: "I will make of you a great nation . . . *and by you all the nations of the earth shall be blessed.*" For twenty-five years the elderly Abraham and his barren wife Sarah wandered around the Near East with nothing to live on but a promise. There was no sign of any descendants and no human possibility of any. And yet, as St. Paul was to write some two thousand years later, "Abraham . . . did not weaken in faith when he considered his own body, which was as good as dead because he was about a hundred years old, or when he considered the barrenness of Sarah's womb. No distrust made him waver concerning the promise of God, but he grew strong in his faith as he gave glory to God, fully convinced that God was able to do what he had promised" (Romans 4:18-21). Because of this, Abraham is called "the father of believers."

At length the elderly couple are visited by three mysterious guests. The beautiful story of the angelic visitation is told in Genesis 18. The angels announce that the promised heir is to arrive at last. Sarah laughs in derision, but the purpose of God is not to be stopped: Isaac is conceived and born.[1] At last, some measure of peace settles over Abraham's life. A lifetime of obedience has been rewarded. We smile upon the two aged parents as the child grows, healthy, normal, and happy.

Then suddenly, and without warning, the unthinkable happens. Its very uniqueness is a cause for wonder. There has never been another story like this in the world. Many times in myth and history people have had to make terrible sacrifices for some greater cause, but never before or since has a man been asked to kill his own child *for no discernible reason whatsoever* except that God wished to test Abraham. The mind reels. What sort of God would do such a thing? we ask. But we are asking the question out of context. The whole story of Abraham, many chapters long, is designed to show that it is the same God whose promise Abraham has known, believed, and obeyed from the beginning. We need to shift our attention away from the modern question "What sort of God would do this?" to the central theme of Abraham's journey. If we look at the story from our own familiar standpoint, it makes no sense from any direction; either God is a monster for ordering the death of a child, or Abraham is crazy because he is willing to kill his own son. But, remember, we are in another country here. The Biblical narrator is not interested in these issues at all. The story is about a life lived in faith and hope for some forty years with no guarantees. It is about *radical trust in the future of God*.

Our daughter and her husband take their two children on occasional airplane trips. It makes me very anxious to have both of my grandchildren and their parents in the air at the same time. A crash would mean the total wipeout of our family future. This is what Abraham was faced with. Isaac was the only legitimate child that he and Sarah would ever have. Whereas in chapter 12 Abraham is asked to cut himself off from the past, in chapter 22 he is asked to cut himself off from the future.[2] In order to receive the full impact of the story, however, we have to probe more deeply. It isn't just his *family* future that is at stake here. It is the salvation of *the whole world,* because that is what God has promised will happen through Abraham's seed. It really does take a huge effort on our part to grasp this. Abraham has lived for decades in the conviction that God was going to use his faith to bless the entire human race for all generations to come. Now God is asking Abraham to wipe the blessing off the face of the earth. Yet even to say that Abraham is about to lose the future is not adequate. We have to go deeper still. The loss of the future means the loss of faith as well. The story takes us out of the realm of ordinary religion into a place where there is no sure footing at all. Here we stare into the abyss. Here we must entertain an understanding of faith that is beyond anything that we have contemplated before. Many believe that the most radical description of faith in the Bible is found in Romans 4:17, where St. Paul writes that Abraham believed in the God "who gives life to the dead and calls into existence the things that do not exist." The author of Hebrews echoes this idea: "By faith Abraham . . . was ready to offer up his only son. . . . He considered that God was able to raise men even from the dead" (11:17-19). This is our guide to the heart of the story.

At times like this I always think of my professor and mentor, Paul Lehmann. Paul and his wife Marion had only one child, Peter, born when they were in their forties. Peter lived to be a healthy twenty-two and then, in 1976, suddenly developed aplastic anemia and died without issue. All who loved the Lehmanns were stricken with sorrow, but there was another dimension as well. Every student of Professor Lehmann over the decades was watching to see what would happen, as though our own faith hung in the balance. Had he ceased to trust in God, we might have given up too. When I think of Paul today, I think of his heroic faith even in the agony of the loss of his human future. I honor him today as one of Abraham's most valiant offspring. Unlike Abraham, he did not receive his son back again from the dead in this life. But trusting in God means to put oneself into God's hands totally, even when the road leads out into Godforsakenness, even when the fulfillment of God's promises seems to have receded into impossibility. Throughout the ages the story of Abraham has been an important one for those whose faith is tested by terrible events, when there is nothing remaining to hang on to except St. Paul's words: Abraham believed in "the God who raises the dead and calls into being the things that do not exist."

The Genesis story presents our father Abraham as a person who was asked to do something that no one else was ever asked to do, precisely in order to demonstrate to the whole world what faith really means. As God tested Abraham God was at the same time working through Abraham's faith to reveal a new thing to the world: an unprecedented example of steadfast loyalty to God throughout a night of humanly impenetrable darkness.[3]

But now listen. We have not yet come to the climax of the story. The narrator emphasizes that Abraham was in the very act, with the knife, in order to make sure there is no doubt about the matter; Caravaggio, Rembrandt, and others have painted the moment just that way, with an angel grabbing Abraham's hand at the last second.[4] At the very moment that we avert our eyes in unspeakable horror, God acts. "Abraham put forth his hand, and took the knife to slay his son. But the angel of the Lord called to him from heaven, and said, 'Abraham, Abraham! . . . Do not lay your hand on the boy or do anything to him; for now I know that you fear God, seeing you have not withheld your son, your only son, from me.' And Abraham lifted up his eyes and looked, and [saw] a ram, caught in a thicket ᵤy his horns; and Abraham went and took the ram, and offered it up as a burnt offering instead of his son" (Genesis 22:11-12).

Abraham himself, guided by faith, had said to Isaac — "God himself will provide the lamb for a burnt offering, my son." What Abraham did not have to do, God did. The ram was *a substitute* for Isaac, provided by God. When Jesus, the only Son of God, was brought to the cross to bear the sin of the world into the godforsaken dark, there was no substitute for him. He became the substitute for us. This is the strange new world of the Bible.

In this age when many clergy and Biblical scholars are suggesting that Biblical faith is unfashionable and retrograde, I am not ashamed to say that, more and more, I am discovering that the alien world of the Bible is the sphere where human beings are truly understood, where we will find our real selves, where we will discern our eternal destiny. I believe the Biblical future is the one future worthy of total commitment. The more I read the Bible the more I want to live by its promises. The telling of the story of Abraham and Isaac today brings you, too, this very day, to the threshold of faith: faith in the Lord of the promise, in the new world to come, and in the life everlasting.

Amen.

Rules of the Freedom Game

ST. JOHN'S CHURCH, SALISBURY, CONNECTICUT

The Ten Commandments have been in the news lately. A judge in a Southern state is in hot water because he refuses to remove a plaque of the Ten Commandments from the wall of his courtroom. The *Register-Citizen* reported that a local schoolteacher is in political trouble because, in attempting to discipline students, she asked them, "Don't you kids know the Ten Commandments?" I think it would be safe to say that, no, they don't know the Ten Commandments, and neither do most church members nowadays. When I was a child, we used to read the Decalogue on a regular basis in the Episcopal Church, the way we did earlier this morning. For reasons that I don't fully understand, it is rarely done now.

To be sure, an argument could be made for de-emphasizing the Decalogue. The gospel of Jesus Christ is not a rule of law. Being a Christian is not a matter of following a code. When the Christian faith declines into legalism or moralism, it is no longer the good news of God, but the bad news of religiosity, which always mutates into repression and intimidation. There is a difference between the Law and the Gospel. St. Paul describes this difference: "We have believed in Christ Jesus, in order to be justified by faith in Christ, and not by works of the Law, because by works of the Law shall no human being be justified" (Galatians 2:16). Any Christian congregation that does not understand this has missed the freedom train. There is nothing more important in the Christian life than understanding Paul's distinction between "the righteousness based on Law and the righteousness based on faith" (Romans 10:3-5). Righteousness based on Law is what FitzSimons Allison calls "teeth-grittin' Christianity."[1] It isn't any fun. It can never relax. It is never sure it is good enough. It always seeks to condemn others. It is constantly overcompensating by veering off into self-righteousness. The Gospel is not like that at all. The righteousness based on faith is free and joyous. It knows it is on the right playing field even if it misses a lot of the goals. Playing the gospel game means that the rules are not burdensome; they make it more fun because everyone agrees on what they are and are therefore free to forget about them. Even more important, when the rules are understood the way they are supposed to be, they actually give us a picture of the ideal game, the perfect game where each person has a position to play and nobody minds losing because there is always another chance to win tomorrow.

There is a special reason for the reading of the rules of the game this Sunday morning. The Decalogue from the Book of Exodus is the Old Testament reading for today, the Third Sunday in Lent. During Lent, the church hears Old Testament lessons of particular gravity and importance. If you were to read all the Old Testament selections in the three-year Lenten cycle, you would find that you had hit a number of high points in the Hebrew Scriptures. I was brought back to the Ten Commandments myself in that way. For a long time, being enamored of the Gospel, I gave little thought to the Law. I was brought back exactly six years ago, when I was called to preach on the Ten Commandments during Lent for the first time. The experience had a powerful effect on me. I began to understand what one Biblical scholar calls "the great and almost numbing loss" suffered by our society since the Commandments fell into the background. This commentator, Walter Harrelson of Vanderbilt, continues: "The loss of knowledge of the Ten Commandments means a loss in understanding what human liberty is, what freedom of the spirit means, and how freedom is to be maintained in the world."[2]

I found many more writings along this line. St. Augustine calls the Decalogue the Christian's charter of freedom. Dietrich Bonhoeffer writes that the commandment of God "not only forbids, but also permits: not only binds, but also sets free."[3] Paul Lehmann says it is important to get the tone right: "The tonality [of the Ten Commandments] does not sound like, 'This you must do, or else.' It sounds, rather, like 'Seeing that you are who you are, this is the way ahead, the way of being and living in the truth, the way of freedom.' "[4]

It will help us to appreciate the Decalogue as a charter of freedom if we understand that the children of Israel had already been constituted by an unconditional covenant of God, first with Noah, then with Abraham. The Commandments were given into a community of people that had already been chosen by God to be his A team. The Commandments can never be detached from their setting in the community that comes into being as a result of God's determination to rescue us from our disobedience and put us on a new playing field of abundant life. The Decalogue is not, therefore, a set of static legal prohibitions. It has often been said that they are not *prescriptive* but *descriptive*. They show the way of life for God's children. They can't be understood apart from the God who gave them. That's why the First Commandment is preceded by: "I am the Lord thy God who brought thee out of the land of Egypt, out of the house of bondage," and only then continues, "Thou shalt have no other gods but me." The Decalogue is neither good common sense, nor practical maxims, nor accumulated folk-wisdom, nor a philosophy of life; it is the revelation of the will of God to reshape us according to his loving purpose. The Ten Commandments can never be grasped apart from the knowledge of God himself.

I have tried to think of a way to illustrate the way that the negatively phrased Commandments ("Thou shalt not . . .") serve as a charter of freedom. I'm going to give an example from my own life. Please don't misunderstand me; when it comes to breaking Commandments, I can stand at the head of the line any day of the week. But there is one aspect of the Commandment "Thou shalt not steal" that occurs to me as an example of the way the Decalogue might function within the family of God. So here goes.

I grew up in an old-line Virginia family that emphasized honor. To be dishonorable was to betray who I was and who my family was.

This was not taught by Law handed down; it was taught in the context of family identity and belonging. It was reinforced, not by thundering legalisms, but by the unthinkability of disappointing the patriarch, my father (and for that matter, my great-great-grand-father Eugene Davis, whose reputation for goodness and rectitude lived on unto the third and fourth generation). The tonality was not "This is what you must do, or else." It was "Seeing that you are who you are (a Virginian), this is the way of freedom."

Let me be more specific. I do not for one minute mean to imply that I have never done anything dishonorable; the opposite is true. But in one small respect I can offer an example: I am apparently incapable of shoplifting. I simply can't do it. Hundreds of opportunities present themselves, but I would rather stand in line at the cash register for an hour than walk off with so much as a pack of Life Savers.

My point in telling this is to try to show how freeing it is. I do not have to go through mental gymnastics on my daily trips to the Salisbury Pharmacy. I do not have to calculate risk against benefit. I do not have to look around to see if anyone is watching. I do not have to worry about alarms going off. Old-guard Virginians don't shoplift; that's all there is to it. That simplifies my life tremendously, and it makes my trips to the store a pleasure rather than a problem.

Take the famous Seventh Commandment, "Thou shalt not commit adultery." This is the butt of good-news-bad-news jokes: "What is the good news? God has reduced the number of Commandments. What is the bad news? The Seventh is still in there." So is the Seventh Commandment an example of God being mean and robbing us of pleasure? When you have talked to a wife whose husband has given her a case of herpes, it might cause you to think again. We clergy hear plenty of stories. For example, there was the young, gorgeous, single woman who picked up a married businessman in a bar and had a one-night stand with him. As a result of that one fling, she became pregnant and decided she wanted to keep the baby. The man had not even given the young woman his last name, but she tracked him down through his company and told him either he would pay child support or she would tell his wife. I have often thought of the heavy cost of that one night of heedlessness. God wants to protect us and our children from such situations. In central Africa, adultery is a way of life — for the men, that is; the husbands come home and transmit AIDS to their wives. I read a story about a Ugandan man who had become a Christian. He said, "In the beginning, Adam had only one wife. God knew what was better." Walter Harrelson ends his commentary on the Seventh Commandment with these words: "Surely no one any longer can seriously challenge the view that sexual faithfulness in marriage is good."

Last week I read an interview with Andrew Young, whose book about the civil rights movement was recently published. I learned from the interview that Mr. Young's much-loved wife of 40 years had died of cancer. The reporter asked him, "You remarried last March, just 18 months after Jean died. . . . Was it difficult to start over again so quickly?" He replied, "I was 22 when I first married; the only life I'd known was married life. I needed a relationship of trust and permanence. . . . After my wife's death . . . everywhere I went, people set me up with women — some of the most beautiful and intelligent women in the world. I wasn't interested. I'd get up in the middle of the evening, go back to my hotel room and read a book. I'm not cut out to be a playboy."[5] Now some people would say that Andrew Young had missed some great opportunities, that he was too straight-arrow. I would say that he was a free man. In the area of sexual behavior, he was immune to temptation. That's what freedom means — not freedom to choose what kind of sin you want to commit, but freedom not to commit sin at all. And it doesn't just mean freedom *from* something, like sexually transmitted diseases; above all it means freedom *for* something, like having, in Mr. Young's case, not only one but two good marriages.

In the film shown here a few weeks ago about the exploits of the 10th Mountain Division during World War II, one man said that in order to function as a soldier you had to forget your religion. I've been thinking about that ever since. I suppose he was speaking hyperbolically, but still, he doesn't understand the meaning of the Ten Commandments or the nature of God's grace. Knowing the Ten

Commandments doesn't mean obeying them in some superhuman way as though we lived in a world without sin. What it does mean is that we will have integrated, not compartmentalized, lives. It is assumed in the Decalogue that there is going to be stealing and adultery and killing in the world, but the difference between God's people and others is that God's people will know that what they are doing is wrong and will always be mindful of the need to come before God in daily prayer and confession, to receive forgiveness and the strength to follow a better way. Thus many Christian soldiers have become devoted workers for peace when the necessity for killing other human beings was past.

There is a delicate balance here. Martin Luther, in a famous phrase, said, "Sin boldly!" He meant that we do not need to forget our religion *at any time,* even when we are in the midst of failing God and our fellow man. God is the one who has given us a place of grace to stand firmly upon even as we continue to be assailed by sin. This gives us a robust freedom of conscience that is perhaps the greatest of all Protestant traits. At the same time, however, Martin Luther loved the Ten Commandments, knowing that God is not sentimentally permissive. God's goodness takes shape in the very real, mundane struggles of everyday life, struggles in which all of us, like little children, need constant guidance and help from our Father in heaven. In today's society, where norms have been loosened to the vanishing point, we need God's good commandments more than ever.

Let no one think, however, of a return to the Ten Commandments in the sense of using them for control and repression. That would be the opposite of a charter of freedom. Later on in the interview with Andrew Young, he shows that he has the balance right. He understands the Law against adultery from the standpoint of the Gospel. He is himself free of this sin, but he is astonishingly forgiving of the adulterous behavior of others, including his mentor Martin Luther King. Mr. Young, a deeply believing Christian, knows the frailty of human nature. He knows the goodness of fidelity and the badness of adultery, but he also knows that each one of us is totally dependent on God's grace and that none of us can obey any commandment without that grace. This is why we say, after the reading of each Commandment, "Lord, have mercy upon us, and incline our hearts to keep this law."[6] If any of us begin to congratulate ourselves on keeping the commandments, we have already lost our way. True prayer to the God of the Commandments begins, "Lord, have mercy on me, a sinner." If we truly understand the nature of God our Father, and if we are coming to know what it means to belong to that Father's family, then the willing embrace of the Father's loving commandments will become, not a burden but a privilege, not bondage but liberty, not a cause for anxiety and fear but an opportunity for growth and movement and life in a free space where the only constraint is a heartfelt wish not to disappoint the kind and merciful Father who loved us so much that he gave his only-begotten Son, to save us from lawlessness and sin and wandering in the dark. And so, knowing the rules, let us go forth to play the game with joy.

Amen.

Exiled into Babylon

ST. JOHN'S CHURCH, SALISBURY, CONNECTICUT

W hen the handsome old Salisbury Town Hall burned to the ground a few years ago, I had only been through town a few times, but even so, I was affected. I can scarcely get my mind around the degree of shock the event must have caused this community.

Now imagine, if you will, something more. Imagine that the Town Hall, the Ragamont Inn, the White Hart, the Academy Building, the Scoville Library, and all the churches are burned at once. Imagine further that they are burned, not just by a couple of local boys gone wrong, but by a rampaging army from an utterly foreign place — from Southern California, say, or Las Vegas. These invaders, having destroyed everything of importance in our town, proceed to carry off, not only all of our local treasures, but also every person with a higher education, leaving the working classes behind to manage as best they can in a ravaged landscape. It would be hard to say who was worse off, those who were taken away into exile, or those left behind to struggle in the ruins. I don't know about you, but I think I would lose my mind if I were dragged off against my will to spend the rest of my days in Las Vegas.[1]

Well, something like this, on a very much larger scale, happened to the Hebrew people in the year 587 BC. The Old Testament readings in Lent take us in chronological order from the heights to the depths. We have gone from the promise made to Noah, through the covenant with Abraham, to the gift of the Ten Commandments in the Sinai wilderness following the Exodus from Egypt. The Exodus and the constituting of the children of Israel (Jacob) into a people is the center of the Old Testament experience. Now we see it all swept away into catastrophe.

A brief account of the disaster is given in today's first reading from the Second Book of Chronicles. This short passage recounts how the prophets of Israel warned the people that they were in danger, but they paid no heed until the Chaldean (Babylonian) army was at the very gates. We are told how the soldiers killed civilians in the Temple itself, how Nebuchadnezzar the king of Babylon looted the Temple and the museums and the historical societies, how the soldiers burned the city of Jerusalem, how the people were carted off hundreds of miles to live in exile in the midst of the colossal idols, the vainglorious architecture, and the mega-showplace called the Hanging Gardens of Babylon. Surrounding them in their new location was all the wealth and pomp of a great world empire, shaming them with their smallness and impotence in the midst of the magnificence of Mesopotamia. This is the setting for the famous lines in Psalm 137: "By the waters of Babylon, there we sat down and wept, when we remembered Zion. On the willows there we hung up our lyres. . . . How shall we sing the Lord's song in a strange land?"

Not even these exercises in imagination, however, can fully bring us into the depths the children of Israel experienced as a result of this calamity. You and I have never known anything like what they went through. The invasion, conquest, and exile of 587 was the greatest crisis in the history of the people, but it was not just a national crisis. Far more important, it was a "theological emergency."[2]

To return to our imaginary invasion of Salisbury by a foreign power: Imagine that for a number of years the town meetings of Salisbury have been forums for competing groups of prophets who get up and contend for the opinion of the citizenry. One group of prophets, the popular group, is much larger than the other. They say, "We are God-fearing, decent people here. We don't have anything to be worried about. Nothing bad is going to happen to us.

Look around; see how nice it is here. This is God's country." The other group of prophets is very small in number. Members of group one groan and roll their eyes at the ceiling when group two gets up to speak. People go out and get coffee or go to the bathroom. Nobody wants to hear what the second group has to say. Would you and I want to hear it? Of course not. Listen to this: "Thus says the Lord of hosts, the God of Israel: 'Behold, before your eyes and in your days, I will make the voice of mirth and the voice of gladness to cease from this place. . . . Because your fathers have forsaken me,' says the Lord, 'and have gone after other gods and have served and worshipped them, and have forsaken me and have not kept my law, and because you have done worse than your fathers . . . therefore I will hurl you out of this land into a land which neither you nor your fathers have known, and there you shall serve other gods day and night, for I will show you no favor'" (Jeremiah 16:9-13). This is a truly terrible saying, and it is no wonder the people did not want to hear it. Because of these words, Jeremiah the prophet was *persona non grata* for most of his life. One of the most interesting and most persecuted people in all the Bible, Jeremiah lived night and day in close proximity to the searing Word of God, which is not a comfortable place to be: "A horrible and shocking thing has happened in the land [says the Lord]: The prophets prophesy lies . . . and my people love it this way" (Jeremiah 5:10-11).

So the setting for the Babylonian invasion was one of heedless optimism, self-satisfaction, feelings of invulnerability — rather like America today. The people, and above all the ecclesiastical establishment — the clergy and the vestries and the boards of deacons — were impervious to the warnings of Jeremiah. The town meetings were increasingly tense as Jeremiah refused to turn down the volume. If you don't repent and return to the Lord, he said, you are going to have to serve false gods in earnest, and then you will see whether they can save you or not. Surely one of the most terrible threats that the children of Israel ever heard is "I will hurl you out of this land into a land which neither you nor your fathers have known, and there you shall serve other gods day and night." This would be equivalent to saying I had to offer sacrifices and burn incense to the gods of Las Vegas for the rest of my life. The truly horrible aspect of this, mind you, is not that the gods of Mesopotamia are in bad taste. That's not the problem. The real problem is that *they cannot save*. They have no power. They cannot grant what they promise. That is how the false gods of this world differ from the God of Abraham, Isaac, and Jacob. The idols dazzle and they seduce and they entice; they demand our money and our attention and our allegiance; they are worshipped by celebrities and moguls and potentates; but they cannot deliver. Jeremiah mocks the false gods: They are made of gold and silver, but they must be fastened down so they will not fall over; they must be carried about because they cannot move on their own; they are gorgeous, dressed in silk and purple, made with beautiful craftsmanship, but they are impotent: "There is no breath in them. They are worthless, a work of delusion; at the time of their punishment they shall perish. Not like these is he who is the portion of Jacob, for he is the one who formed all things, and Israel is the tribe of his inheritance; the Lord of hosts is his name" (Jeremiah 10:14-16).

When Jerusalem was destroyed by the Babylonians, nothing less than the faith of Israel was at stake. That was the theological emergency. Many, if not most, of those left at home in the ruins turned away from the pure worship of the Lord of hosts and took up with the local cults. Those who were carried off into exile were even more beset. Here they were surrounded by temples and palaces that made the Jerusalem temple look like a backwoods cabin. The Babylonian gods had armies and empires; the God of Israel had apparently been routed by them. How could anyone imagine that the religion of Israel would survive? The fact that it did, and the way that it did, is an authentic miracle.[3]

Imagine the people of Salisbury in exile in Las Vegas, say — a modern Babylon. Imagine that we refuse to play the games, eat the food, drink the drinks, or bow down to the gods of the place. We are like Daniel and his friends in Babylon; they infuriated Nebuchadnezzar by setting themselves apart for the service of the one true God. They would not worship the monarch of Babylon. They would not pray to his idol, even though it was attended by celebrities and bathed in lights and clothed in money. Further, these faithful Jews humbled themselves before the true God. They confessed the sins of Israel and acknowledged their fault. They asked God for forgiveness and begged for his mercy. They knew they did not deserve God's help, but they remembered his mercies of days gone by and called upon his loving-kindness. They devoted themselves to prayer and fasting. A few — a very few — of the Jews in Babylon were like that. They were the ones through whom God spoke to give the world the most audacious theology the human race has ever known.

The prophet Ezekiel was one of these, and there were a few others. The greatest of them all, however, was a man whose name we do not even know. We call him the Second Isaiah. His writing appears in chapters 40–55 of the book of Isaiah, and it is the most sublime sustained piece of poetry in the Old Testament. Out of despair he wrests hope; out of exile he declares return; out of utter failure he projects vindication. His prophecy astonishes because it affords an unimpeded view of a horizon hitherto unseen. There is nothing else quite like it in all the Bible.[4] It is absolutely amazing that such a voice could emerge from a tiny group of resident aliens from an insignificant defeated nation in the midst of the mighty culture of Mesopotamia. Even more extraordinary is the fact that we do not hear the voice of the Second Isaiah at all. Perhaps it is just as well we do not know his name. The voice we hear is the voice of God: "I am the first and I am the last; besides me there is no god. Who is like me? Let him proclaim it, let him declare and set it forth before me. Who has announced from of old the things to come? Let them tell us what is yet to be" (44:6-7). "I am the Lord, and there is no other" (45:5).

Here is what this great prophet of the exile teaches: God is Lord over the Babylonians and the entire created universe; God has accepted the tears and prayers of his exiled people; he has declared their suffering to be over; he is preparing a highway in the desert for their return. "I, even I, am he who blots out your transgressions for my own sake, and remembers your sins no more" (43:29). God has not been humiliated by the Babylonian gods. Israel was punished for her sins, but now God announces a new thing: Israel will become a light to the nations. Here in the work of the Unknown Prophet of the Exile we see for the first time a sustained description, in the most exalted terms, of God's universal purpose for *all* the peoples of the earth.

But we have not yet reached the deepest place of all. Not only does this prophet lift the eyes of Israel out of her own little plight onto the world stage where the Lord of hosts is working — even through pagan kings and armies — to make his purposes come to pass; he is also the prophet who, more than any other, has articulated the central role of redemptive suffering in the divine plan. In the mysterious but crucial passage from chapter 53, the prophet describes the Suffering Servant of the Lord: "He was despised and rejected of men. . . . He was wounded for our transgressions, he was bruised for our iniquities; upon him was the chastisement that made us whole, and with his stripes we are healed. All we like sheep have gone astray; we have turned every one to his own way; and the Lord has laid on him the iniquity of us all." No Christian can hear this without thinking of Jesus Christ, and this passage is appointed to be read on Good Friday. In the context of the exile in Babylon, however, Isaiah's Servant signifies especially the central role of suffering in God's plan of redemption. It is precisely through exile, through humiliation, through submission to God's will, that the divine mercy makes itself known.

The theme of exile is carried throughout the Bible. In the New Testament, those who come to faith in Christ are repeatedly told that they will never feel at home in this world. "For here we have no lasting city, but we seek the city which is to come," says the Epistle to the Hebrews (13:14). We are strangers on the earth. A satisfied Christian is a contradiction in terms. Who can be satisfied when a tree falls on a van and kills four bright young spirits?[5] Who can be satisfied when God is not known, when Christ is not loved, when God's children are not fed or clothed or protected? When one of you said to me the other day, "I don't like this world the way it is!" it was spoken out of the exile in Babylon.

And so this morning, to all of you who sometimes feel that you are in exile, to all who suffer unjustly, to all who are willing to listen to the prophets who tell the truth, to all who long and work for a better world, to all who cry out, "How long, O Lord?" the Word of the one and only God to his suffering people in Babylon will strike your heart with a brand-new immediacy: "Fear not, for I have redeemed you . . . you are mine. When you pass through the waters I will be with you; and through the rivers, they shall not overwhelm you; when you walk through fire . . . the flame shall not consume you. For I am the Lord your God, the Holy One of Israel, your Savior. . . . Because you are precious in my eyes, and honored, and I love you" (Isaiah 43:1-4).

Amen.

The New Covenant

ST. JOHN'S CHURCH, SALISBURY, CONNECTICUT

Text: Jeremiah 31:31-34

Do you remember a song called "My Ma Told Me Not To Put Beans In My Ears"?[1] The idea is a familiar one; the child never thought of putting beans in his ears until he was forbidden to do it. Then, of course, he was immediately seized with a desire to attempt the experiment as soon as possible.

The lure of the forbidden was just as strong in St. Paul's day as it is in ours. Paul writes, in the seventh chapter of the Epistle to the Romans, "If it had not been for the law, I should not have known sin. I should not have known what it is to covet if the law had not said, 'You shall not covet.' But sin, finding opportunity in the commandment, wrought in me all kinds of covetousness . . ." (Romans 7:7-11). Here Paul spells out for us the relationship of sin and the law. The commandment gives sin an opportunity it did not have before. As soon as the hapless human creature is told not to do something, the urge to rebel becomes overwhelming.

The story told by the Old Testament is a story of rebellion. It begins with God's goodness in creation followed by the primal disobedience of Adam and Eve, who cannot resist the forbidden fruit. The narrative continues with the unconditional covenant made by God with Abraham, violated repeatedly by various forms of disobedience in the lives of Abraham's offspring. God does not give up;

he sends Moses to deliver the people of Israel from their bondage in Egypt. In the Sinai wilderness he gives them a new start, declaring them to be his people and giving them the Ten Commandments which were to be their charter of freedom. Before the tablets even have a chance to cool off, however, the rebellious people are already making a golden calf to worship behind Moses' back. Still, God does not give up. He brings them into the promised land in spite of their repeated betrayals. True to form, they no sooner settle in than they start casting sidelong glances at the forbidden gods of Canaan. God sends them prophet after prophet to warn them, but they continue to disobey the commandments, especially the first one: "Thou shalt have no other gods but me." Those of you who were here last Sunday know what happened next; two mighty pagan powers from Mesopotamia, first the Assyrians and then the Babylonians, swept over Israel, destroyed the Temple of Solomon, ravaged her towns and cities, and carried off her people into exile.

This brings us up to date in our Lenten series from the Old Testament. The readings during Lent are chosen because of their special importance to our faith. The lesson from Jeremiah today is one of the most crucial passages of all.

It's important to understand the historical context. Without the Hebrew prophets, you and I would not be here in church today. Without the Hebrew prophets, the faith of Israel would have perished from the earth. Today's lesson is taken from a letter written by Jeremiah to comfort the Jews whose institutions and culture had been destroyed by pagan invaders. Jeremiah was one of the two great prophets (the other being Ezekiel) who lived through the Babylonian invasion and exile. We must try to understand the plight of the exiles. Being driven away from home was bad enough. Far worse was the overwhelming sense that they had been abandoned by God. How were they to cope with this terrible, life-threatening feeling? They were faced with two unacceptable theological alternatives: Either God was too weak to defend them against the foreign powers and their gods, or he had cast them aside permanently because of their disobedience to his commandments. In the midst of this acute dilemma, here is what Jeremiah wrote: "Behold, the days are coming, says the Lord, when I will make a new covenant with the house of Israel and the house of Judah, not like the covenant which I made with their fathers when I took them by the hand to bring them out of the land of Egypt, my covenant which they broke. . . . This is the covenant which I will make with the house of Israel after those days, says the Lord: I will put my law within them, and I will write it upon their hearts; and I will be their God, and they shall be my people . . . for I will forgive their iniquity, and I will remember their sin no more" (Jeremiah 31:31-34). This key passage gives us the term "New Covenant," or "New Testament." At the Last Supper, when Our Lord says, "This is my blood of the new covenant," or "new testament" (I Corinthians 11:25), he is thinking of Jeremiah's words.

Why did there need to be a New Covenant? What was wrong with the old one? Was it too harsh? Was it too difficult? Was it too unloving? Was it too — you know, *too Old Testament?* No, there was only one thing wrong with the old one; it didn't have the power to create obedience. Sin was in league with the commandment — because, Paul says, "apart from the law sin lies dead." As the apostle famously continues in Romans 7, "I can will what is right, but I cannot do it. For I do not do the good I want, but the evil I do not want is what I do." So the story of Israel, which is the story of us all, tells of a people who have "suffered shipwreck on God and his commandments."[2]

In his celebrated *Confessions,* St. Augustine wrote of his struggles to obey God's law. "O God!" he cried, "Make me chaste! . . . but not yet!" No more eloquent account of the incapacity of the unaided human being to obey God has ever been written. He compares the paralysis of the human will to being locked in a room. The prisoner can *will* to get out, but that's no help. Only the person outside with the key can set him free. Augustine felt that he was helpless before the demands of the Law.

So what does God do in the New Covenant? Does he soften the old covenant? Does he make it easier? Does he announce that he used to be the mean God of the Old Testament but has now decided to be the all-forgiving God of the New Testament? Does he say, "That's okay, Augustine, that's okay, Fleming; you don't really have to follow any of those commandments; I was just kidding"? None of the above. If anything, he ups the ante considerably. Remember the Sermon on the Mount? Jesus says, "You have heard that it was said to those of old, 'You shall not kill; and whoever kills shall be liable to judgment.' But I say to you that every one who is angry with his brother shall be liable to judgment" (Matthew 5:21). And he said, "You have heard that it was said [to those of old], 'You shall love your neighbor and hate your enemy.' But I say to you, Love your enemies and pray for those who persecute you" (Matthew 5:43-44). And of course, thanks to Jimmy Carter, we all know the line about how looking on a woman lustfully is the equivalent of committing adultery in one's heart. So, no, God does not weaken the Old Covenant in the least when he makes a new one; he makes it a lot stronger.

All our lives, if we have any sense of what it means to be a Christian at all, we must wrestle with the discrepancy between what we are and what God wants us to be. This conflict rages within us. Each of us must cope with the consequences of our bad actions, or our cowardly inactions. This is part of what it means to come under God's judgment; we must live with our various failures. Even if we are successful in hiding our sins from others, God sees and knows our inmost being. "O God to whom all hearts are open, all desires known, and from whom no secrets are hid. . . ." We are in a bad fix before God. Our story is one of prolonged and habitual disobedience. That is what the Babylonian exile means; we are at an impasse.

Well, if the New Covenant isn't any less demanding than the old one, what good is it? If we can't obey the old one, what is the use of having a new one? If the new one isn't any easier, what is the difference between them? Now hear the Word of the Lord: "I will make a new covenant with the house of Israel and the house of Judah, not like the covenant which they broke. . . . This is the covenant which I will make with the house of Israel after those days, says the Lord: *I will put my law within them, and I will write it upon their hearts.*" What is the difference between the Old Covenant and the new one? Just this: the new one will be written in our hearts.

This is not the same thing as the somewhat hackneyed distinction between the "letter" and the "spirit" of the law. The New Covenant operates in a far more powerful way than that. I refer to the sermon of two weeks ago on the Ten Commandments: when God's law is written in our hearts by the Holy Spirit, we discover that God's will and our will is one and the same. Not only will we *not want to* be perpetually angry with our brother, not only will we *not want to* commit adultery, we won't commit adultery, we won't nurse anger, and we won't even notice that we don't do it. That's freedom! Our wills have blended into God's will.

Impossible, you say. Precisely. It's as impossible as unlocking the door from the inside with no key. It has to be done by divine intervention. Something has to work upon us from beyond ourselves. That is exactly what God announces through Jeremiah in his New Covenant. "With men it is impossible, but not with God," said Jesus, "for all things are possible with God" (Mark 10:27).

We can all agree, I'm sure, that racial division in America is one of the most formidable problems facing us. Here are two stories about two Christian women, one white, one black, in whom the New Covenant has been at work. The white woman was a member in the church of my childhood, located in rigidly segregated Southside Virginia. Her teenage son was killed by a car full of intoxicated joyriding black youths. I will never forget one day in my mother's living room (this was decades before the civil rights movement really took hold in the area). The bereaved mother said, "I don't understand why I don't hate those drunken colored people." She paused. "I guess God has given me a forgiving heart." *All things are possible with God.*

An article about the second woman, Jean Griffith Sandiford, appeared in the December 18 *New York Times*.[3] Her son was Michael Griffith, attacked for no good reason ten years ago in Howard Beach, Brooklyn, by a band of white teenagers. His mother, who was frequently seen reading her small Bible during the trial, says that the pain of her son's death has not diminished over the years. "Sometimes I sit here and cry," she said. But speaking of the three men still in prison for the attack, she said, "At night I pray for them. I ask God to forgive them. When I talk to people about that, they say, 'You're crazy; how can you feel that way about somebody who killed your son?'" Yes; crazy. St. Paul wrote to the Corinthian church, "The message of the Cross is foolishness to those who are perishing, but to us who are being saved it is the power of God. Has not God made foolish the wisdom of the world?" (I Corinthians 1:18-19) These two women are examples of the New Covenant at work. They did not even know how they had received this power that they had in their hearts, but they knew it was "not their own doing, but a gift from God" (Ephesians 2:8). This is the way the New Covenant works; God writes it on our hearts. It becomes like breathing. It happens, because God gives it. The urge to violence and revenge went no further because of those women's reactions. The cycle of bitterness came to a halt before the power of their deeply internalized Christian faith.

These two women were women of prayer. They sought God's will precisely at the point when human nature wants to go in another direction. The Lord's will, Jeremiah teaches, cannot be stopped by the disobedience and sin of human beings, but as people of the New Covenant, our part is to pray daily that our wills would be conformed to his. This is true prayer — not prayer that God would give us things, but prayer that we would seek his will above all else.

Next Sunday is Palm Sunday. The Lord goes his sorrowful way. In the Garden of Gethsemane he kneels on the ground in agony. He sweats drops of blood in his anguish (Luke 22:44). He prays, "Not my will, but thine, be done." In him all the history of Israel is summed up. Our disobedience becomes his burden to carry, like the scapegoat going away into the wilderness to Satan. "The Lord has laid on him the iniquity of us all" (Isaiah 53:6). In Jesus, the Son of God, the New Covenant is fulfilled. When you come forward to receive his "blood of the New Covenant," you may rest secure in the knowledge that he gives himself to you. God has seen us foolishly putting those beans in our ears, and he has come with the key to our prison doors. He is working through his judgment to recreate our wills and give us "the obedience of faith" (Romans 1:5).[4] Here are his tender words to us, spoken through Jeremiah: "Is Ephraim my dear son?[5] Is he my darling child? For as often as I speak against him, I do remember him still. Therefore my heart yearns for him; I will surely have mercy on him, says the Lord" (Jeremiah 31:20). Dear people of God and heirs of the Covenant, do not fail to receive this mercy into your heart today, with joy.

Amen.

His Dereliction, Our Deliverance

CHRIST CHURCH, GROSSE POINTE, MICHIGAN

And they went to a place which was called Gethsemane; and he said to his disciples, "Sit here, while I pray." And he . . . began to be greatly distressed and troubled. And he said to them, "My soul is very sorrowful, even to death; remain here, and watch." And going a little farther, he fell on the ground and prayed that, if it were possible, the hour might pass from him. And he said, "Abba, Father, all things are possible to thee; remove this cup from me; yet not what I will, but what thou wilt."

Mark 15:32-36

Eloi, eloi, lama sabachthani? (My God, my God, why hast thou forsaken me?)

Mark 15:34

Palm Sunday is a very strange day. Its proper name is the Sunday of the Passion, because the story of Jesus' suffering and death is always read. A case could be made that this is the most important Sunday of the year to come to church. It's deeply encouraging to see so many of you here, because it's a tough Sunday. It begins in celebration, and it ends in catastrophe. We come in joyful, and we go out stricken. This day is not for the faint of heart. I once knew a woman who wouldn't come to church on Palm Sunday because she couldn't stand being asked to shout "Crucify him!" I always felt very sad for her. She had missed the whole point. She could have come to church every other Sunday of the year and she still would have missed the whole point.

What is the point? Let us take our cue from St. Mark, since this is his year. There is something the evangelist St. Mark wants you to know. Did you ever think about that? We would not be here today if it were not for the fact that the Bible was written by people who were willing to give their lives in order to get the message out, not just for their own time, but for all time. We have just heard Mark's Passion narrative. Mark's Gospel moves toward this climax as toward its sole reason for being. His entire book is structured so that its meaning is concealed until the moment of Jesus' death on the cross. Mark wanted his readers to understand the meaning of this death more than he wanted anything else in the world. Each day this week, we will move deeper into the heart of these events. Not everyone is willing to enter into the Passion. If you are willing, you may count yourself blessed, because that willingness means that the Lord is moving in your heart to draw you to himself. And so this sermon comes with an invitation: are you willing?

Let us follow Mark. He deliberately frames his dramatic account with two sayings of our Lord in Aramaic, one at the beginning of the Passion story, and one at the end: In the garden of Gethsemane Jesus prays, "Abba, Father, all things are possible to thee; remove this cup from me; yet not what I will, but what thou wilt"; and from the cross, he cries out, "My God, my God, why hast thou forsaken me?"

Both these sayings have caused offense, the second — the Cry of Dereliction — in particular. It's important to realize how remarkable it is that Mark and Matthew preserved it and passed it along. They could have just left it out. Luke, as a matter of fact, omits it altogether. Mark, however, clobbers us over the head with it. Let's try to understand why he does this.

Matthew, Mark, and Luke[1] all tell us that when Jesus came into the Garden of Gethsemane after the Last Supper, just prior to his arrest, he was assailed by dreadful emotions. Mark uses very strong words. In one translation[2] it says that he was "horror-stricken and desperately depressed." The scene is traditionally called "the agony in the garden."

The trouble with traditional names of that sort is that they roll off the tongue with the ease and thoughtlessness of familiarity. It requires a great effort of the imagination to recapture some of the intensity of Jesus' struggle. We need to try to realize how deeply shocked the disciples must have been to see their supremely self-possessed Master overtaken by such a tempest of emotion. Their reaction was to withdraw into sleep, very much like a depressed person today. They simply could not cope with that much pain.

The prayer of Jesus in the garden is famous — perhaps too famous, for it is hard for us to hear it with open ears. Repetition threatens to make the story stale. We must work hard at recovering its original impact. "Abba, Father, all things are possible to thee; remove this cup from me; nevertheless, not my will, but thine, be done." It would not be too much to say that this brief prayer encapsulates the greatest struggle the world has ever known.

What exactly *was* going on in the Garden of Gethsemane? There are two lines of interpretation. The most obvious one is that Jesus shrank from the thought of death, and particularly from the thought of a degraded, debased, public death. But this way of understanding the agony in Gethsemane has not satisfied everyone. You may not be aware that from the very beginning of the Christian era the episode has caused scandal. In 170 AD a learned pagan named Celcus wrote a diatribe against Christianity. He demanded to know how a person reputed to be the divine Son of God could "mourn and lament and pray to escape the fear of death?" The question has arisen again and again as to why Jesus should have undergone such a horrendous inner struggle when many historical figures — Socrates is often mentioned — have gone to their deaths with great peace and serenity. Why the discrepancy? This question demands an answer. I don't mind telling you that I struggled for years with this question before I found the interpretation that seemed to me to point in the right direction.[3]

The struggle of Jesus in the garden is linked to what happens the following day, on Good Friday. As he hangs on the cross, Jesus becomes so totally identified with human sin that he cries out, "My God, my God, why hast thou forsaken me?" There is a key passage in the prophet Habakkuk: "Thou art of purer eyes than to behold evil, and canst not look on iniquity" (1:13). St. Paul says that God made Jesus *to be sin* (II Corinthians 5:21). If this is true, then God the Father must avert his eyes and Jesus must experience abandonment. The dread of Jesus in the garden is not the dread of death; it is the dread of the Godforsakenness of sin. We must understand that the Jesus who prays in the garden has never experienced sin. He has looked upon it and lamented it; he has denounced it; he has forgiven it; but he has never yielded himself to its power — not until Good Friday. All during the night of Maundy Thursday, the Lord wrestles, through prayer, with his destiny until he is sure that the will of his Father and his will are one will — even to the point, and this is all but unthinkable, of submitting to total abandonment.

There are a lot of things that you and I fear in this world; loss of power and loss of love are close to the top of the list. Fear of abandonment is perhaps the greatest fear of all, because being abandoned means the loss of power and the loss of love forever. When we see people doing desperate things, it is because of this fear. Politicians will sell their souls, mighty men will torment the helpless, corporate executives will fake documents and shred files, club members and gun owners and flag wavers and residents of exclusive communities of all sorts will go ballistic if there is the slightest threat to their way of life, and it is all because of fear. When Jesus rose from his knees in the garden he had overcome fear, and he proceeded to relinquish every form of power known to this world, every source of love, and above all his closeness to his Father. The New Testament speaks of Jesus predicting his own Resurrection, but I think it is not wrong to say that when he rose to his feet in Gethsemane he was preparing to shoulder a weight that for all he knew might truly crush him forever — a weight not only of death, but of God's eternal condemnation.

IT is important to understand that we do not see in the Cross a wrathful Father doing something terrible to an innocent son. Nothing could be further from the truth of what is going on in the Garden of Gethsemane and on Calvary. What we see is that Jesus, the representative man, our substitute, not only *shows us how* human will aligns itself with God's will, but also *makes it happen,* in his own person; and then, in the greatest act of love that has ever taken place, he gives his own person to us. The death of Jesus on the cross is the Father and the Son acting *together,* with one will, for one purpose — to deliver you and me from the condemnation that the Son of God bore away from us.

In your book of daily meditations by Christ Church members, Bruce Birgbauer has written something very deep: He says, "Most people have difficulty with the concept of sin." This is true. This difficulty keeps people away from the Cross. It prevents them from entering into the meaning of Holy Week. Mr. Birgbauer goes on to say that being a Christian leads us into "recognizing that each of us, including myself, sins in thought, word, and deed *on a daily basis.* Busy-ness, lack of patience, failure to be thoughtful, a sharp tongue — all are evidence of our sinful nature." He writes further that we need to acknowledge that "we are all sinful creatures deserving of no special treatment before God."[4] The great words of Thomas Cranmer are applicable here; we ask God to look upon us "not weighing our merits, but pardoning our offenses." I return to the woman who would not say "Crucify him!" I remember her exact words: "I just can't do it!" It was very important to her to think of herself as one of the righteous. She could not confront her own darkness. How sad this is. If she but knew it, there is great power in the act of repentance. When we acknowledge our solidarity with other sinners, we experience God's mercy as never before. This is the prayer Jesus commended: "God have mercy on me, a sinner" (Luke 18:13).

The Passion narrative of St. Mark comes to its climax with an epiphany. A Roman centurion — a pagan, a foreigner, a hated oppressor, one of those who nailed Jesus to the Cross — is the first person in the gospel to make an unequivocal, public declaration of faith. As Jesus draws his last breath, Mark tells us, the centurion declares, "Truly this man was the Son of God." We cannot know the true meaning of Jesus until we see him on the Cross. St. Paul says the same thing: "I was determined to know nothing among you except Jesus Christ and him crucified."

Every year, Holy Week presents us with a challenge and an invitation. The meaning of Christ's Cross is as near to you as your own heart. His "perfect love casts out fear" (I John 4:18). This is no time, and this is no week, for us to hold back. There is no better moment than this very day to give ourselves to him without reservation. Let us not withdraw from his pain; let us come before him this Good Friday, and let us come understanding the magnitude of what happened there. The weight of our sin, yours and mine, was assumed by him. Let us come in the full knowledge of our own culpability — for *as we do, in that same moment*, we shall recognize in this staggering event of *his dereliction* the overwhelming joy of *our deliverance.*

Amen.

Strange Ending, Unthinkable Beginning

ST. JOHN'S CHURCH, SALISBURY, CONNECTICUT

Trembling and bewildered, the women went out and fled from the tomb. They said nothing to anyone, because they were afraid.

Mark 16:8

We extend a very special welcome today to those who do not often come to church. This sermon is written with you in mind. It's always fascinating to try to figure out what Easter means to people who aren't usually here. As a matter of fact, it's revealing to inquire what Easter means even to people who come all the time. I was in a gift shop in an Episcopal church recently, looking for Easter cards. There was a big selection to choose from, but I was saddened to see that there was not one card with any reference to the Resurrection of Jesus from the dead. All the cards had flowers, bunnies, and butterflies on them. The messages were along the lines of "Happy Spring!" And this was in a church bookstore!

Well, resistance to the real message of the Resurrection is deeply entrenched, not only in the culture, but in human nature. As most of you know, I was in Grosse Pointe, Michigan, for Holy Week. There were Easter bunny banners and Easter egg trees in people's yards all over the place. Obviously we are just going to have to get used to this, but I must admit I find it startling to see Easter decorations on Good Friday. I used to think Easter was immune to the Christmas syndrome, but I guess that's not the case. Maybe it's a good thing; Christian believers are going to have to work much harder to understand the difference between generic Easter and real Easter. My host and hostess in Grosse Pointe struck a blow for real Holy Week by putting a simple palm branch on their door. Maybe the scarcity of true Resurrection proclamation will make it that much more powerful when it is heard. There is all the difference in the world between the return of nature's glory in spring and the resurrection of the dead. "Renewal," "revival," "rebirth" — these are the wrong words. *Resurrection,* in the Christian tradition, means something else.

Now don't get me wrong. I delight in filling my house with flowers and eggs during the Great Fifty Days of Easter, beginning on Easter Day. Everyone at St. John's is thrilled with the hyacinths that Betsy Smith has given to the church for you to take home, especially in light of her own bereavement. These are wonderful symbols of our Resurrection hope. Still, it is helpful to remember that in the Southern Hemisphere, it is beginning to be winter. Maybe an early New England Easter with bare branches is a good thing. "Bloom in every meadow, leaves on every bough" are still a long way off. This can be a reminder that the real message of Easter Day has nothing to do with the return of spring greenery. In fact, the wonderful hymn we are going to sing after this sermon is built on the imagery of autumn: "Christ is risen, Christ the first-fruits of the holy harvest field, which will all its full abundance at his second coming yield . . . then the golden ears of harvest will their heads before him wave, ripened by his glorious sunshine from the furrows of the grave."[1]

The furrows of the grave — that is all the women could see, that is all they could think about as they went to the tomb of Jesus at the break of day on the first Easter Sunday morning. What do you suppose they were thinking as they walked along the path? Do you think they were expecting anything? Maybe the flowers were blooming and the birds singing as they walked along. Do you think they took comfort from that? I know a woman whose child died in the spring. She says that each year the flowers and the fragrances are a torment to her, bringing back all the pain of the season of her child's death. Do you think it is likely that the women going to the tomb looked out over the fields and said to each other, "Maybe the Master is going to come back like the wheat that springeth green"? Not on your life. There is nothing in nature that could have prepared them for the Resurrection.

Among the four gospel accounts of Easter morning, Mark's is the most unsettling. We are told that the women saw the stone rolled away and they saw that the body of Jesus was not there. They heard the message of the young man, or angel: "He is risen! He is going ahead of you into Galilee. There you will see him." They were so undone by this sequence of events that they turned and ran without waiting to hear another word. It's quite dramatic; if we were filming it we would show the women grabbing up their skirts and rushing headlong from the scene even before the last syllables of the angel's announcement die away. "Trembling and bewildered . . . they said nothing to anyone because they were afraid."

The early church saw that this ending was problematic. Two alternative endings were written and were stuck on to the Gospel of Mark; we can read them in most Bibles. What interests me this morning is this final verse 8. Most scholars now believe that Mark intended to end this way, but whether he did or not, this last verse makes a powerful impression. Matthew and Luke have toned it down considerably. The impression given by Mark is one of real terror and utter inability to cope with the news just received.

One reason that the New Testament accounts of the Resurrection command respect is that the women's discovery is described in such a bald fashion. There is nothing seductive in the tale, certainly not in Mark. What a contrast to the photographs on the greeting cards! They are in soft focus; they are suffused with golden light; they are designed to make a pretty display. But what about an Easter card with a picture of panicky women running pell-mell down the road? They "fled from the tomb," Mark says, "for trembling and astonishment had come upon them."

Now I don't know if you are aware of this or not, but in this century the New Testament proclamation of the Resurrection has been under such concerted attack that a great many Episcopal clergy no longer believe in it. I have made a habit of collecting Easter sermons over the years, and it is not easy to find anyone preaching straightforward sermons about the Resurrection. Maybe we are like the women; the message is so staggering that we can scarcely bring ourselves to say anything about it. Over and over in these sermons and messages, the same words appear, year after year: *renewal, revival, rebirth.* These words are used far more than the word *resurrection.* We hear of a new season, new growth, new life. We hear of sap rising in the trees, the singing of birds, the warmth of the lengthening days. We hear of "a new season in the earth and in the heart of humanity." We hear that "the early Christians came to understand that love is stronger than death."

Seriously, now: does this really grab you? Is it possible that ideas like this would have taken hold of a tiny band of utterly demoralized, beleaguered, disgraced, scattered disciples and transformed them into a mighty power that within a few years would be shaking the foundations of the Roman Empire? One journalist who wrote a story about Easter recently described it as a "spring festival" celebrating "the ancient myths of the Mediterranean imagination." Is that what turned the disciples around? Is the miracle of Easter simply this, that the disciples "came to understand" something? Or did something *actually occur* in the darkness of the tomb in the middle of the night that was over against all human understanding altogether? Is that perhaps what Mark wants us to know?

If the greeting card racks are any indication, it really does look as though the message of the Resurrection of Jesus from the grave is going to become once again, as it was in New Testament times, the central motivating factor in the faith and life of a very few. Maybe this is the way that God wants it to be in our time. Who knows, maybe this kind of radical message might be more appealing today to those who do not regularly come to church. Maybe those of us who come all the time have become so anesthetized to the news of the Lord bursting from the tomb that we no longer hear it as it was meant to be heard. I am glad that Mark is the gospel appointed for this year. The strange ending of his Resurrection story might be for us just the extra thrust we need, like the booster on a rocket, to propel us out into a much more world-transforming view of our Lord's victory than we had before.

While I was in Grosse Pointe, the wife of a leading Detroit banker was struck by a hit-and-run driver in a supermarket parking lot and left to die. She and her husband, a devoted couple for forty years, both active Episcopalians, had just finished building the "dream house" where they were planning to move for their retirement. The Detroit papers were full of stories about how utterly devastated her husband was. Ordinary words of comfort were not reaching him. The funeral was to be yesterday. What would give that husband real hope and strength? Messages about generic life after death? Thoughts about springtime in the heart? Hopes for a renewed future? What about this: "Christ has been raised from the dead, the first fruits of those who have fallen asleep. For as in Adam all die, even so in Christ shall all be made alive" (I Corinthians 15:20, 22). Or this: "Christ being raised from the dead dieth no more; death shall have no dominion over him" (Romans 6:9). Or this: "The trumpet shall sound, and the dead shall be raised incorruptible. . . . Death is swallowed up in victory . . . through our Lord Jesus Christ" (I Corinthians 15:52-57). The reason those messages are not found on greeting cards, not even in church bookstores, is that they all speak of death and you can't mention death on a greeting card. But the proclamation of the New Testament is precisely this: that Christ has entered death and descended into hell for our sakes and has wrested supremacy away from them forever.

This is not the same thing as the immortality of the soul, or life after death. Belief in life after death is so commonplace as to be meaningless. Those poor misguided souls in Rancho Santa Fe believed in life after death.[2] We do not say in our creed, "I believe in life after death." We say something qualitatively different: "I believe in the resurrection of the body," or "the resurrection of the dead." No other faith has ever spoken of the resurrection from the dead of a historical person, let alone a person who had been publicly put to death in the most gruesome and degrading way possible. The immortality of the soul is a commonly held religious belief in all cultures, but the Resurrection, as St. Paul wrote to the Romans, is the gift of the God who "calls into existence the things that do not exist" (Romans 4:17). Resurrection means that something utterly new and unlooked for has been done by God in the midst of a dying world. This is not just human wishes about immortality carried out into infinity. This is an unlooked-for reversal of everything that human beings would have had any reason to expect. Behold, says the Lord God, "[I will] show thee great and mighty things *which thou knowest not* (Jeremiah 33:3)."

No wonder the women in St. Mark's gospel were terrified. This terror may be what Mark wanted the church to grasp. I realize that this goes against the grain of what people expect to hear on Easter Day. In some ways it is easier to go to anoint a dead body than it is to deal with a living God. Perhaps it is easier to scatter ashes into a lake than it is to commit the body of our most dearly loved one to the Lord, "ashes to ashes, dust to dust . . . in sure and certain hope of the resurrection of the dead." The news of the raising of Jesus of Nazareth is stupendous in every way, but not least is the stupendousness of its implications for life in this world. If the Resurrection is God's ultimate word to us about our destiny, and I believe it is, then there is reason for us to tremble, because recognizing this utterly new truth means that we will sooner or later be led to relinquish our dependence upon all those things that in this world meant life, truth, beauty, security, power, and wealth — even our careers, our loved ones, our very lives. If we merely surround the Easter message with daffodils and write Peace and Love on it, we have robbed the angel's announcement of its world-overturning power. That, I think, is what Mark wants us to know. "They fled from the tomb . . . because they were afraid." And even as they were fleeing, the risen Lord was going before them into Galilee; that is, he was already creating the new conditions that would transform their fear and trembling into indescribable joy. There was nothing in nature that could have prefigured this. It is a mighty event from beyond nature, from the Creator of nature. We could not have predicted it. We have no human right to hope for it. The Biblical story of creation tells how, for our disobedience and rebellion, God decreed death. But the decree has been set aside. It has been set aside in Christ. The tomb is empty. "He is not here" — he is not in nature, he is not in the ground, he is not in the trees, he is not in the sap rising — *"He is not here — he is risen."*

How do I know this? I don't "know" it exactly, the way I "know" that my daffodil bulbs are going to sprout. The Resurrection is not of that order of knowledge. It is a gift of faith.

I know it because my grandmother told me fifty-five years ago, and because one year ago on Easter Sunday a preacher whom I trusted told me again.[3] I trust the witnesses. That's what we all are, in the last analysis — witnesses. The Christian faith, in the last analysis, is built on trust in the witnesses. That's what the preacher is today, and that's all the preacher ever is — one who testifies to the truth. "He is not here; he is risen; behold, he goes before you. There you will see him, just as he told you."

Alleluia! The Lord is risen indeed!

THE SECOND SUNDAY OF EASTER 1996

Believing Without Seeing

ALL SAINTS' CHAPEL, SEWANEE, TENNESSEE

Blessed are they who do not see and yet believe.

John 21:29

Here are pictures of Jesus on the most recent covers of three newsmagazines: *Time, Newsweek,* and *U.S. News and World Report.* [1] As a secular friend said, "Hey, your man made it!" The *Newsweek* article is the best. Kenneth Woodward, that fine religion reporter, tries his best as a good journalist to disguise his faith in the Resurrection, but it sneaks through. He says, "That Jesus rose from the dead is a statement of Christian faith . . . and implies a bond of trust between those who live in the presence of Christ today and those who first carried the Easter message 2000 years ago."

There are several different ways of extending the greetings of the season to one another. "Happy Easter!" is the most familiar salutation. I have always envied the way that one of my favorite professors was able to say, with a two-fisted handclasp and a clear gaze straight into the eyes, "A blessed feast of our Lord's Resurrection!" [2] On the other end of the scale, we have hit a new low with "Have a nice Easter." To my ears this sounds something like saying to the astronaut leaving for Venus, "Have a nice trip."

The best Easter greeting, of course, is the oldest one: "Alleluia! Christ is risen!" To which the answer is "He is risen indeed! Alleluia!"

[138]

To this day, the Greek Orthodox say *Chrystos anesti* to each other as naturally as you and I say "Happy Easter," and what's more, they say it for fifty days.

I have a vivid memory of the first Easter Sunday I spent in New York City in 1982. I had just joined the staff of Grace Church at Tenth and Broadway. It was very different from any previous Easter Sunday in my life. I have always associated the Day of Resurrection with a good deal of hustle and bustle around the house, all four of us getting dressed, having breakfast, excited about going to church (this was in Greenwich, Connecticut). The crocuses would always be blooming, if not the daffodils. The grass would be greening in the front yard, and the short drive, all together, to the church, through suburban residential areas, was always replete with signs of spring. Well, this year was a startling contrast. I got up by myself, dressed by myself, drank my Carnation Instant Breakfast by myself, and drove into the city by myself.

Usually on Sunday I am very thankful for the absence of traffic going into the city, but on this Easter morning the empty highway, combined with the overcast, made the morning seem dreary and depressing. I tried singing "Welcome, Happy Morning!" to myself, and that helped some, but as I came down the FDR Drive and got off at 23rd Street, things seemed even gloomier than before. Six days a week, the streets and sidewalks of Manhattan pulsate with life; but early on Sunday mornings, the place is eerily empty. As I passed the bleak intersection of Park and 21st, I glanced over at Calvary Church. Not a man or woman to be seen, not an open door, not a single sign to show that it was the Day of Resurrection. I was beginning to feel really bummed.

I turned left off 14th Street. There are few sections of Broadway more dead-looking on Sunday than the blocks immediately north of Grace Church, consisting as they do of rows and rows of antique stores locked and bolted with iron gates pulled down over their fronts like mausoleums, or prisons. Again, there were virtually no people to be seen anywhere, and even the fact that there were plenty of parking spaces seemed to me to bode no good. It appeared to me to be the first lifeless Easter Sunday that I had ever experienced.

However!

As I slowed down and moved into the right lane in order to park across Lower Broadway from Grace Church, I glanced over at the entrance. The door was wide open, and in the doorway, dazzlingly silhouetted in his impeccable navy blue suit and white shirt, stood a parishioner named David Crum with his hands full of service bulletins and, in his buttonhole, the sparkling white carnation that identifies the Grace Church usher. My heart lifted, more than I can find words to say. As I got out of the car, my arms full of vestments and paraphernalia, I was seized by this irresistible impulse and I shouted — all the way across Broadway — "David! The Lord is risen!" And David, God bless him, without a moment's hesitation shouted back "He is risen indeed!" And as I sprinted across the street, ironbound shops and lifeless sidewalks forgotten, I knew that Easter had truly come.

On the evening of the day of Resurrection of our Lord Jesus Christ, the disciple Thomas had a lot more to feel depressed about than a few empty sidewalks. He had not seen anything to convince him that Jesus had truly risen from the dead. As the Gospel of John presents this disciple, he was a congenital pessimist to begin with — devoted to Jesus, but certain that things would turn out badly. In chapter 11, when Jesus says he is going back into Judea where his enemies are, Thomas says gloomily, "Well, we might as well go back too, and die with him." In chapter 14, when Jesus begins to speak of going away to prepare a place for them, Thomas says morosely, "Lord, we don't know where you are going, so how can we know the way?" Thomas was a believer in Murphy's law, so to speak. He sensed that Jesus was going to die and that they would be left without any future.

When Jesus actually did die, and it turned out to be the worst possible kind of death — not a heroic martyrdom of some sort but the shameful death of a condemned criminal of the lowest class — it must have seemed to Thomas like a confirmation of his darkest fears. I think many of us can sympathize with the way that Thomas went off to hug his misery to himself, refusing to be comforted. When the disciples were gathered together in that room where the risen Lord first appeared to them all, Thomas was not with them; he was so angry and bitter and broken up that he could not, or would not, seek fellowship — very much like many of us, don't you think, when we are mad at God or mad at the world and we stay away from the Lord's Supper? Thomas stayed away, and he missed it! — he missed the visit of the Lord who had risen from the dead.

The next day, the other disciples went to Thomas and they said, "Thomas! He is risen!" Try to imagine this, not as a seasonal greeting or even as a piece of startling new information, but as the transmission of the most genuinely earth-shaking message that the world has ever heard. I think we can assume that the other disciples crowded around Thomas, perhaps grabbing him by the shoulders to get his attention, saying "Thomas! Don't you hear? Don't you understand? Jesus is risen! He is risen *from the dead!* We have seen him!" It is a million miles away from "Have a nice Easter."

Thomas's response is consistent with his personality. He says, "I don't believe it, and unless I see the print of the nails, and place my finger in the mark of the nails, and place my hand in his side, I *never will* believe it." We have all known people like Thomas, perhaps we are like Thomas ourselves, creating our own conditions for faith. I won't believe unless God gives me a sign, whether it be a sunburst on Lower Broadway or a direct appearance of Jesus himself. We want to create our own conditions for faith. Sometimes the conditions we set are conditions we believe *will never be met.* Thomas has come down to us as "doubting Thomas," but that is really a misnomer; Thomas is not just a doubter, he is "downright obstinate" (Calvin), a "stubborn disbeliever" (A. MacLaren). He has already made up his mind that he is not going to accept this news into his heart.

Thomas, however, is not completely hardened by any means. Like many of us who stay away from worship for a while, hope against hope draws us back. One week after the Resurrection, the disciples are once again gathered in the house with the locked doors, and this time Thomas is with them. Once again Jesus appears in the room — as actor Tom Key says in *The Cotton Patch Gospel,* "Jesus came through — and I mean *through!* — the door!" Once again the

Lord bestows upon them his promised peace, and then he turns directly to Thomas, singling him out. Imagine that! Remember how Jesus did that all the time during his life, turning his attention to one individual person, knowing that person's heart better than he knew it himself. Imagine Thomas's state of mind, seeing the Lord right in front of him with his own eyes. If I had been Thomas I would have been completely overwhelmed, so overpowered by the unexpected graciousness and maybe also fearsomeness that I would forget all about my impertinent demand to touch his wounds.

Jesus doesn't let Thomas forget it, though. "Thomas," he says, [speaking his own words back to him] "Put your finger here, and see my hands; and put out your hand, and place it in my side; do not be faithless, but believing." In his boundless graciousness, Jesus actually grants to Thomas the signs which he so presumptuously had demanded. It is a perfect example of the way grace goes before knowledge of sin; Jesus' willingness to meet Thomas's conditions exposes the disciple's effrontery far more effectively than any rebuke would have done. Jesus does not meet him halfway; Jesus meets him all the way and from beyond all the way. Thomas must have been very ashamed to hear the Lord speaking his own stubborn, faithless words back to him again, but his joy and wonder cause him to forget himself altogether as he utters the words which are generally acknowledged to be the highest titles given to Jesus in the New Testament — "My Lord and my God."

Modern commentators are agreed that, despite the tradition in painting and sculpture, Thomas did not actually touch Jesus. As soon as Jesus made the offer, Thomas realized that it was not needed for faith. The appearance of Jesus transforms him completely; where previously his idea of faith was intellectual assent to a set of observable facts, now it becomes personal trust in a living Lord. Where previously he had assumed a "show me!" posture, now he humbly acknowledges his total dependence on the Risen One. "Do not be faithless any more, but believing," Jesus says to him. Being a believer is not a matter of accepting data; it is an attitude, a stance of the whole person yielding himself in trust to the One who gives faith, who confirms faith, who brings faith to completion.

The words that Thomas speaks — *My Lord and my God* — are the supreme titles given to Jesus in the Bible. "Nothing more profound could be said about Jesus."[3] These titles are the very same titles given in the Old Testament to God himself, Lord God of Hosts, Maker of heaven and earth. The fourth Gospel has come full circle; the proclamation of the Prologue, "The Word was with God and the Word was God," reaches its true destination on the lips of Thomas, a mere human being who would now be entrusted with carrying that proclamation to the world.

And so it comes about that Jesus says an amazing thing. Gently, looking at Thomas, he asks, "Thomas, do you believe because you have seen me?" And then, looking over Thomas's head and past the disciples and through the walls of the room and across time and space, the Lord looks up and out and across the generations into the future and, speaking to you and to me, he utters the last Beatitude: "Blessed are they who have not seen and yet have believed."

Is there anyone here today who is wondering if the Resurrection could possibly be true? Do you have conditions that must be met before you will believe? Or, perhaps, do you believe vaguely in something called "life after death" without ever having considered putting your trust in the only One who has ever come back victorious from the grave? What would it take to convince you? What would it take? Stigmata? the Holy Grail? the Lost Ark?

No. As Thomas came to realize, that is not God's way. Seeing alone does not create faith. We learned that in the ninth chapter of the Gospel of John, the story of the man born blind. He is the one who first uttered those unforgettable words, "was blind, but now I see" — while at the same time the religious leaders could not see anything at all. Seeing alone does not create faith. "We live by faith and not by sight" (II Corinthians 5:7), writes St. Paul, and Hebrews says "Faith is being certain of what we do not see" (11:1). Thomas saw the nail marks, but none of those who came to believe later saw them; they came to believe because of the apostles' testimony — *Now is Christ risen from the dead.* That is the way the Resurrection faith spread like brushfire through the Mediterranean world 2000 years ago; that is the way it still is spread today — one person telling another, one bearing witness to another, "He is risen! He is risen indeed!"

This morning I have nothing to show you in the way of proofs — no legal arguments, no signs, no stigmata, no miraculous relics. Magical proofs have I none, but what I have I give you: what I have is no less than what the first apostles had, what the Christian church has had from the beginning — the gift of faith. The church was not built on seeing with the eyes, but on the "bond of trust between those who live in the presence of Christ today and those who first carried the Easter message 2000 years ago."

And so this morning, through the word of this merely human witness, the risen Lord looks at you this very day — looks past Thomas and the other disciples through the walls of All Saints' Chapel and across eternity and says, "Blessed are they who have not seen, and yet believe."

Alleluia! Amen.

Hear! See! Touch!

ST. JOHN'S CHURCH, SALISBURY, CONNECTICUT

That which was from the beginning, which we have heard, which we have seen with our eyes, which we have touched with our hands. . . .

I John 1:1

A friend of mine lost her husband; he died of heart disease when they were still middle-aged. The men from the undertaker arrived to take the body away. The wife had had plenty of preparation for her husband's death and up to that point had been remarkably stoical. When they began to take her husband's body out of the house, however, she was overwhelmed with grief and for the first time began to cry and sob. The home health care nurse tried to console her; "It's only his body," she said. "His soul has gone to heaven." My friend wept even more uncontrollably, saying, "But it's his body I want!"

Bodies matter to us. There is a sense in which we really cannot separate a person from his body. If the body of someone we care about is subjected to indignity or brutality, it fills us with horror. Think of all the money and effort spent on recovering the bodies of those killed in the Oklahoma City bombing and on TWA flight 800. When Itzhak Rabin was assassinated a couple of years ago, his young granddaughter touched the heart of the world when she spoke about him. The most compelling part of what she said was her evocation of his "warm hands" and how she would never feel them again. Bodies matter.

Thousands of years of philosophical and religious teachings have, however, made some inroads against this basic fact of our nature. We are encouraged to believe that the body is "just" a temporary dwelling, a way-station, or even an illusion — that it has no lasting significance. It seems to me that we Americans are singularly confused about this. One the one hand, we seem to be one of the most body-conscious civilizations that ever existed; untold billions are spent each year on health clubs, exercise equipment, diet books, body sculpting, cosmetic surgery, and revealing fashions. On the other hand, Americans seem to be eager for "out-of-body" experiences as never before; modern religiosity emphasizes the "spiritual," so bookstores have whole sections on the supernatural, the transcendental, the mystical. The concept of reincarnation seems to have a fascination for many Americans who are perhaps not entirely aware of its philosophical basis in indifference to the body. No wonder we are suffering from a collective breakdown in cultural values; we are being bombarded by contradictory messages from every side.

This confusion has entered the church. Burial in the ground was the only Christian tradition for two thousand years; only in this century has cremation become fashionable. The traditional Christian burial service with the coffin present in the church and an interment in a cemetery is more and more infrequent. More and more people seem to want to get the body off the stage. And yet the medical profession is struggling with a highly problematic increase in resistance to autopsies; people seem reluctant to release the bodies of their loved ones for this worthy purpose. We are indeed confused.

The New Testament church found itself in the midst of a society that, like ours, was mixed up about the importance of the human body. On the one hand there was the overwhelming preponderance of gnostic religious teaching about the insignificance of bodily life compared to the mystical marvels of "spiritual" experience. On the other hand, there was the massive testimony of the Hebrew Bible and the Jewish tradition which was virtually unanimous: the person is a psychosomatic[1] unity of body and spirit; bodily existence is the only kind that matters; a person without a body is unimaginable. Here were two opposing views. Many early Christians did not know what to think. The popular religious beliefs of that day, as of our day, were very tempting. Surely it was more "spiritual" to think of the body as being on a lower plane of existence. One could not really expect to find the presence of the divine in human flesh; it would be distasteful somehow, unworthy, beneath God's dignity. It would compromise the deity to be trapped in something so corruptible, so material, so earthy, so — well, so *fleshy.*

In particular, this was an issue of critical importance with regard to Jesus of Nazareth, a man who was now being hailed by the young, new church as Messiah, as King, as Lord. It was claimed of him that he was the Son of God *incarnate* (from the Latin: *in carno, carnis,* flesh). Could this be believed?

The first Epistle of John was apparently written to a church that was split into hostile factions, some maintaining that Jesus was God in human flesh and others insisting that he was not — that God could not possibly have come in real flesh. The opposition said that it *looked* as though he did, but he didn't really. It *seemed* like a body, but that was an illusion. The underlying conviction of these gnostic opponents was the age-old "religious" belief, still alive and well today, that bodily life was of a lesser order than "spiritual" life. This was directly counter to the Hebrew conviction that there isn't any such thing as real human life without a body.

So the author of our Epistle for today wrote a message to counteract this confusion and to set perplexed Christians straight on what the Incarnation really was. He begins with these words:

"That which was from the beginning, which we have heard, which we have seen with our eyes, which we have looked upon and touched with our hands, concerning the word of life — the life was made manifest, and we saw it, and testify to it, and proclaim to you the eternal life which was with the Father and was made manifest to us — that which we have seen and heard we proclaim also to you" (I John 1:1-3).

This is a fascinating passage on many levels. It's somewhat

garbled in Greek and difficult to translate into English, but the basic message is clear: God's life has appeared in the world in Jesus Christ, in a form that could be heard, seen, and touched. In another passage from this same letter, the author drives the point home:

"Beloved, do not believe every spirit, but test the spirits to see whether they are of God; for many false prophets have gone out into the world. By this you know the Spirit of God: every spirit which confesses that Jesus Christ has come *in the flesh* is of God, and every spirit which does not thus confess Jesus is not of God" (4:1-3).

The message is reinforced by the gospel reading from Luke this morning. After his Resurrection, Jesus appeared to his disciples, who were scared to death because they thought he was a ghost — and in the Hebrew mind, a ghost was not a good thing to be: "And he said to them, 'Why are you troubled, and why do questionings rise in your hearts? See my hands and my feet, that it is I myself; handle me, and see; for a spirit has not flesh and bones as you see that I have'" (Luke 24:38-9). "That which . . . we have heard, which we have seen with our eyes, which we have . . . touched with our hands . . . that which we have seen and heard we proclaim also to you."

It is no accident that these passages are read during the Easter season. We are forcefully reminded of the Christian proclamation of the resurrection of the *body,* as we say in the Apostles' Creed.

To this day there is great resistance to the doctrine of the resurrection of the body in general, and the Resurrection of Christ in particular. This resistance isn't just doubt that such a thing happened. It's also because it seems so "unspiritual." The Resurrection of the body doesn't seem "religious" enough. Surely, what we call "life after death" isn't so mundane and prosaic as to include muscle and bone, lymph glands and blood vessels — not to mention what St. Paul calls "the less honorable parts of the body" (1 Corinthians 12:23).[2] To be sure, Paul makes it clear in his teaching about the Resurrection that our bodies will be *changed;* they will be different, as Jesus' body was different. Yet the New Testament message of the Resurrection is one that takes bodily life seriously. There are early Renaissance paintings of heaven, not as naive as they might look; what they show is not a bunch of white-gowned, winged figures floating about in the clouds, but a group of recognizable human beings, grabbing each other, hugging each other, fairly knocking one another's hats off for joy.

Bodies matter. The Hebrew and Christian Scriptures are in no doubt about it. Our bodily life is just as important as our so-called "spiritual life." That's why sexual ethics are so important in Biblical faith; bodies matter. They are not to be treated casually or disposably.

The ultimate proof that bodies matter is that Jesus had one. The First Epistle of John insists on this, as does our gospel reading from Luke. Last week we heard the story of Thomas, who says he won't believe until he sees and touches the wounds in the Lord's body. Faith in Jesus means that he really lived, really died, and really was raised from the dead into a new kind of authentic bodily existence that still bears the scars of his life as one of us.

The temptation to spiritualize Christianity has always been a problem. The first Epistle of John was written in large measure to counteract this tendency. The rest of true Christian faith is the claim that the Son of God took on human flesh. We need to understand what this means. Jesus didn't just come and inhabit a human body for a while, sloughing it off when he was finished with it. He actually became united to our mortal condition. He became a bloody dead body, publicly displayed as unwanted rubbish — that's exactly what crucifixion was supposed to indicate. He became one with our condition in his total nakedness and helplessness. It was not a mythic religious ritual; it was the most irreligious thing that ever happened. The Christian claim that the eternal Creator God paid the penalty for our sin in his human flesh remains unique in all the world.

But now let us ask ourselves what good it really does in the last analysis to believe this? Suppose a hijacker was going to shoot all the hostages on a plane and one of the commandos who was supposed to rescue everybody climbed into the plane, laid down his gun, and said "Shoot me, too"? We might be amazed at the gesture, but what earthly good would it do? It would not save a single hostage.

The extraordinary message of the New Testament is that Jesus has not just entered our condition in order to die alongside us. He has not entered into bodily human life merely in order to share it with us. In entering human flesh, he has actually overcome the enemy. He has won the definitive and final victory over all the ills that flesh is heir to. St. Paul declares, "As we are united with him in his death, so we shall be united with him in his Resurrection." The gospel depends on this; a Jesus without flesh and blood is not the Lord and Savior of Christian faith.

Faith is the right word. The truth of the Resurrection of our Lord is apprehended in this life only by faith. But there is nothing more powerful than faith.[3] It has immediate and practical consequences. It makes a difference in how we live and how we die. I just got back from Birmingham, Alabama. They have a wonderful museum there that tells the story of the civil rights movement, and the role of the Christian gospel in it. When the demonstrators and protesters sang "We Shall Overcome," it was with the unconquerable faith — preached nightly in the black churches — that the overcoming of oppression derives its strength from the overcoming of Jesus. The victory of the Resurrection is enacted over and over again in the flesh-and-blood conflicts of this present world. That includes you and me in our own mundane struggles against such things as bitterness, resentment, impatience, envy, small-mindedness. In spite of all the ambiguity and vulnerability of our fleshly nature, we are precious in the Lord's sight. For us he has assumed that vulnerability; for us he has undergone its consequences; for us he has been raised out of the grave. On behalf of all victims and hostages everywhere, including ourselves in all our various bondages, at this moment as we are gathered for the proclamation of this message, let us in heart and mind embrace the wounded hands and feet of our dear Master and Savior, Jesus Christ, our Lord and our God. "As we are united with him in his death, so also shall we be united with him in his Resurrection."

Amen.

Ascension Day in Pretoria

GRACE CHURCH, NEW YORK CITY

The Psalm appointed for Ascension Day is #47. Here are a few verses from it:

> Clap your hands, all you peoples;
>> shout to God with a cry of joy.
> For the Lord most high is to be feared;
>> he is the great king over all the earth.
> He subdues the peoples under us;
>> and the nations under our feet. . . .
> God is king over all the earth;
>> God sits upon his holy throne. . . .
> The rulers of the earth belong to God;
>> and he is highly exalted.

And here is the latest report from South Africa:

> The power that had belonged to whites since they first settled on this cape 342 years ago passed today to a Parliament as diverse as any in the world, a cast of proud survivors who began their work by electing Nelson Mandela to be the first black president of South Africa. . . . Mr. Mandela appeared on a high balcony at the old Cape Town City Hall, gazed out at the bay where he spent more than a third of his adult

life on an island prison, and spoke his presidential theme of inclusion. . . . Afterwards Archbishop Desmond Tutu, the irrepressible Anglican Primate of Southern Africa, who serves as a kind of national toastmaster, sprang to the microphone and gleefully shrieked, "We are free today! We are free today!"[1]

And from Francis X. Clines's "Reporter's Notebook," under the subhead, "A Jubilant Archbishop":

More prominent than the red of Leninism was the clerical purple of Christianity sported by Archbishop Tutu. . . . The Anglican Primate of Southern Africa arrived at Parliament in a state bordering on delirium. "It's a transfiguration!" he shouted of the power shift. Rabbi Jack Steinhorn . . . part of the multi-denominational phalanx led by the Archbishop, shrugged and smiled. "We're the God squad," he explained as the archbishop fairly whirled on into the Parliament.

And on Monday, the *Washington Post* featured on the top of the front page a large photo of Nelson Mandela and Archbishop Tutu side by side, Mandela listening as Tutu addresses the throng. It is hard to resist the happy thought that God planned the whole thing for the feast of the Ascension which the church celebrates tonight and tomorrow.

It is a day and a time for us deliberately and consciously to rid ourselves of the idea that the Ascension of Jesus into heaven is a faintly comical conception that even the finest painters have had trouble portraying; no matter how great their skill, Jesus' feet as he rises off the ground never look quite right, and the artificiality of the renditions just emphasize the difficulty. The meaning of Ascension Day is not that Jesus went up into the clouds as though a puppeteer on high had jerked a string. The meaning of Ascension Day is that Jesus the Son of God reigns over all things. The Epistle to the Hebrews explains it: "[Christ] reflects the glory of God and bears the very stamp of his nature, upholding the universe by his word of power. When he had made purification for sins, he sat down at the right hand of the Majesty on high" (Hebrews 1:3).

And so the people of God rejoice on this day in a way that would be incomprehensible if all we believed was that Jesus went sailing up into the sky. In fact, in the reading for Ascension Day from the book of Acts, the angels warn against such an interpretation when, in today's Gospel, they say, "Men of Galilee, why do you stand looking into heaven?" The place to look for Jesus is right here and now in the events of this earth. The Holy Spirit, given at Pentecost, will be at work not far off in the empyrean but in the human story. Only the eyes of faith can see it, however. There were no news reports of Jesus' Ascension in the *Jerusalem Times*. There were no evening broadcasts or tabloid headlines announcing that a recently crucified rabbi had levitated out of sight. The Ascension is not accessible to scientific investigation. The work of God in human history remains, as always, discernible through faith alone. God has planned it that way. Faith is a very creative thing; God has enlisted us as partners in faith and hope. That is what Nelson Mandela and Archbishop Tutu and, it should be said, former President de Klerk have been engaging in — a work of faith and hope. Bishop Tutu never gave up on his vision of transfiguration. It kept him going when, humanly speaking, there seemed to be no hope. It was his strength again and again when he was tempted to slip into espousing violence. He is one of the greatest Christian witnesses of our time or of any time.

Bishop Tutu has credibility of a special sort because he has looked evil in the face for many years, when there was no human reason for hope. He never sought to gloss over the hard truths of human life. Nor can *we* afford to be starry-eyed. *Time* magazine this week has a horrifying cover. There is a quotation on it. It reads, "There are no devils left in Hell; they are all in Rwanda." It would be a gross understatement to say that Africa has not become a paradise overnight. Nor will the euphoria in South Africa last. There will be disillusionment and violence; white people will keep on discriminating against black people just as they do here in the United States. The human heart is, as we read in Ecclesiastes, "full of evil, and madness is in men's hearts" (9:3). But the world will not forget the sight of Nelson Mandela and F. W. de Klerk clasping hands over their heads in a gesture of victory. The world will not forget Nelson Mandela's words about his former enemy, "one of the greatest reformers, one of the greatest sons of our soil."[2] The world will not forget that Mandela invited his former jailer to his inauguration. Human hope is made of such moments — no, on second thought, not human hope, but *divine* hope, the hope against hope (Romans 4:18), the hope that is in Christ Jesus risen and ascended to the right hand of power. "Clap your hands, all you peoples; shout to God with a cry of joy. God is king over all the earth; the rulers of the earth belong to God."

Every account of Bishop Tutu mentions his unquenchable high spirits. For a number of years I have kept a photo in my office. It was taken about ten years ago when apartheid was still in full cry. It shows four men, all of them larger-than-life Christians. Two of the men are physically large as well; they are the Archbishop of Canterbury, Robert Runcie, and Terry Waite. One of the men is medium-sized; he is Allan Boesak. The fourth man is very short. He is in the center of the picture. He is Desmond Tutu. All of these men are laughing uproariously. It is clear that Bishop Tutu has just told a joke. It is, for me, a picture of heavenly reality. They have their heads thrown back and looks of joy on their faces. Death has no dominion over them. "Clap your hands, all you peoples; shout to God with a cry of joy."

C. S. Lewis wrote in *The Screwtape Letters* that the one thing the devil could not endure was being laughed at. The unquenchable joy of Christians even *(especially!)* under oppression is one of the most powerful weapons in the arsenal of the "God squad." One of the most rapturous news stories I have ever read in my lifetime is the Francis X. Clines story on the front of the *Times* today.[3] On the day of the new president's inauguration, Clines rode the commuter train from the Soweto ghetto into Pretoria. He tries to maintain some degree of reportorial decorum, but it is obvious that he is completely bowled over by the celebration on the train. During the three-hour ride, the black South Africans who ordinarily ride the train to go to their jobs in the white enclaves of Johannesburg danced the "toyi-toyi" in the aisles. Clines writes that the train was "traditionally a sardine-can affair for the ostracized black underclass of apartheid, but today a vehicle of historic exultation. . . . Whatever the exuberance level of the formally choreographed proceedings, most of the watching world missed the full truth of South Africans' joy, not being aboard the toyi-toyi train." "Clap your hands, all you peoples; shout to God with a cry of joy. For the Lord most high is . . . the great king over all the earth."

Seeing Jesus at the right hand of power over all the rulers of the earth requires discernment. As Christians in training for faith, we learn to read and watch the news with Biblical vision. Praying with the Christian Church in the name of the Lord who is risen and ascended means discerning his presence and power even in the midst of the most dreadful things that human beings do to one another, and it means resisting them. May God grant that we too will resist them in the streets and subways and workplaces of New York, by extra efforts to show respect for our neighbors of color, in honor of Nelson Mandela, in celebration of the South African miracle, and above all in the name of our risen and ascended Lord Jesus Christ.

And that leads me to bring the message of the Ascension home to every individual here tonight, for the struggle between good and evil is not just something taking place overseas in a foreign country, but something that is taking place in each individual heart as well. Jesus is not only Lord of the rulers and political movements of the world; he is Lord of each Christian and each Christian community. We too are given works of faith and hope to do. A few of us are called to do these works on a grand scale, but most of us will be fighting the good fight on the personal and local scene. I spoke recently to a Christian woman who has struggled long and hard against her own personal demons and is sometimes afraid she is losing the battle against her own worst impulses. I have tried to reassure her that her faithfulness to the risen and ascended Lord, her faith in him and her allegiance to the community that bears his name, are signs that he is Lord in her life and will not let her go. It seems to me that, again, there is an analogy to the South African situation here. In the article about the euphoric three-hour dance on the train from Soweto to Pretoria, Clines writes of the songs that the Soweto people have been singing during their long captivity — songs of resistance, songs of defiance, songs of hope and promise in spite of the seemingly hopeless circumstances, songs "intended to snatch courage from intimidation." Since the train windows were open, the ecstatic sounds could be heard by those living alongside the tracks. It is hard to believe, but Clines testifies that he saw white suburbanites waving V-signs and fists of triumph as the train passed with its load of joy. What interested me most of all is that these are the same songs that the Soweto people have been singing all along. One song of encouragement to Nelson Mandela (they always call him "Mr. Mandela") was first sung when his 27-year imprisonment was only half over. Another song from many years ago speaks of liberation in the present tense, as though it had already happened, so that even in their chains the slaves were singing, "We have cleansed this land," as though, Mr. Clines reports, it were "an accomplished fact." This is surely a marvellous image of Easter and Ascensiontide faith. We do not see Jesus reigning from his throne — not yet — but in faith and hope the reality of his victory is already present, in the small and seemingly insignificant triumphs of the human spirit, whether it be at the level of geopolitics or at the level of the individual's struggle with himself.

I leave you tonight with one final image of the Ascension of the Lord. At the end of the Inaugural ceremonies, the warplanes of the South African government rose into the air. These planes are part of a defense force that was originally built, in large part, to keep someone like Nelson Mandela from seizing power. Now it is Mr. Mandela who tells the planes what to do. As the ecstatic crowd cheered and danced, the planes flew over in formation and from their tails there streamed clouds of vapor in rainbow colors. "The kingdom of this world has become the kingdom of our Lord and of his Christ" (Revelation 11:15). Verily, verily, Jesus Christ is "Lord of the dance."

Amen.

Faith Overcomes the World

GRACE CHURCH, NEW YORK CITY

For whatsoever is born of God overcometh the world: and this is the victory that overcometh the world, even our faith. Who is he that overcometh the world, but he that believeth that Jesus is the Son of God?

I John 5:4-5

People who don't have faith, or say they don't, often seem to be interested in faith nonetheless. Over the years I have collected a number of clippings from various sources in which the writers announce that they are atheists or unbelievers and then proceed to tell a story of faith that has impressed them. I have a number of friends and conversation partners who are like this, too. They don't seem to believe anything, but they persist in hanging around with people who do. In this respect they are exactly the opposite of the cynical clergy I know who not only don't believe much of anything but also won't have anything to do with their evangelical brethren.

The other day I was chatting with an old friend, a militant atheist. He said that he wasn't too happy about having a sixty-seventh birthday. I agreed that getting older was something nobody liked. He said, rather sarcastically, "Well, it's different for you. You have eternity to look forward to." My immediate reaction to this was indignation. I protested, "That doesn't make any difference! I still don't like getting older!" The more I think about it, however, the more I think I wasted an opportunity. The next time I see him I am going to reintroduce the subject and say yes it does too make a difference. Faith in Jesus Christ and the eternal life that he gives makes a great deal of difference.

Part of me has always resisted this because it sounds as though the only reason to believe in God is the promise of eternal life. It's important to remember that the Hebrew people believed in the God of Abraham, Isaac, and Jacob for thousands of years without any promise of a life beyond the grave. The promise of resurrection was an unimaginable act of God's grace that human beings had no right to expect. The idea of believing in Jesus in order to gain eternal life seems somehow repugnant; in the Old Testament, faith in God is the right thing to have just because God is God and there is no way to live a fully human life in this world without him, never mind a life after death which the ancient Hebrews didn't believe in anyway. So it has always seemed to me more than a little manipulative to dangle "life after death" in front of people in order to convert them. I recently read Brian Moore's novel *Black Robe,* about the Jesuit mission to the Huron Indians of Canada. It's a good book, better than the movie, but ultimately I found its depiction of Christianity depressing because the chief message of the missionaries to the Indians (in the book, anyway) is that they will "go to heaven" if they are baptized. That seems to me to be a fatal diminishment of the gospel message, and one can scarcely blame the Hurons if they didn't much like it.

There is no such reduction of the gospel in the first epistle of John. The lectionary takes us through this letter during the Easter season. The genius of the Gospel and the Epistles of John is that they show how the life of faith in Jesus Christ includes not only the promise of eternal life but also a radically transformed life *now,* with power given through the Holy Spirit right this minute. Christian faith is not mere assent to propositions like "There is life after death." Faith is not what we see defined all around us as "spirituality"; that can mean almost anything. Faith is not a mere set of beliefs. Christian faith is a way of life. Dietrich Bonhoeffer, who endured two years of imprisonment by the Nazis before he was hanged, was a great exemplar in our own time of all-encompassing faith. Bonhoeffer wrote: "Faith means the finding and holding fast of this foundation [the life, death, and resurrection of Jesus Christ]. It means casting anchor upon it and being held fast by it. Faith means founding my life upon a foundation which is outside myself, upon an eternal and holy foundation, upon Christ."

Faith is a way of life. More important still, it is *Christ's* way of life. I will never forget something that was said to me years ago by a woman in the parish where I first served. She was an attractive person and she was very nice to me, so I liked her well enough, but none of that stays with me. What I remember is her telling me that a new couple had come to town — Episcopalians — and that I should make a point of cultivating them. She leaned across and said to me, in a conspiratorial tone, "They are, you know, *successful people.*" In two words, she had described her entire worldview. She and her husband were successful, their friends were successful, and everybody else was a lower form of life. I think I was supposed to be flattered that she considered me to be among the successful. She had cast her anchor upon success and expected to be held by it.

Now I am going to be very honest and tell you that I am not beyond being seduced by the world of the successful. I have found myself more than once in my life looking around a room to see who might be more interesting than whom. That is one of the reasons I need the life of the Christian church. Only in the midst of the worshiping community can we find the reinforcement we need to live the life of faith in Jesus Christ on a steady basis, because as Flannery O'Connor wrote to a wavering friend, "Some people when they lose their faith in Christ, substitute a swollen faith in themselves. . . . Let me tell you this: faith comes and goes. It rises and falls like the tides of an invisible ocean. . . . Leaving the Church is not the solution."[1]

I need the church, and so do you, because as Wordsworth famously wrote, "The world is too much with us." Who can overcome the world of getting and spending? Who can overcome the world of poses and competition and vanity? According to today's *New York Times* Styles section, our world is presently being defined by . . . guess who? Who is on the talk shows these days telling us who we are and what is good for us? Gianni Versace, Karl Lagerfeld, and Calvin Klein, that's who. I am as interested in fashion as the next person, but when I think of being enslaved by it all my life, it scares the wits out of me. I do not want to be driven all my days by some human notion of success, which in the end may or may not include you and me.

Some of us are in a stage of our lives where we are seriously in danger of being slaves to fashion, whether in clothes or "successful" careers or the latest spiritual fads. Others among us are at a very different point; one of our most devoted parishioners, for instance, is making no secret of her terminal cancer. The last thing she is thinking about is fashion and fads. Because we are all part of one another here in that organic whole called the Body of Christ, we see both horizons at once, through the eyes of the various members among us — through some we see the near horizon of daily life with its manifold temptations, and through others we glimpse that far horizon that John calls "eternal life." And so we are looking at our corporate life in two ways at once: in the light of the life, death, and resurrection of Jesus on the one hand, and, on the other, in light of — or rather, we might say, in the *shadow* of — what John calls "the world," which means all the forces that stand in opposition to God's purposes. And this is what John has to say about all of this to all of us in the lesson for today. "For all that is begotten by God conquers the world. Now this is the conquering power that has conquered the world: this faith of ours. Who then is the one who conquers the world? None other than the person who believes that Jesus is the Son of God." (Translation by Raymond E. Brown.)

There was a story illustrating all of this in the Easter Day issue of *The New York Times*. The noted journalist Francis X. Clines does not state his own position, but one imagines that he is not a believer, for he begins, "An atheist at the funeral could envy the power of religion in the life of Amy Federici, one of six people murdered by a gunman in random rage last winter on a Long Island commuter train. The 27-year-old woman's church farewell was a dark starburst of grief and sanctity. . . . The talk was of [Amy's] incandescent virtue and not of anything remotely resembling vengeance. Her parents . . . prayed by her coffin to set this tone." It appears that the reporter was sufficiently impressed that he went back again several months later to visit the family. This is what he reports: "A hard winter has since passed. For all the bulwark of religion, grief is enduring." The mother and father say that they have never before felt "such wrenching pain. . . . Both are Christians convinced they will see Amy again, but their loss is profound across temporal life, a life in which they now pray for the man accused of the slaying. 'We are burdened for his soul,' say the parents, who write letters to the other families caught in the railroad tragedy, to the parents as well of the yeshiva students mortally wounded in the [recent] Brooklyn Bridge shootings, and to dozens of others. . . . The mother is haunted . . . by the attention paid to her family. 'Why us? . . . Look at all the little ones killed in playground shootings . . . the answer in part is because we're white and this shooting came from across the lines from city to suburb.'" More puzzling is the terrible, undiscriminating embrace of the mass media, as though there were no difference between it and the Amy Fisher story. "The fact is," says the mother, "America has a passionate love for violence." In addition to its other activities, the family has actively taken up the cause of gun control.

Clines continues, "Mercifully transcending all, today is Easter. It hasn't arrived soon enough for [Amy Federici's family]. 'It's all about overcoming death,' [Amy's mother] explains. 'We live forever. Starting now.' For us the aftermath has been multifaceted, and with great beauty in many ways.'"[2]

You never know when something good might spring forth from the pages of the newspaper. This *Times* piece was obviously written especially for Easter Day. You will see right away that the Federicis are a most striking illustration of the faith that overcomes the world. The faith of this family binds together the now and the not-yet, both the unremitting struggle that is this life and the Christian hope for the world to come. "We live forever. Starting now," the mother said with dead-on theological accuracy. "This is the conquering power that has conquered the world: this faith of ours. Who then is the one who conquers the world? None other than the person who believes that Jesus is the Son of God." We can see also that this sort of faith makes a deep impression on unbelievers. That is one reason that John writes, "If any one says, 'I love God,' and hates his brother, he is a liar; for he who does not love his brother whom he has seen, cannot love God whom he has not seen." John passionately believes that Christians must demonstrate faith by love; this is a primary theme of both the Gospel and the first Epistle. It is no good saying to an unbelieving world, "See how much we love God," if the world can see that we do not love one another. Amy Federici's parents are a living example of faith showing itself through love, not in wishful thinking and psychological denial, but through the struggle and into the very jaws of death, like Christ himself, the One who said "In the world you will have tribulation, but be of good cheer, for I have overcome the world" (John 16:33).

Faith in Jesus Christ does make a difference. It makes all the difference in the world. Trusting Jesus' promise of eternal life means a significantly transformed life here and now — not necessarily a "successful" life as the world counts success, but a life grounded in the power of God to overcome every enemy, whether it be cancer or homicide or just the daily grind. And so if anyone has wandered in here today off the street, or if anyone here is wondering if faith is for you, we testify to you that although this is no perfect congregation, some years of training in the faith that shows itself in love is making a difference. We are God's work in progress. John writes, "Beloved, we are God's children *now;* it does not yet appear *what we shall be,* but we know that when he appears we shall be like him, for we shall see him as he is." We are inexpressibly grateful this morning to testify that "Faith means the finding and holding fast of this foundation [the life, death, and resurrection of Jesus Christ]. It means casting anchor upon it and being held fast by it. Faith means founding my life upon a foundation which is outside myself, upon an eternal and holy foundation, upon Christ." Then like Dietrich Bonhoeffer, like Amy Federici's family, we will be ready to meet anything that comes. "Now this is the conquering power that has conquered the world: this faith of ours. Who then is the one who conquers the world? None other than the person who believes that Jesus is the Son of God."

Amen.

The Apostolic Flame

ST. JOHN'S CHURCH, SALISBURY, CONNECTICUT

*Now we have received not the spirit of the world, but the Spirit
which is from God, that we might understand the gifts bestowed on us by God. And we impart this in words not taught
by human wisdom but taught by the Spirit. . . .*

1 Corinthians 2:12-13

Last week I read in the *Times* that in one single day — one 24-hour
period — the "Deep Blue" Website received 22 million hits.
Twenty-two million! I must admit that I was staggered by that. This
is the thought that ran through my mind: What is the use of trying
to preach sermons to little congregations in little churches, or even
in big congregations in big churches that seat thousands of people?
What is any of that compared to 22 million people logging on to
just one site on the Internet in just one day? For a few minutes I
felt very foolish and small.

Then the Lord reminded me of the power of the Holy Spirit,
and I was restored to confidence once more. How many people do
you think were gathered in that room on the day of Pentecost?
Thousands? Hundreds? Probably not more than a few dozen. But
the Holy Spirit descended upon them. Do you know where to find
the very first mention of the Holy Spirit? I think you will recognize

it: "In the beginning God created the heaven and the earth. And the earth was without form, and void; and darkness was upon the face of the deep. And the Spirit of God moved upon the face of the waters. And God said, Let there be light: and there was light" (Genesis 1:1-3). So the Spirit who was present and powerful when the Creator God spoke trillions — yes, *trillions* — of comets into being is not going to be put in the shade by the World Wide Web.[1]

What is the Holy Spirit, and what does it do? Well, first of all, we were reminded a few minutes ago in our multilingual reading of the lesson that the Holy Spirit speaks all the different languages on earth. Anything we do liturgically on this day of Pentecost, however, is only an approximation, because in the Spirit everybody understands everybody else. Pentecost is the first salvo in God's great plan to undo the effects of the Tower of Babel. I think today of the young man whose memorial service was held here this past week. He wanted to learn as many languages as possible so he could understand people better. Working hard to understand another person is a work of love. Communication and understanding are gifts of the Holy Spirit. In particular, the Holy Spirit gives us the power to understand who Jesus is and what he has done for us. Jesus himself said so, in the Gospel of John: "The Counselor, the Holy Spirit, whom the Father will send in my name, he will teach you all things, and bring to your remembrance all that I have said to you" (John 14:26).

I wonder if you noticed anything strange a few moments ago. I said "What is the Holy Spirit and what does it do?" We need to make a course correction right away. The Holy Spirit is not a *what* and not an *it*. Just before his death, Jesus said, "I will pray to the Father, and he will give you another Counselor,[2] to be with you for ever, the Spirit of truth, whom the world cannot receive, because it neither sees *him* nor knows *him*; you know *him*, for *he* dwells with you, and will be in you" (John 14). The Spirit is personal. The Spirit is a "who," not a "what." Jesus does not call the Spirit "it." He calls the Spirit "he." There is a fashion nowadays for calling the Spirit "she," but with all due respect, there is no Biblical warrant for this. The Holy Spirit is the living, personal Spirit of Jesus, therefore a "he." I admit it's tricky, because the Spirit can't be pinned down in any sort of human categories. We know this from Jesus' own words to Nicodemus: "The wind blows where it wills, and you hear the sound of it, but you do not know whence it comes or whither it goes; so it is with every one who is born of the Spirit" (John 3:8). Nevertheless, we call the Holy Spirit a "he," because the Holy Spirit is the living presence of Jesus himself. "He [the Spirit] will glorify me," said the Lord to his disciples, "for he will take what is mine and declare it to you. All that the Father has is mine; therefore I said that he will take what is mine and declare it to you" (John 16:14).

Another fashion in describing the Holy Spirit is to liken him to school spirit, or team spirit, or community spirit. This is helpful in one sense: you can't really accomplish very much if you don't have spirit. Spirit is that extra dimension that makes the difference. The great Spanish dancer Pilar Rioja builds her dance programs around the Spanish conception of that extra dimension, which they call *duende*. *Duende* is like the Holy Spirit in that it is mysterious, invisible, unbidden, yet essential to a living, breathing performance. This sermon, for instance, will be dead on arrival if the Holy Spirit is not working both in me and in you. Yet, on the other hand, the Holy Spirit is not at all like *duende,* or like team spirit, because the Holy Spirit is very specifically the third person of the Trinity — "proceeding from the Father and the Son" as we say in the Nicene Creed. Thus everything that the New Testament says about the Spirit is determined by Jesus. The Holy Spirit is not just any kind of spirit that happens to blow through. St. John writes, "Beloved, do not believe every spirit, but test the spirits to see whether they are of God . . . every spirit which confesses that Jesus Christ has come in the flesh is of God, and every spirit which does not confess Jesus is not of God" (1 John 4:1-3). Similarly, when St. Paul says, "God's love has been poured into our hearts through the Holy Spirit which has been given to us" (Romans 5:5), he doesn't mean romantic human love. He means the self-sacrificing love of Jesus that poured itself out on the Cross.

It has been said that Jesus departed from his disciples in one place at one time in order that he might be with all of us in all places in all times. This is the work of the Holy Spirit, who makes the Lord a living presence with his people wherever they are. It is the Spirit who draws us together on Sunday morning for worship. It is the Spirit who teaches us how to "love one another as [Jesus] has loved us" (John 15:12). It is the Spirit who makes Jesus present with us as we come to receive him at the altar rail. In every Eucharistic service, there is a prayer to the Holy Spirit,³ because the mysterious transaction that occurs whenever the people of God gather for the sacraments cannot happen without the Spirit. It is he whose power confirms in us the Way of Jesus, who is himself the Truth; the Lord himself said so: "When the Spirit of truth comes, he will guide you into all the truth" (John 16:13).

As surely as we are all gathered here today, the faith of the Christian Church depends for its existence on the reality and power of what happened on Pentecost. If it never happened, we should shut down St. John's this very day and convert the building to secular use.

You have heard me speak many times of the stunning stained-glass windows all around the walls of our church. They portray the Twelve Apostles. These were the most ordinary people in the world until the Holy Spirit got hold of them. They had never done anything distinctive or significant in their lives. Two things happened to transform them from feckless disciples into world-changing apostles and evangelists. Those two things were the Resurrection of Jesus from the dead and the descent of the Holy Spirit at Pentecost. The Holy Spirit is the power of the Resurrection at work in human beings. These men went out from Galilee and from Jerusalem into the far reaches of the Roman Empire and gave their very lives so that you and I would confess the name of Jesus Christ today in Salisbury, Connecticut. This happened, not because they were remarkable people, but because they were seized by an irresistible power greater than anything in cyberspace. If it were not for the anointing of those disciples by the Spirit, the message of Jesus Christ would have disappeared from the face of the earth. They were changed, that day of Pentecost, from disciples to apostles. The word *apostolos,* in Greek, means "one who is sent." It doesn't mean "one who *thinks* he is sent"; it means one who *is* sent. The true test of an apostle was his commission from the living presence of Christ himself. It couldn't be simply imagined. The apostle's words had to be, as Paul himself said, "words not taught by human wisdom but taught by the Spirit" (I Corinthians 2:13). We here in Salisbury have just as much stake in this as the first-century Christians of Ephesus or Corinth. Is the message you have heard at St. John's from God or not? Is this fellowship where many of your children and grandchildren have been baptized and your loved ones given to God in their deaths just another human association? Does our faith arise from our own religious longings or is it given from beyond ourselves altogether?

You know that we rattle off some words every Sunday: "I believe in one holy catholic and apostolic church." Take a new look at that word *apostolic.* It means that the Holy Spirit of God really did descend upon that group of insignificant men and women,[4] and it means that the message they carried to the world really is the truth about God's only-begotten Son, Jesus Christ. "We impart this [gospel] in words not taught by human wisdom but taught by the Spirit." If the church isn't *apostolic,* then the entire Christian faith and everything that arises out of it is a fraud from beginning to end.

Since it is Pentecost, I am going to ask you to do something I have only done three or four times before in my twenty years of ministry. You don't have to do this; it is an invitation, not an order. The purpose of this invitation is to solemnize your sense of participation in the apostolic flame that descended on the day of Pentecost. If you feel moved to do so, simply stand up in your places and take up your Biblical inserts. Please turn to the Epistle lesson from I Corinthians (12:4-13) and just hold it in your hand for a minute.

The conversion of the apostles was not for them. It was for you. Here is what Paul said to one of his congregations: "There are varieties of gifts, but the same Spirit." This means that you and your gifts, whatever they are,[5] are part of the indispensable whole that the Spirit is bringing into being. "To each is given the manifestation of the Spirit for the common good." Maybe you never thought about yourself that way before. Paul doesn't say "to some"; he says, *"to each."* That means that every one of you has a gift from the Spirit to offer to all the others "for the common good." If you don't know what your gifts are yet, you may confidently expect to find out, because "the Spirit which is from God [teaches us to] understand the gifts bestowed on us by God" (that's from I Corinthians 2:12). Then in the final sentence of today's reading Paul says: "By one Spirit we were all baptized into one body — Jews or Greeks, slave or free." When we have a service of Holy Eucharist before a church meeting, as we do today, it is a powerful movement of the Spirit to demonstrate in our midst that we are not just another group assembled to do business, but a fellowship gathered by a force that is not our own. Paul writes that apostolic authority is given by the Spirit for one purpose only: *for building you up* (II Corinthians 10:8). You too receive power from God today, power for life, power for service, power for ministry, power for love. May you be granted such an abundance of gifts that, through you, Christ our Lord may yet do such great things with this congregation that we cannot presently even imagine them, by the great might of his Holy Spirit.

Amen.

The Multicultural Good News

GRACE CHURCH, NEW YORK CITY

Jesus came and spake unto them, saying, "All power is given unto me in heaven and on earth. Go ye therefore, and teach all nations, baptizing them in the name of the Father, and of the Son, and of the Holy Spirit . . . and lo, I am with you always, even unto the end of the world."

Matthew 28:18-20

A few days ago, as I was beginning to think about this sermon for Trinity Sunday, I heard an agnostic friend refer to the activity of the Christian church as "proselytizing." That made my blood rise just a little; without really thinking, I said, "Not *proselytizing!* That's the wrong word." "What word would you suggest, then?" said my friend. Again, without really thinking, I blurted out, *"evangelizing."* It was on the spur of the moment, but the more I have thought about it, the more I think the Holy Spirit was teaching me. The word *evangel* is a New Testament Greek word, lying at the heart and center of our faith. It is not a word that human imagination came up with; it is a God-given word. It means "good news." Evangelizing, therefore, means, "telling good news." It is the opposite of bad news. Proselytizing sounds like bad news to me, and who wants to hear that?

Christian evangelizing is not the same thing as "religion." Religion is not good news. An exhortation to "be religious!" is not going to put a smile on very many people's faces. When somebody says "religion" to me, it immediately makes me think of all sorts of things I don't like to do; for instance, as soon as I try to meditate about something, I fall asleep. Religion comes as bad news to the irreligious, so it creates a separation between those who are self-consciously religious and those who are not. The good news of the Christian gospel, however, is *for everyone.* St. Paul writes that Christ died *for the ungodly* (Romans 5:6), which pretty much puts religion out of business. A few years ago, when our family was undergoing a crisis, I received a letter of consolation from a friend. It was a lovely letter, and I have kept it because of its heartfelt empathy, but there was one thing in it that bothered me. She said, "You are being saved by your spirituality." That's a mistake. I am not saved by my spirituality. I am not saved by my religion. I am not saved by doing the right thing or praying the right prayer or having the right attitude. I am saved by *God* — the God who in Christ is reaching out for the unspiritual, the irreligious, the ungodly. "I did not come to call the righteous, but sinners," Jesus said (Mark 2:17).

Christianity is taking its lumps these days. This is the era of multiculturalism. We live in a strange time when, on the one hand, religious tolerance is prized, but on the other hand, actual Christian faith is regarded by the cultural tsars with suspicion, scorn, or outright hostility. I see evidence for this everywhere. In many circles that I frequent, it is considered perfectly proper to discuss various forms of gnosticism, tribal rituals, Zen, and almost anything else — and indeed, to espouse them — but a genuine declaration of Christian faith is off limits. The writings of T. S. Eliot, W. H. Auden, and Flannery O'Connor are prized by Christians, but today, their reputations among the cognoscenti must be defended as though their Christianity were a defect.

This is the way it is today, even in ultra-religious America; authentic Christianity meets with antagonism from the ruling class — that is, from the media and entertainment industry. In particular, there is hostility to what is often called Christian proselytizing. It is all right for a celebrity to be a Scientologist or a Buddhist (just look at the stories in the magazines), but it is not all right to be a testifying Christian. And yet there is no true Christianity without testimony. Christianity is a missionary faith. It is an *evangelizing* faith. It always has been and it always will be, because good news demands to be told. It is selfish to keep good news a secret. Good news has the quality of joy. It wants to share itself. It wants to go beyond its own good fortune to include others. That is what the word *evangelical* means in its truest New Testament sense — the good news of God's salvation for all people. Jesus makes this explicit in the Great Commission, our text for Trinity Sunday: "Jesus came and spake unto them, saying, 'All power is given unto me in heaven and on earth. Go ye therefore, and teach all nations, baptizing them in the name of the Father, and of the Son, and of the Holy Spirit . . . and lo, I am with you always, even unto the end of the world.'" These words of our Lord are found in a strategic place, for they are the concluding words of the first book of the New Testament, the Gospel of Matthew. They are words in which Jesus turns over the good news about himself to the church. In this moment depicted by Matthew, the gospel (the *evangel*) becomes no longer simply the history of Jesus, but the driving force behind the church's service to the world. Withholding this good news would be a betrayal of God's gift. It has been given to us precisely in order that we should give it away. That is what *evangelism* means. It would be the lowest form of selfishness to hold the good news to ourselves; to do so would be a denial of our Lord who gave himself away to the last breath, to the last drop of blood, in order to reconcile the whole world to God. Christians over the centuries have been ready to risk everything for this. Five missionaries from Grace Church have put their comfort and security on the line to serve right now in Liberia, in Cambodia, in Nepal. They are enacting the words of Jesus in the Book of Acts: "You shall be witnesses to me in Jerusalem, and in all Judea, and in Samaria, and to the uttermost parts of the earth" (Acts 1:8).

In the meantime, back here in New York, we are part of the most multicultural society on earth, but many thoughtful people are worried about the way things are going. There is an increasing fragmentation of American society into ethnic and political-interest groups. There is much bad news on this front. We desperately need to be brought together. Historian Arthur Schlesinger worries about the current tendencies wherein "the new ethnic gospel [note that phrase] rejects the unifying vision of individuals from all nations melted into a new race." The way Schlesinger uses the word "gospel" here is interesting, because it clearly does not mean "good news."[1] It just means "message." An ethnic "gospel" is bad news for the American dream. Gunnar Myrdal wrote in 1944 that Americans "of all national origins, regions, creeds, and colors [hold in common] the most explicitly expressed system of general ideals" of any country, and furthermore, he wrote, the schools teach these ideals and *the churches preach them.*"[2] The church has always had this noble calling in America, even though we have often betrayed it. The American vision of many people made one through their new life in the United States continues to have power because it is grounded — whether consciously or not — in God's great plan for the redemption and reconciliation of all humanity. This is not blind patriotism, nor is it what is called proselytizing. It is announcing the good news of God's future Kingdom in terms that can begin to take shape in human society right here and right now.

When the church is really being the church, it is more multi-ethnic, inclusive, and universal than any other body on this planet. Last year I went to the Billy Graham rally in Central Park. I was not prepared for what I saw there. It was by a long way the most truly multicultural group I have ever seen gathered in New York City — more than a World Series game, more than a rock concert, more than any political rally, more even than the great antinuclear march of 1982. I could hardly believe my eyes. There were many thousands of African-Americans, many thousands of Asian-Americans, thousands of Latinos, hundreds of people who appeared to be Middle Eastern, and also people of the Indian subcontinent. There appeared to be an equal number of men and women and a significant number of gay people. A few days later I was told by a Jewish friend that he even knew some Jews who had attended. There is no "religion" that can pull all this together.

Here is a little parable of multicultural Christianity. Many of you know William, who more or less lives on my doorstep on Fourth Avenue. He's been there off and on for four years at least. William appears not to have had a bath for a very long time, so if cleanliness is next to godliness, he's a long way over on the wrong side of the fence. Yet William is one of God's people, and if only he would take his medicine, it would become clear that he knows the Bible at least as well as you and I. His greatest sin is that he sleeps all day and preaches from the Bible at the top of his lungs all night right underneath my bedroom window. As many of you know, William's habitual greeting is "Praise the Lord Jesus Christ." This is what he says to people who give him money, or something to eat, or who say hello, and often he says it to people who are just walking by. William is no fool; he's got the Fourth Avenue scene figured out. When Rosh Hashanah and Hanukkah come around, he hollers out, "Praise the Lord Jesus Christ! Happy Jewish holiday!" I find this utterly disarming. Not only is it true that the most unlikely messengers may at any time be preachers of the gospel, but also it is quite possible to speak the name of Jesus and still be respectful of others.

Last year on this very Sunday — Trinity Sunday — two Jewish friends of mine dropped in for our 11 o'clock service. I was a bit shaken to see them. I thought, Oh my God, here it is Trinity Sunday and they're going to hear this very explicit Christian sermon and they're going to be deeply offended and then what am I going to do? I forged ahead and delivered my Trinitarian, Christ-centered, evangelistic sermon, and then my friends stayed for the entire social hour and talked to everybody and we are better friends now than ever, even though they still say they don't believe in God.

There is something at the heart of the Christian gospel that makes it work for everybody, especially the ungodly and the irreligious. I am reminded of a favorite episode from the ineffable comic strip *Pogo*. Howland Owl is selling detergent, but he figures there won't be any market for the detergent unless he sells a second product along with it. The purpose of the second product is to increase the demand for the detergent. Albert Alligator looks suspiciously at the second box and says "What's the secret ingredient, friend?" and Owl says in a stage whisper, "D-I-R-T." To this day, in our family, if my mother or sister or I taste a good dish or observe something well carried out, we'll ask, "What's the secret ingredient, friend?"[3]

Well, there are two secret ingredients in our preaching this Trinity Sunday. The two of them together will break the multicultural logjam every time. The first one was suggested to me by the program we saw last Sunday about how to get along in Chinese culture. The narrator said something very simple but very profound: "Relationships are very important in China." That brought me up short, because ever since Tianenmen Square, I have been accustomed to thinking of China as a godless, repressive, tyrannical society with no respect for human rights. How quickly we consign our fellow human beings to moral oblivion! The Christian gospel is infinitely more radical and more inclusive than anything you or I would dream up. The Christian gospel is good news for the godless, which reminds us to be more careful about stereotyping others.

The first secret ingredient is *relationships*. Yet, not just any relationships. True relationships originate in God himself. That is what the Trinity signifies. God the Father, God the Son, God the Holy Spirit: God is in relationship within himself from before all time. The Father loves the Son, and the Son loves the Father, and the love that pours out between the Father and the Son takes shape as the Holy Spirit. That's what makes the living God unique. That's what differentiates God from all the non-gods, the made-up gods.

The doctrine of the Trinity is often criticized for being an abstraction. But it isn't an abstraction. In the final analysis it is an *event*. The Trinity *has happened* among us. The incarnation of Jesus Christ, the Second Person of the Trinity, into the world by the power of the Holy Spirit is good news for every person and every ethnic group on earth. Not only does God display his purpose of goodness and mercy toward humanity, he is also bringing into being an actual new community of transformed relationships, a community that can't fail because it is derived from the eternal relationships of the Father, Son, and Holy Spirit. The Trinity is the wellspring of a new humanity.

What's the second secret ingrediment, then? It's D-I-R-T. Not just William's dirt, but my dirt, your dirt, the dirt of China, Liberia, Nepal, Bosnia, the Middle East, and all the ethnic hatreds in the United States of America. That's the lowest common denominator. This is what makes the whole world kin — our need to be cleansed from our dirt. This is the *evangel* that the church proclaims. All the dirt was assumed by God himself in the person of his Son as he died on the cross for the sin of the world. All the broken and fractured relationships of human history are bound up in the Second Person of the Blessed Trinity as he took our dirt upon himself and bore it away. In Christ, we are washed clean and made into a new fellowship where relationships are grounded in the love of Christ for the *un*-lovely, the unwashed, the *un*righteous, the *un*godly. The preaching of the Word and the Sacrament of the Holy Eucharist today are not for the "religious" and the "spiritual." They are for all the unclean: those who do not know how to pray, those who have forgotten their duty, those who have had bad news, those whose relationships are in ruins, those who know their need for unconditional love — and also, wonderful to tell about, even for those who don't think they need anything at all, for God loves even the rich, the smug, and the selfish; and he evangelizes them through the small, the weak, and the lowly. In God there is enough strength to overthrow the pre-tensions of the lofty and to raise the poor from the dust. In him all races meet. In him all threads are woven together. In him there is news so good that we cannot possibly keep it to ourselves, for he has gone before us with the Great Commission to all the peoples of the earth, and lo, Jesus is with us always, even to the end of the world.

Amen.

Saved!

ST. JOHN'S CHURCH, SALISBURY, CONNECTICUT

By grace you have been saved through faith.

Ephesians 2:8

The trial of little Megan Kanka's murderer, contrary to expectations, attracted very few spectators. Various reasons for this were proposed. One reporter suggested that perhaps people could tolerate only so much information about the assault on a seven-year-old girl. Yesterday's paper detailed the horrific childhood of the murderer. I will refrain from expatiating on these ghastly circumstances except to say that, if true, they certainly explain how a person could become a brutal child killer. However, it was not these articles that caused something to snap in my mind. It was another report, on the inside of the paper. A lovely 11-year-old Chinese schoolgirl was strangled and thrown into the East River in New York. The journalist described how her classmates were gathered together by their teachers and told of the news. They were then given flyers to take home, reminding them not to talk to strangers. It was that relatively innocuous detail, more than any of the others, that made me feel deeply depressed and angry. This is the truth about the human condition: *children are not safe.* And do not think that this is true only in cities, or in low-income groups, or in bad neighborhoods.

After all, JonBenet Ramsey came from a prosperous suburban Episcopal family.

There is a problem with Anne Frank's sentence about people being basically good at heart. It was lifted from its original context and made into an inspirational slogan where it has done damage by reinforcing a sentimental view of the world.[1] The Bible teaches us that the world is full of evil. True or not true? I was taking my walk through the countryside yesterday and admiring the beauty of the day, but there were dark reflections in my heart. I was thinking about all the bodies of innocent victims that have been thrown into rivers and buried in woods. I thought about the CIA and its willful destruction of documents detailing its role in the deaths of so many people in Guatemala whose only crime was being on the wrong side of the political fence. I thought of all the suffering in — for instance — East Timor, much of it supported by American policies. I thought about the faces I saw in a series of photographs taken of victims of Pol Pot in Cambodia, young people facing the camera just before they were murdered.

You may well ask why I am hitting you in the face with all this on a June morning. The point is to drive home the fact that the world needs to be saved. It is easy to forget this when one is enjoying life in an idyllic New England village. I like to escape just as much as the next person; I often try to pretend that nothing is wrong. On the other hand I force myself to read and pray about unpleasant things, so that I will not just live in an artificial world of imaginary goodness all the time. The world in and of itself is not a good place, not since the disobedience of the first human beings. This is one of the primary teachings of the Bible and of Christian theology. I am a charter member of The Friends of the Earth and a committed environmentalist, but Christianity differs from certain environmentalist beliefs in that it does not teach of a pristine natural world free from the taint of humankind. According to Scripture, the creation is fallen along with Adam and Eve. St. Paul writes that "the whole creation is groaning in travail as it waits to be set free from its bondage to decay" (Romans 8:21-22). Annie Dillard is my favorite nature writer because she does not flinch from the nasty aspects of animal life; one of the most horrifying passages of literature I can think of is her account of a frog being killed by a giant water-bug; "it was a monstrous and terrifying thing."[2] Nature is "red in tooth and claw"[3] because it, too, suffers from the effects of the Fall.[4]

Ordinarily when the Christian church speaks of salvation, we Americans will assume that the salvation of the individual is meant. The Bible, however, speaks first and foremost of the need for the salvation of the whole created order, the whole human race. In this highly individualistic culture of ours, we need to be frequently reminded of the communal nature of human need. "No man is an island, entire of itself . . . any man's death diminishes me, because I am involved in mankind."[5] Thus Paul says in the second chapter of Ephesians that "we Christians were by nature children of wrath, like the rest of mankind." This is a sweeping statement, and it is meant to be. The Biblical writers see us all as heirs of a vast cosmic dislocation. There is no exemption from this for anyone. It's amazing and encouraging to note how, even though it is highly unpopular to talk about sin these days, the idea does continue to crop up in unexpected places. A couple of weeks ago I read an article in *The New Yorker* about the art critic Robert Hughes, who is writing a book about Goya. This is what he has to say about the Spanish painter: "Goya had a deeply Catholic sense that man was a fallen and sinful creature, which I share. He doesn't paint pictures that say, 'Here are all these people hacking one another to death, but it's all going to be O.K. in the end, chaps!'" That one comment brings us close to the Biblical frame of mind. Ecclesiastes, a very important Old Testament book, says "the hearts of men are full of evil, and madness is in their hearts while they live, and after that they go to the dead" (Ecclesiastes 9:3).[6] So that gives us the general idea of the condition of the world according to the Bible.

Now, if you can take any more of this, we turn to the predicament of the individual. Working with families over 22 years of ministry has been revealing and in some ways disillusioning. I have learned from my own psychotherapeutic supervision that even the most healthy family is "dysfunctional" — to use the currently fashionable term — in some ways. I particularly remember one family that struck me as unusually wonderful — remarkably loving and open with one another. Later I found out that two members of that family were recovering alcoholics and that two others — a married couple — were on the verge of separating. I realized I had been foolish not to notice the signs of damage that had been done. Frankly, it is a miracle of God's grace that any of us grow up sane. It is only because of God's mercy that the world has not simply spiraled down to self-destruction. I mean that with utmost seriousness. This is the picture the Bible gives us of the situation. The goodness and beauty that we perceive around us, the recovery from illness, the moments of intimacy and harmony, are all pure grace from God, not one iota of it deserved by us or ours by right.

The second chapter of Paul's letter to the Ephesians pictures the situation of the whole human race collectively and individually. First Paul says "you" — "*you* were dead through trespasses and sins," meaning someone other than his own group. Then he says "we" — "*we* were by nature children of wrath"; and then he says that *you* and *we* are in the same boat as "the rest of mankind." So you see that there is no exemption for anyone. All of us in our natural condition are prisoners of our own desires; we live "in the passions of our flesh, following the desires of body and mind."

The phrase "children of wrath" in this context is not really so hard to understand. It means that we were *deserving of* wrath — the consequences of selfish lives and ungodly ways. Now most people will deny that they are children of wrath. The usual way of getting ourselves off the hook is to divide up mankind into groups, with ourselves in the best group and everybody else in the worst groups. You and I naturally congratulate ourselves and our friends that we are not serial killers or child molesters. But who can say what we would have been without the grace of God? If our parents had been like the parents of Megan's murderer, who can tell what we would have been? There is a famous saying that needs always to be understood in its original context: "There but for the grace of God go I." It is attributed to a sixteenth-century Englishman, John Bradford, who, when watching malefactors being taken off for execution, did not say, "They are getting what they deserve," but rather, "There but for the grace of God goes John Bradford."[7] This insight was a profound factor in the transformation of the disciples of Jesus after the Resurrection, especially Peter, and it is part of the central message of Paul — gratitude to the Lord for saving us in spite of ourselves. And so the letter to the Ephesians brings us this truly thrilling news: "We were by nature children of wrath, like the rest of mankind. But God, who is rich in mercy, out of the great love with which he loved us, even when we were dead through our trespasses, made us alive together with Christ (by grace you have been saved)."

We have been saved. Not "we might be saved," or "you could be saved," or "maybe you will be saved," or any other kind of "saved" that has an "if" attached to it. Not "saved if you are good," or "saved if you are proper," or "saved if you are better than somebody else." Just *saved.* Saved not by our efforts, saved not by our virtues, saved not by our merits, but by the grace of God. Saved by the Father who, as Thomas Cranmer's Eucharistic prayer puts it, does not weigh our merits, but pardons our offenses.

The world in and of itself is not a good place. It is full of our offenses. The worst scourge of all, wrote the poet Gerard Manley Hopkins, is to be left with nothing more than our "sweating selves."[8] But the Christian gospel is that we have not been left to ourselves. We "were dead through the trespasses and sins in which [we] once walked. . . . Among these we all once lived in the passions of our flesh, following the desires of body and mind. . . . But God, who is rich in mercy, out of the great love with which he loved us, even when we were dead through our trespasses, made us alive together with Christ . . . by grace you have been saved."

And so a meager little group of perfectly ordinary people become the advance troops for God's great plan of liberation. These advance troops, these commandos, are the church. What we are called to do and be is to stand our ground on the space of grace we have been given to hold for the King, and not to retreat from it. We, the people called into being by the Holy Spirit, have daily opportunities to enact the victorious grace of God over all the hostile powers and sinful desires that afflict the human race.

Even the smallest, simplest actions can have effects that reach down the generations. I went to New York City this week to do another memorial service. That night I spent two and a half hours with the family of the woman who had died of cancer. They told many, many stories, but I remember one in particular. Please notice two things. The story is about the grace of God enacted in human life, but it is not a story with no dark undertones. Unconditional love does not mean that there is no rebuke, no call to account. The point is that when we truly experience the mercy of God, a new situation is created where judgment is not destructive, but powerful for transformation into a new, creative, and constructive life.

The daughter of the woman who died is the one who told the story. Let's call her Elaine. Elaine came home late one night after some sort of youthful troublemaking, the details of which I forget and are of no importance. Her mother met her at the door with a facial expression that every child fears to receive from a parent — tight, hard, judgmental, cold. As Elaine tells it, the mother took one look at her ashamed and exhausted daughter and her whole face softened. Every hard line relaxed. The look of judgment transmuted into a look of unconditional love. Just as in the story about the prodigal son coming home to his father, before Elaine even got a chance to say, "I know I've been bad, you don't have to tell me," the mother said, "You go get some sleep. I'll talk to you later." Many years later after her mother had died, the daughter related that story as a turning point in her life. As she told us, "Mother *did* talk to me later" — but she did so out of the new situation that had been created, one of love and not of condemnation. Thus we see that the grace of God is mediated into human life, by simple, quotidian acts of love from mother to daughter, wife to husband, friend to friend.

I read something else in the paper this past week. I read that a couple went to Russia, picked up two Russian children that they were adopting, and then reportedly proceeded to abuse the children on the airplane all the way home. Many of the passengers on the flight were so outraged that they stayed at Kennedy Airport for a long time after landing to make sure that the parents were arrested and the children were taken into safe custody.[9] A small thing for them to do, perhaps, but most of us would be exhausted after a flight from Russia and in a hurry to get home. Most of us would have excused ourselves for various reasons. The people who stayed at the airport did not do this. They did not abandon the field of battle.[10] They held on to a piece of territory in the world for humanity. This is a small signpost of the mercy of God in a world that left to itself would have no children left. Small actions on behalf of the oppressed and defenseless will make up our resistance movement against the Prince of Darkness until the day when God's liberation is complete and his banners fly over us, a day when there will be no need to keep the children safe because there will be nothing but love in the heavenly Father's house, for ever and ever.

Amen.

Saved for What?

ST. JOHN'S CHURCH, SALISBURY, CONNECTICUT

> *We are to grow up in every way into him who is the head,*
> *into Christ, from whom the whole body, joined and knit*
> *together . . . when each part is working properly, makes bodily*
> *growth and upbuilds itself in love.*
>
> *Ephesians 4:11-16*

The events of the past week have given more evidence, not that more was needed, for the truth of the Biblical teaching that the world needs to be saved. A grandson sets his famous grandmother on fire, and a teacher beloved by his students in one of the most chaotic public high schools in the Bronx is murdered for his ATM card.[1] One way to interpret such things is to conclude that there is no God and that human existence is a cruel joke. Some of the greatest writers and thinkers have come to this conclusion. I myself find it very difficult to defend faith in God in the face of such events. As for finding answers, it is not only difficult, it is impossible. The Bible gives no answer to the problem of evil. It simply tells us that the whole world is in "bondage to decay" (Romans 8:21) and that we are all "by nature children of wrath" (Ephesians 2:3) and that the human race is deserving of condemnation. In William Golding's classic novel *Lord of the Flies,* after the boys marooned on the island have morphed into murderous little beasts, they are rescued by a

[183]

naval vessel, a cruiser. The author then ironically asks, "And who will rescue the adult and his cruiser?" The message of the Bible is that there is no rescue from within this sphere. Rescue must come from beyond. And that is exactly what has happened. "We all once lived in the passions of our flesh, following the desires of body and mind, and so we were by nature children of wrath, like the rest of mankind. But God, who is rich in mercy, out of the great love with which he loved us, even when we were dead through our trespasses, made us alive together with Christ — by grace you have been saved!" (Ephesians 2:3-5). This was the message of last week's sermon ("Saved!"), which concluded with a summons to all of us Christian soldiers to stand our ground, to hold on to the piece of territory God has given us to defend and not to retreat from it, even at the risk of our own comfort, our own reputations, if need be our own lives. And thus we proceed from the great gospel message *Saved!* to the question, *Saved for what?*

The primary answer to the question "Saved for what?" is found repeated many times in the first chapter of Ephesians. We are saved *for the praise of his glory* (1:14). God's glory is not so much God's magnificence as it is his mercy. "In him we have redemption through his blood, the forgiveness of our trespasses, according to the riches of his grace which he lavished upon us" (1:7). Even more glorious, we will not just be forgiven, we will be transformed; we will be perfected. Paul says, "We [will] be holy and blameless before [God]" (1:4). One of the scandals of Christianity is found here. The grace of God is capable of making us "holy and blameless." One of the strongest arguments against the death penalty from a Christian perspective is that such a sentence indicates that retributive punishment is the last word in human affairs, whereas the Bible shows us that God mercifully withheld such punishment from us. If Timothy McVeigh[2] were to repent, which seems unlikely but is always possible in God, then it would be just as true of him as it is of you and me that he would be saved by "the immeasurable riches of God's grace" (Ephesians 2:7). Putting McVeigh to death is a way of saying that you and I are deserving of God's grace but murderers are not. This is to misunderstand the very nature of grace. Grace is *undeserved:*

that is the whole point. Don't get me wrong; I am in favor of life sentences without parole in many cases, certainly in this one. But death sentences give the impression that some wretches are beyond the reach of God's grace, and if that were true, then "amazing grace" would not only not be amazing, it would no longer be grace.

Saved for what, then? In Dostoevsky's novel *Crime and Punishment,* the axe-murderer Raskolnikov goes off to prison, but is sustained by the love of the prostitute Sonya, who reads to him the story of the raising of Lazarus in the gospel of John. The last sentences of *Crime and Punishment* read this way: "Raskonikov did not [yet] know that the new life . . . would cost him great striving, great suffering. But that is the beginning of a new story — the story of the gradual renewal of a man, the story of his gradual regeneration, of his passing from one world into another, of his initiation into a new, unknown life." The saving grace of God is "the beginning of a new story" for us, the story of our "gradual regeneration" through suffering love. It is the story of our passing from the world in which we are ruled by "the devices and desires of our own hearts" into the world of God's purposes. It is the story of our passing from the world where "we have left undone those things which we ought to have done, and we have done those things which we ought not to have done," into the new and hitherto unknown world where we are being made *holy and blameless* before God. That, we are told in the first chapter of Ephesians, is God's great plan.

But now comes another shocker. It is God's plan to accomplish the rescue of the world *through — you and me!* Paul tells us in Ephesians that it is God's *eternal purpose* to make his new world come into being *through the church* (3:10-11). What a crazy idea! How can we take it seriously? I assure you this is one of the questions that troubles me most, in view of the church's dismal performance in many instances. Yet the apostolic message is clear. Let's take a look at some of the descriptions of the church in Ephesians. For instance: "You are no longer strangers and sojourners, but you are fellow citizens . . . and members of the household of God, built upon the foundation of the apostles and prophets, Christ Jesus himself being the cornerstone, in whom the whole structure is joined together and grows into a holy temple in the Lord; in whom you also are built into it for a dwelling place of God in the Spirit" (2:19-22). Here is the image of the church as a structure with each member an integral part and Christ as the cornerstone, a dwelling of the Holy Spirit.

Another description of the church is in the fourth chapter. Paul begins, "I . . . beg you to lead a life worthy of the calling to which you have been called, with all lowliness and humility, with patience, forbearing one another in love, eager to maintain the unity of the Spirit in the bond of peace. There is one body and one Spirit . . . one Lord, one faith, one baptism, one God and Father of us all" (4:1-6). Here the apostle is thinking of the way that all Christian congregations are continually threatening to pull apart into factions. This must not be, he says, for there is only "one Lord, one faith, one baptism." Paul is not thinking here of the different denominations that we have today. He has in mind the cliques and parties that develop within all congregations, including this one. Wherever such divisions persist, the church is failing its commission. On the other hand, whenever there is renewed fellowship, deepening respect, developing affection, there are the signs that God's plan is working the way it is supposed to. At the conclusion of our reading for today, Paul says, "Speaking the truth in love, we are to grow up in every way into him who is the head, into Christ, from whom the whole body, joined and knit together by every joint with which it is supplied, when each part is working properly, makes bodily growth and upbuilds itself in love" (4:15-16). Notice the phrase, "when each part is working properly." Paul, you see, is not into denial. He recognizes that more often than not, the church will not be "working properly." But he knows that when it does work properly everyone will recognize it and will be exhilarated by it. That's one of the reasons for having parish parties, for instance. When all the different members are making their contributions and everyone is having a good time, we recognize that something extraordinary is happening. It's not like having a party at the club or in one's home, because there, the guests are selected. In the church, when it is working properly, people who thought they had nothing in common suddenly discover that they have one Lord, one faith, one baptism.

At the end of this service we are going to sing "Onward Christian Soldiers." This hymn always seems to be a great favorite, yet there is much capacity for misunderstanding it. One verse goes like this, "We are not divided, all one body we, one in hope and doctrine, one in charity." One is tempted to say, "What nonsense!" Right here in this congregation this morning Person A is having mean thoughts about Person B. How incredibly hypocritical to sing such a hymn! One of my favorite Christian jokes, however, concerns a young man who is railing against the church as he speaks to an older man, a priest. The young man says, "I can't stand the church! It's full of hypocrites!" To which the wise old priest says with a twinkle, "Well, there's always room for one more!" The unity of the church and the blamelessness of its members is present now only by faith. It exists in its fullness as that future reality which God is bringing to pass. It is right to speak of the present struggle of the church as a battle in which we are all soldiers. The Epistle to the Ephesians is full of battle imagery: "Be strong in the Lord and in the strength of his might. Put on the whole armor of God, that you may be able to stand against the wiles of the devil. For we are not contending against flesh and blood, but against the principalities, against the powers, against the world rulers of this present darkness. . . . Therefore take the whole armor of God, that you may be able to withstand in the evil day, and having done all, to stand. Stand therefore . . ." (6:10-13). There is definitely a battle going on. There is a battle against racial prejudice in America. There is a battle against greed and materialism in America. There is a battle against economic injustice and lack of opportunity for many of our people. There is a battle against uncaring institutions that rob people of self-respect and dignity. Christian soldiers really do need to march "as to war." The trouble is that we don't sufficiently know how to do it. We don't have enough faith and trust in the great things that God is doing. We keep falling back on the ungodly weapons of fear, apathy, retribution, vengeance.

One of the wisest and most mature commentators among us is Russell Baker. He wrote yesterday in the *Times* of the problems of men and women in the military, noting sadly that because "there is a more mature quality in the female nature than in the male," it had been hoped that feminism would be a "maturing influence" on the "essentially boyish, game-playing nature of American [male] life." Now, however, Baker writes that the entrance of women into the military has resulted in the Kelly Flinn situation which, "no matter how the Air Force rationalizes it, was about a boyish, game-playing system determined to keep women from flying a glamorous killing machine." Well, the Epistle to the Ephesians has as one of its great concerns not only the warfare of Christian soldiers, but also the relations of men and women. In probing this matter of becoming the church *working properly,* we might find some illumination in unlikely places.

A great deal has been written recently about male bonding in the military. I have read at least five articles about it in the last month. Many students of human behavior have noted with increasing conviction that most men have great difficulty conducting mature, sustained, deeply-felt relationships with anyone. Women have to do most of the emotional work in most marriages. Men's whole lives are spent resisting intimacy. I observed this firsthand on Friday at the local graduation; the girls were unashamedly hugging and shedding tears, whereas the boys were cracking jokes and pretending to be cool. There is nothing new about this, you will say. No, but what is new is that we know more now about the dangers of men's being distanced from feelings. The recent articles I mentioned have focused on the special nature of male bonding in wartime. A level of intimacy is achieved that is rare for most men in most other settings. Much opposition to women in combat is based on this factor. When men tell their war stories, something more is present than just bravado and machismo. There is an awareness of the preciousness of comradeship. Men will tear up as they speak of the sacrifices of their fellows. It seems to be very difficult for men to achieve this level of deep relatedness in any other setting. The Promise Keepers movement is very controversial, but my impression of it is largely positive. It is a Christian response to the craving for real relationships of love among men who have come to know Christ. If local churches were *working properly,* there would be no need for

Promise Keepers. Ultimate tears are shed in joy and gratitude and awe as men and women reflect upon the consummate sacrifice of the Son of God, who laid down his life, we must remember, not just for his buddies, but, most of all, *for his enemies.*

The Christian community, when it is *working properly,* offers men and women a way of being related to one another that cuts across all the things that divide us. After all, wars do end, and the intimacy of the battlefield fades or disappears. The members of the fraternity grow older and develop different interests. The wives put an end to at least some of the games. The locker rooms, the team sports are for the young. Not everyone likes to go duck hunting. Not everyone likes to play golf, or bridge, or poker. The community choruses in Salisbury come closer than anything secular I can think of to put together all ages and walks of life, but not everyone can sing. It is the church and only the church, when it is working properly, that is "joined and knit together in every joint, that makes bodily growth and upbuilds itself in love" across every barrier of race, age, class, and experience. There is nothing else in human life — literally nothing — that levels distinctions and creates new relationships like the knowledge that one has been saved by grace. It causes even the most dessicated heart to bloom.

"By grace you have been saved." Saved for what? Here's what. Saved to be a beachhead for God's great reclamation project to save the world from sin and death. Saved to be a dwelling place of God's unconditional love for sinners of every description. Saved to be messengers of the gospel of Christ "not only with our lips but in our lives." Saved to beat our "swords into plowshares, and our spears into pruning hooks" (Isaiah 2:4) for a new kind of warfare whose colors will never be put into a museum or stored in an attic or relegated to a closet, but will grow brighter as they are united with the victorious majesty of our Lord Jesus Christ for ever and ever. As another military-style hymn puts it, "For not with swords' loud clashing, nor roll of stirring drums, but deeds of love and mercy, the heavenly kingdom comes." Saved for what? Saved so as to live in this life in such a way that, in the life to come, our severed friendships being restored to an intimacy and ease that we can only now begin to imagine, we shall dance and sing in harmony forever to the praise of God's glorious grace.

Amen.

The Words of Eternal Life

ST. ANDREW'S DUNE CHURCH, SOUTHAMPTON,
LONG ISLAND, NEW YORK

After this many of his disciples drew back and no longer went about with him. Jesus said to the twelve, "Do you also wish to go away?" Simon Peter answered him, "Lord, to whom shall we go? You have the words of eternal life; and we have believed, and have come to know, that you are the Holy One of God."

John 6:66-69

A few years ago my husband and I were spending the weekend at a summer colony not unlike this one. The summer chapel service there was always packed. Many people attended the summer chapel who never went to church anywhere else. At a dinner party the conversation turned to this subject. One couple said that, for them, the summer chapel service was a social occasion and a time for the lusty singing of hymns, but that they weren't believers in any sense of the word. Why not? I inquired. "Because," said the wife, firmly and decisively, "I don't need it."

I thought about that this week when the news came of the fiery end of TWA Flight 800. I heard the President say on the radio that we could not get through such terrible times without faith in God. I wondered about that. There is always a suspicion about religion, that it is just made up by us in order to make an unbearable situation bearable. If this is true, then the person who says she doesn't need religion is more honest, more courageous, more sophisticated than the rest of us weak and benighted souls. Clearly, that is what the woman at the dinner party thought.

The most powerful argument against Judeo-Christian faith that I know of is that of Sigmund Freud. He was that rarest of beings — a committed, consistent, principled atheist. In his essay, *The Future of an Illusion,* he argues with great forcefulness that religious faith in general and Judeo-Christian faith in particular are "born from man's need to make his helplessness tolerable." Reading *The Future of an Illusion* is a sobering experience. It is the strongest argument against religious faith in existence, as far as I know. One comes away feeling like rather a fool for continuing to be a believer. He writes, "Religious ideas . . . are illusions, fulfillments of the oldest, strongest, and most urgent wishes of mankind. The secret of their strength lies in the strength of those wishes." And, "Where questions of religion are concerned, people are guilty of every possible sort of dishonesty and intellectual misdemeanor. . . . They give the name of 'God' to some vague abstraction *which they have created for themselves.*"[1]

I don't have any way of knowing about you, but speaking for myself, every time there is a catastrophe I question my faith all over again. This particular airline crash hit me harder than most, probably because my husband flies to Europe constantly. Am I a Christian because I want to believe that everything is going to turn out all right? Have I projected a God out of my own need? Freud and many others — including quite a few of my most interesting friends — say yes. Freud's reputation is undergoing the inevitable revision right now, but he will always command respect, not only for his desire to help humanity but especially for his great discoveries. I admire his insight into the nature of religion: namely, that it is based on wishes rather than reality. A system of faith based on human wishes can, as he suggests, be very strong indeed, but in the last analysis, it cannot deliver the goods. This is one of the prophet Isaiah's powerful themes: the gods that we make for ourselves are a joke. The prophet mocks them: "The man makes a god, his idol; he falls down to it and worships it; he prays to it and says, 'Deliver me, for thou are my god!' (44:17) . . . then they lift it upon their shoulders, they carry it, they set it in its place, and it stands there; it cannot move from its place; if one cries to it, it does not answer or save him from his trouble" (46:6-7).

A long line of Christian theologians and Biblical scholars insists that the Judeo-Christian tradition is *not religion.* The dictionary gives a number of definitions of religion, all of them originating as human activities: worship, belief, ritual. We are so used to thinking of religion that way, whether we are believers or not, that it comes as quite a shock to discover from the Scriptures of the Old and New Testaments, from the Hebrew prophets to the Apostle Paul, that *God is not interested in religion.* Religion is a human construct, allowing people to create a God after their own image instead of the other way round. Religion makes God more manageable by setting up conditions that God will be bound by. At the risk of sounding crass, we can put it this way: religion is a human means of putting God in our debt, as though God owed us something for our faith. If God is, in this fashion, a construction of our own, then we are indeed deceived and the whole Biblical enterprise is false. Such a god cannot deliver the goods. Such a god "stands there; it cannot move from its place; if one cries to it, it does not answer or save him from his trouble."

It has often been noted that in times of disaster there are more people in the churches than usual. Is this because we have more "need" for "religion" at such times? Is it because our human weakness is more obvious and our wishes for a way out are more pressing? If so, then the really strong and honest people are the ones who do not pray even in foxholes, do not go to church even in times of crisis. If our god is only a projection out of our own religious longing, then truly, "I don't need it." I don't need wishful thinking. I don't need bogus consolation. I don't need a phony prop, and neither do you.

In the Gospel of John, there is a moment in the ministry of Jesus when a number of his disciples turn away from him. Early in his ministry Jesus had more disciples than he did at the end. His huge popular following did not stay the course, because he did not fit the people's idea of what the Messiah should be. This turning away begins at the end of the sixth chapter, after the great discourse on the Bread of Life. The religious authorities take offense at him. They "murmured at him, because he said, 'I am the bread which came down from heaven.' They said, 'Is not this Jesus, the son of Joseph, whose father and mother we know? How does he now say, "I have come down from heaven"?' Jesus answered them, 'Do not murmur among yourselves. No one can come to me unless the Father who sent me draws him; and I will raise him up at the last day. . . . No [one] has seen the Father except him who is from God; he has seen the Father'" (6:41-46). Jesus' claim to be "from heaven" is shocking to those who know that he is just a local boy, but worse still, he identifies himself as the One who reveals God. Here is the crucial distinction between "religion" and the confession of Jesus Christ; he is not the fulfilment of human wishes, but the One who reveals a God whom none of us could ever have imagined. In the evangelist's words in the preface, we hear once again the teaching of the Old Testament that God is inaccessible to human religious aspiration: "No one has ever seen God." Then John announces the unique revelation of "the only Son, who is in the bosom of the Father, he has made him known" (1:18). This has never been an easy message to assimilate. It was offensive to religion in Jesus' time and it is offensive now. Better to have a New Age god or goddess than this Son of Man who offers his own body and blood. "The [religious authorities] therefore strove among themselves, saying, 'How can this man give us his flesh to eat?' Jesus said unto them, 'Verily, verily, I say unto you, Except ye eat the flesh of the Son of man, and drink his blood, ye have no life in you. Whoever eateth my flesh, and drinketh my blood, hath eternal life'" (6:52-54).

Jesus thus becomes even more specific, and now he angers not only the pooh-bahs but his own disciples: "'The one who eats my flesh and drinks my blood abides in me, and I in him. . . . This is the bread which came down from heaven . . . he who eats this bread will live for ever.'" This he said in the synagogue, as he taught at

Capernaum. Many of his disciples, when they heard it, said, 'This is a hard saying; who can listen to it?'" (John 6:55-60) It can't be said too often: the *specificity* of Jesus, the "scandal of particularity" as it is called, goes against the grain of ordinary religiosity. Not only do the leaders react against this concreteness, many of Jesus' own disciples react against it too. And so we read, "After this many of his disciples drew back and no longer went about with him. Jesus said to the twelve, 'Do you also wish to go away?' Simon Peter answered him, 'Lord, to whom shall we go? You have the words of eternal life; and we have believed, and have come to know, that you are the Holy One of God'" (6:66-69).

Let me propose a little mental exercise. Picture yourself at a cocktail party. One of the waiters comes up to you with a platter of very fattening *hors d'oeuvres*. Your response is to say, "No, thank you." If you are feeling especially determined, you might even say, "I don't need that!" But imagine that your host comes up to you with his hand outstretched. Would you say "I don't need *you*"? It sounds quite different, doesn't it? It personalizes it. It makes it seem less a statement about oneself and one's own needs and more like a personal rejection. And that, indeed, is what it is.

I have often thought about that woman at the dinner party, and many other people that I know. If it is "religion" that she doesn't need, then she is in good company with the Hebrew prophets. But if it is the Lord Jesus Christ and his words of eternal life that she is rejecting, then that is a different matter.

Truly, Christian faith would not be worth much if it is based solely on human need. A god built on that foundation cannot deliver broken bodies from the sea. Why should we take Jesus' word for it? It might not even be Jesus' word at all; the so-called "Jesus Seminar" delights in announcing periodically that Jesus never said or did the things claimed for him in the Bible.

Why do we come to church and sing the hymns and say the prayers and pledge our money? Is it because we "need" to convince ourselves of a happy ending? Do I need to believe in Jesus and the Virgin Birth and the Resurrection and all the rest of it in order to avoid facing the pain of existence? Your rector was out on the water with the Coast Guard for two days after the TWA catastrophe. He has been face to face with horror. Human nature easily forgets the truth of its situation when placed by the seashore; the rolling breakers delight us, and the sunshine replenishes us with a sense of well-being. Then someone's flight bag washes up on the strand and we realize that it belonged to a human being with hopes and dreams like yours and mine, loved and cherished by someone on the ground, bound for a rendezvous with the City of Light, and now suddenly and without warning all those longings and aspirations are completely obliterated. I was struck by the admonition to the rescue workers: *Don't look at the faces.* This is an acknowledgment that anyone with any feelings can understand; if we look at the faces, the reality of what has happened will overcome us with its force and we will be unable to do our jobs. The rescue worker is not sustained by wishful thoughts about the celestial destiny of the victims. He is simply putting one foot in front of the other as he goes about his grim but necessary task. There are many times in all our lives when we too must do this.

Not long ago I heard that the husband of the woman who didn't need "it" had died suddenly and prematurely of a heart attack. As far as I know, she has not changed her mind about the Christian faith. Most likely she would consider it a craven capitulation to start seeking religion now. If "religion" is what we were talking about, I would agree. But that is not what the church offers. The church offers something quite different.

Why do terrible things happen? I do not know. Have I any proof that what the church proclaims is true? Only the faith of those who have put their trust in Jesus as the Son of God. Is this wishful thinking? Maybe. I do not believe so. With all due respect to the religions of the world, there is no other story like the Christian story. Today's passage means a great deal to me. I wouldn't be able to count the number of times that I, too, have felt like drawing back from the stance of faith because horrible things happen and I just don't see any evidence that the Christian promises are true. But then I hear the Lord saying to me, "Do you also wish to go away?" and I find myself answering with Peter, "Lord, to whom shall we go? You have the words of eternal life; and we have believed, and have come to know, that you are the Holy One of God."

The eternal God who created the heavens and the earth has come down from his throne on high into his creation and has submitted to the fury of its rebellion and wickedness by his own free will in order to deliver us from everlasting sin and death. In a reversal that has no parallel in the history of religion, the selfsame God of whom the Psalmist says, "The voice of the Lord is upon the waters; the God of glory thunders upon many waters. . . . The Lord sits enthroned over the flood" (Psalm 29:3, 10),[2] this incarnate God has given his very self in order that we should be saved from the flood, and in so doing has submitted himself to the power of the deep. In the cross of Jesus, the flood has gone over the head of its Creator.[3] There is no other story like this. We do not proclaim "religion" today. We come together to hear the living voice of a living Lord, who has passed through the domain of death and hell and emerged victorious, bearing the keys with him. He has the words of eternal life. May we all today put our trust in him, as we come to know that he is the Holy One of God.

Amen.

Affliction, with Joy

ST. JOHN'S CHURCH, SALISBURY, CONNECTICUT

*Render therefore unto Caesar the things which are Caesar's;
and unto God the things that are God's.*

Matthew 22:21

*You received the Word in much affliction, with joy inspired
by the Holy Spirit.*

I Thessalonians 1:6-7

The Nobel Peace Prize was awarded last week to two people that most of us had never heard of in a country that many of us know little about. The Nobel committee, choosing two men from East Timor instead of better-known candidates from more prominent countries, made no bones about its timing, stating that they made these selections this year because they feared the struggle of East Timor was in danger of being forgotten at precisely the moment when there might be a possibility of a peaceful settlement. "The Nobel committee issued a blunt attack on the Indonesian Government, accusing it of 'systematically oppressing the people of East Timor.'"[1] *One-third* of the population of the small country is estimated to have died under Indonesian rule, making President Clinton's financial ties to Indonesia questionable indeed.

One of the two men is José Ramos-Horta, who now lives in Sydney, Australia. His activities in the independence movement led to his exile in the 1970s. He returned to the country, only to flee again at the time of the Indonesian invasion in which his two brothers and his sister were all killed. Since then he has not ceased to travel the world to speak on behalf of those being oppressed by harsh military rule in East Timor. He has known the cost of speaking out against Caesar.

As one of my clergy colleagues said in a gathering this week, "Rendering unto Caesar is the easy part." The hard part is deciding and acting on what belongs to God. Of all the brilliant strokes executed by Jesus of Nazareth in his debates with his enemies, the one we read today is arguably the most stunning. Let us hear it again from a different translation:

"The Pharisees went and plotted to entrap him in what he said. So they sent their disciples to him . . . saying, 'Teacher, we know that you are sincere, and teach the way of God in accordance with truth, and show deference to no one; for you do not regard people with partiality. Tell us, then, what you think. Is it lawful to pay taxes to the emperor, or not?' But Jesus, aware of their malice, said . . . 'Show me the money for the tax.' And they brought him a denarius [the coin for the tax]. And Jesus said to them, 'Whose head is this, and whose title?' They said, 'The emperor's.' Then he said to them, 'Give therefore to the emperor the things that are the emperor's, and to God the things that are God's.' When they heard it, they were amazed; and they left him and went away."

We need to remember that Judea in the time of Jesus was an occupied country under the Roman Empire and the Jews were subject people. No one likes paying taxes to a hated occupying power. Add to this the fact that the Roman coin portrayed the face of Caesar and an inscription claiming divinity for him, and you get some idea of the abhorrence of the religious leaders for the payment of the tax. So the question they asked of Jesus was meant to trap him either way he turned. If he had said, "It is lawful to pay the tax," he would have alienated his own people. If he said, "It is *not* lawful to pay the tax," he would have been inciting revolt against the Romans. Either way, he would have been caught. We should try to imagine the drama of the scene as Jesus holds up the denarius, the hated coin of the upper classes, and, standing in the temple where any sort of authorized idolatry was unthinkable, asks the leaders of that temple to identify the loathed inscription. Ironically, though Jesus' dazzlingly adroit rejoinder vanquishes the scribes and Pharisees temporarily, it ultimately contributes to his death, because it sets everyone against him, religious leaders and secular rulers alike. The rejection of Jesus by just about everybody is a major theme of the New Testament. He makes enemies in every group, whether Romans or Jews, Pharisees or Sadducees, liberals or conservatives. One of the reasons he was such an infuriating person is that he himself belonged clearly to no group, but continually slipped from everyone's grasp, as he does in the story today. Once again we see why he is called in the New Testament the "stumbling-stone." The only people he does not antagonize are those who are so poor and friendless that no one else ever takes their part.

Human rights groups around the world have hailed the Nobel prize winners on behalf of the poor and oppressed people of East Timor. We have spoken of the first of the two prize winners. The other is the local Roman Catholic Bishop, Carlos Ximenes Belo. He is one of those all-too-rare Christians who saves the reputation of Christianity for all the rest of us. A Washington journalist wrote that Bishop Belo "could have [left] the country, but he has put his neck on the line and stayed. He has constantly risked his life — constantly." The Catholic Church is seen by many to be all that stands between the ordinary people of East Timor and the brutality of the Indonesian military. Many baptized Christians in that largely Catholic country have to make daily decisions about what belongs to the emperor and what belongs to God.[2]

In today's Epistle, the apostle Paul says something strange. He says to the Thessalonian Christians that they have received the Word of the gospel "in much affliction, with joy inspired by the Holy Spirit, so that you become an example to all the believers in [the other churches]." What a curious thing, to suggest that *affliction* and *joy* go together! But this is one of the central messages of the

Christian faith, that unearned suffering is redemptive. When Paul wrote to the Philippians, "Rejoice in the Lord always, and again I say rejoice" (4:4-13, our Epistle last week), he was *writing from prison.* Our closing hymn last week was "Rejoice, ye pure in heart," with the chorus, "Lift up your heart, lift up your voice, rejoice, again I say, rejoice!" Everybody loves it. One person said to me, "We should end every service with that hymn!" Not a bad idea! But we should never forget that Paul writes, "Rejoice *in the Lord.*" This is not ordinary rejoicing. This is not rejoicing in good health, or pleasant company, or a windfall in the stock market, or even in the indescribably glorious fall foliage of New England. This is a far deeper sort of rejoicing, the sort that is linked to affliction. When Paul wrote, "I rejoice in the Lord greatly," he wrote as a man whose days are numbered. He knew that Caesar, who in Paul's time was Nero, was after him. When he writes to the Philippians that he "shares the sufferings of Christ, becoming like him in his death" (3:10), he means it literally. It is in this context, that of certain martyrdom, that Paul writes to Timothy, "I have fought the good fight, I have finished my course, I have kept the faith" (II Timothy 4:7). Those are not just fine-sounding words. They were written by a man who was in the very act of giving up his life for Jesus Christ.

Paul was indeed executed by Nero in Rome — beheaded by Caesar. Even paying taxes is easy compared to discerning in this world what belongs to Caesar and what belongs to God. Over the centuries, the Christians who are best remembered are those who have defied Caesar in their own time and paid the ultimate price for it. Dietrich Bonhoeffer in Nazi Germany, Father Aleksandr Men in Russia, Archbishop Romero in El Salvador, Martin Luther King in Memphis, Archbishop Luwum in Uganda — their names are in the church calendars now; their sacrifices will give life to the church generation after generation. They met affliction with joy. Bonhoeffer's last recorded words before he was hanged by the Nazis were, "This is the end; for me, the beginning of life."

I don't think any of us here today are going to be called to be executed for Jesus' sake (although you never know). We are more likely to be summoned to less dramatic types of affliction, less visible forms of suffering for Christ's sake. Sometimes this mundane, low-profile suffering is just as heroic as the more celebrated agony of the Christian martyrs. Some ordinary Christians are called to expend themselves unstintingly in ministry to the poor and defenseless whom Christ loves. Some endure loss and deprivation patiently and without bitterness for the sake of others. Some make genuine personal sacrifices in order to serve the common good; this can be as great a matter as making a large *anonymous* financial gift to the community or as small as giving over the control of a favorite project at the Fall Festival. Most of all, perhaps, some are called — indeed we are all called — to Christian maturity, which involves patient, consistent postponement of personal gratification in order to serve the needs of others. But there can be no denying that the discernment required to distinguish between Caesar and God is often the most dangerous of all Christian tasks. Many are the preachers who have lost their jobs or reputations by suggesting that segregation, or apartheid, or the Confederate flag, or the Vietnam war, or the welfare cuts, or the tax structure, or the struggle for human rights around the world, might not be in the spirit of Christ. Discerning the spirit of the times is one of the most challenging of all Christian callings; it takes courage to risk one's reputation. I sometimes wonder what I would do if I were a pastor in North Carolina, where my position would depend on the support of tobacco company executives. Cozying up to worldly power is always a dangerous proposition for a Christian. Even an admirer of Billy Graham, as I am, might question whether he did not spend rather too much time in the White House. It is far easier to seek for tax loopholes and then pay the rest than it is to face up to what is owed to God.

I come into the church a lot during the week to pray for the congregation and the ministry of this parish. One day recently I looked around me at these windows of the Twelve Apostles with their symbols. All of these people gave their lives in order that you and I might know the gospel of God's amazing grace in Jesus Christ. They gave everything they had for generations of Christians yet to come, for you and for me, for our children, and for our grandchildren. The Epistle to the Ephesians teaches that the Church is "built upon the foundation of the apostles and prophets, Christ Jesus himself being the cornerstone, in whom the whole structure is joined together and grows into a holy temple in the Lord . . . you also are built into it for a dwelling place of God in the Spirit" (2:19-22). That is an awesome thought. Look around you and think how those first Christians gladly gave themselves up to affliction, imprisonment, exile, and death in order that this congregation here today might become "a dwelling place of God in the Spirit." We are surrounded, here, by a great fellowship of those who were joyful in the midst of affliction. They were led to realize that Caesar, ultimately, has no claim on us at all. The real calling is not from Caesar; it is from the Lord. When we take up our offering, we say, "All things come of thee, O Lord, and of thine own have we given thee." *All things* come from thee, O Lord. Render unto Caesar? That's the easy part.[3] Our calling is, rather, to renew our understanding of what it means to follow Christ. Thus in the last week of his life our Lord, by means of his parables and teachings, led his flock to be prepared for his death. The redemptive power of suffering on behalf of others was demonstrated for all time in the Cross of Christ.

And so: whatever sacrifices you are making in order to serve the need of someone else, whatever indignities you are suffering on behalf of the church, whatever the cost to yourself as you seek to carry out the task that God has laid before you, take heart! As a dear Christian friend wrote to me last week, "He knows." The Lord knows what we are enduring, the Lord knows what we are suffering, the Lord knows what we are sacrificing, and he stands with us to vindicate us. He is on our side. "His love foretells our trials; he knows thine hourly need; / He can with bread of heaven our fainting spirit feed."[4] Caesar is not Lord. Jesus is Lord. Let us honor him, not only with our lips, but in our lives.

Amen.

Clint's Got It

ST. PAUL'S CHURCH, RICHMOND, VIRGINIA

*God has consigned all men to disobedience that he may have
mercy upon all.*

Romans 11:32

Here's a question for you. If you were asked to state an idea that
was specifically Christian, that was not typical of any other
system of belief, what would you say?

One might begin by proposing the Incarnation of Jesus, the
one and only son of God, as an actual, historical human being. That
would be a good suggestion; there really isn't anything else exactly
like it in religion.[1] Another indisputable choice would be the cross
of Christ itself; in spite of the fact that crosses have been temporarily
appropriated by the fashion designers, the Crucifixion of the Son of
God remains the unique and central feature of authentic Christian
faith. Today, however, I have yet another theme in mind. Like the
cross, it is entirely unique to Christianity, and it divides us even
from Judaism. This motif pops up in the most unlikely places. When
it does, we need to take note of it, because wherever it appears, and
in whatever context, we can identify it as specifically Christian,
whether the speaker or writer is aware of it or not.

Take, for example, the Clint Eastwood movie *The Unforgiven*,
one of the more violent movies of our violent age, which contains

the following bit of dialogue: Clint Eastwood's young sidekick has just participated in the shooting and the painful, prolonged death of another man. He is shaken, but he reassures himself by saying, "He had it coming." He receives no comfort from Clint, who utters this deathless line, "We all have it coming."

That is a uniquely Christian idea, whether the screenwriter knows it or not. We find it in a more elevated context in Shakespeare's *Hamlet*. The Prince of Denmark tells Polonius to take good care of the visiting Players. Polonius, in his fatuous way, replies:

My Lord, I will use them according to their desert.

Hamlet retorts,

God's bodkin, man, much better: use every man after his
   desert,
and who shall 'scape whipping?

In the Psalms, we hear, "If thou, O Lord, were to mark what is done amiss, O Lord, who could stand?" (Psalm 130:3). The implied answer, of course, is *no one*. No one can stand before God because of all that is wrong with us. In his letter to the Romans, Paul says it *twice* in this crisp and unmistakable way: "There is no distinction." First he says, "There is no distinction; all have sinned" (3:22-23), and later he says, "There is no distinction between Jew and Gentile" (10:12) — that is, between righteous and unrighteous, between godly and ungodly. It can't be said too often that this puts "religion" out of business, because if there isn't any difference between the religious and the unreligious, then there is no point in going through the motions. We *all* have it coming, and there is nothing — *nothing* — that we can do to change that fact of our lives before God.

In that case, why bother with church at all? Here's why. In a later section of Romans, Paul writes that "We shall all stand before the judgment seat of God" (14:10). The role of the Christian church is to believe this and to act upon it. The role of the church is to stand forward and take the first place in line. Peter puts it well in his first epistle: "The time has come for judgment to begin with the household of God" (I Peter 4:17). This means that Christians do not shrink from the knowledge of our fault, our sin, before the blazing holiness of God. As we acknowledge our weakness in his sight, we are making a testimony before the world that he alone is God and that human destiny is in his hands, not ours. This is what happens every time we say the General Confession.

The reading from Romans today contains the climactic verse of the entire letter: "God has consigned all men to disobedience that he may have mercy upon all" (11:32). Many theologians and preachers have been afraid of this verse, recognizing how radical and irreligious it is. They have skipped over it lightly, or ignored it altogether. Others, however, have pointed to it as the heart of the gospel. Martin Luther wrote, "Take to heart this great text!" I have been meditating upon it for many years now, and more and more it seems to me to be, with the rest of Romans, to be the deep irreducible core of our faith, the uniquely Christian idea. And so the way to be a Christian is not to *escape* judgment and responsibility, but to *embrace* it in the name of and for the sake of the whole world, that world of sinners for whom Christ died. So our truest solidarity with our fellow human beings is not joining them in the club, the bank, or the boardroom, but repenting our sins among our fellow sinners, because we know that if it were not for God's salvation of the *un*godly (Romans 4:5), no one of us could stand before him.

Many of you will have seen *Schindler's List* by now. I think it is our Christian duty to see it, as a tiny fraction of what we owe to our fellow human beings. There has been much debate about Oskar Schindler's highly ambiguous character, and if you are interested, I urge you to get the book by Thomas Keneally, which is very well written and fills in a lot of what is missing in the film. The point that is of interest for this sermon, however, is that in the 1960s Schindler was invited to Israel and was officially declared a "Righteous Person." This is an official Israeli designation based upon the Hebrew idea that there would always be a righteous remnant among the Gentiles.

A friend of mine saw *Schindler's List* and, afterwards, remarked to a Jewish acquaintance that Schindler had performed a remarkable feat. My friend reported, "He looked at me with stony eyes and said, *'Why were there not more Schindlers?'*" Why, indeed? This agonizing question, human nature being what it is, will be with us till the end of time as we know it. What would you have done? What would I have done? *Who can count himself righteous?* The question does not bear much investigation, and we turn away.

We are speaking today of an important point of difference between Judaism and Christianity, one that can be discussed very profitably in Jewish-Christian dialogue. I am pretty certain about this because in New York City I am having significant, if informal, interfaith conversation with Jews almost every day. As we have already said, the difference is best expressed in that pithy statement of Paul, the Hebrew of the Hebrews: "There is no one righteous, no, not one," and "There is no distinction between Jew and Gentile; all have sinned."

If I know human nature at all, the designation, Righteous Person, did not lie easy in the soul of Oskar Schindler. He must have known better in the depths of his spirit. The "Schindler Jews" always supported him and never abandoned him, but his last years were spent in a "mean, cramped apartment" in a grubby district of Frankfurt, in a state of mind described by one of the Jewish survivors as "discouragement, loneliness, disillusion." In a far less dramatic and newsworthy way, there are many in our Christian congregations who are publicly hailed as good, righteous, spiritual people but who can never be free of the fear that they are not good enough. Maybe you yourself are one of those people. Maybe I am. Many clergy and other Christian leaders know the feeling of being held up as models when we know down deep that we do not deserve it.

The Christian theme of common solidarity in sin and unrighteousness is a uniquely liberating message. It is infinitely more freeing to acknowledge the profoundly ambivalent motives underlying even our finest actions than it is to be constantly engaged in a process of self-deception, trying to convince ourselves that we are good enough.

There is a line in *Much Ado About Nothing* which precisely

illustrates our text ("God has consigned all men to disobedience in order that he may have mercy upon all"). Dogberry, the comical constable who always gets his words mixed up, says to one of the malefactors in his custody, "O villain! Thou wilt be condemned into everlasting redemption!" These are immortal words. Think of it! You and I, no matter what sorts of villains we may be, are "condemned into everlasting redemption." There is nothing in "religion" equal to this message. There is nothing else in all the world like this declaration of freedom from sin, freedom from guilt, freedom from failure, freedom from condemnation, *not on account of our deserving,* but on account of God's mercy — as we say in the great phrase from Thomas Cranmer's prayer book, "not weighing our merits, but pardoning our offenses."

"We all have it coming." There is more freedom in that utterance than in all the "belief systems" of the world put together. It is our charter of salvation. Happy is the man who is found, not grasping at prerogatives and perks, but on his knees with hands outstretched before the Lord. Happy is the woman who cherishes the forgiveness of sins far more than the relentless struggle to think well of herself.[2] Happy is the family where faults are readily acknowledged, forgiveness is offered, and reconciliation produces new life. True self-discovery and human fulfillment are to be found in the knowledge that God is both just and merciful, and that he has found the way, through our Lord and Savior Jesus Christ, to "condemn us into everlasting redemption."

Amen.

How to Dress for a Wedding

ST. JOHN'S CHURCH, SALISBURY, CONNECTICUT

> *. . . Those servants went out into the streets and gathered all whom they found, both bad and good, so the wedding hall was filled with guests. But when the king came in to look at the guests, he saw a man there who had no wedding garment; and he said, Friend, how did you get in here without a wedding garment? And he was speechless. Then the king said to the servants, Bind him hand and foot, and cast him into the outer darkness where men will weep and gnash their teeth.*
>
> *Matthew 22:1-14*

In cultures the world over, weddings are generally the biggest parties that families ever give. God loves parties. Did you know that? From one end to another, the Bible is full of imagery about parties. We read in the book of the Exodus: "Moses and Aaron went to Pharaoh and said, 'Thus says the LORD, the God of Israel, Let my people go, *that they may hold a feast to me* in the wilderness'" (5:1). Feasting is built into God's plan from the beginning. It is built into God's plan for the ending as well, for as we read in the last book of the Bible, "Blessed are those who are invited to the marriage supper of the Lamb" (Revelation 19:9).

It's a little difficult for us Episcopalians to get on board with this feasting business. I'll never forget my first Bar Mitzvah. Dick and I left our house at nine-thirty in the morning and yet had to leave before the third course was served because we had ignorantly made four o'clock appointments. After that I had no further trouble understanding why Jews complain that there is never enough to eat at WASP weddings. Indeed, the Episcopal idea of a party is decidedly pinched in comparison with that of other cultures. In a recent *New Yorker* article, Henry Louis Gates, Jr.,[1] wrote that as a black Episcopalian he had always felt uncomfortable with the wild and woolly carryings-on at the Pentecostal church down the road, but that he had never doubted that the real thing was more likely to be there than at his own church.

And Jesus said, "The kingdom of heaven may be compared to a king who gave a marriage feast for his son." This is not an ordinary wedding; this is a royal wedding. The misfortunes of the British royal family have taken a lot of the gloss off such weddings lately, but we still can understand that an invitation to a royal wedding is no small thing. A whole country will buzz about the wedding plans for months in advance, and it is well understood that there will be two kinds of people: the small elite group of those who are invited to attend, and the very much larger group of those who are not. Among the wedding guests themselves, there will be a further pecking order: those on the A list will get the best seats while the B list will have to content themselves with poor sight lines and the company of other second-tier folk. Pecking order or no, however, it would be inconceivable that anyone invited would refuse to come altogether, as they do in Jesus' parable of the royal marriage feast.[2] Unlike most of Jesus' other parables, this one is not at all realistic. Realism is not the point. The thrust of the parable lies elsewhere.

"The kingdom of heaven may be compared," Jesus said, "to a king who gave a marriage feast for his son, and sent his servants to call those who were invited to the marriage feast; but they would not come.[3] Again he sent other servants, saying, 'Tell those who are invited, "Behold, I have made ready my dinner, my oxen and my fat calves are killed, and everything is ready; come to the marriage feast.'" But they made light of it and went off, one to his farm, another to his business. . . ."[4] Hospitality in the ancient Near East, and in the modern Middle East for that matter, is a major cultural preoccupation. Offenses against hospitality are considered grave indeed, more than you or I can readily imagine. Today's parable is usually called "The Parable of the Marriage Feast," but one wise commentator calls it "The Parable of God's Rejected Invitation," and that is a much more helpful title.[5] Even at our distant cultural remove we can understand what it feels like to work for days on a lovely dinner party with place cards, flowers, polished silver, scrubbed floors, carefully chosen wine and beautifully prepared food, only to have guests call at the last minute and offer some feeble excuse for dropping out. In order to understand what Jesus is getting at, we need to reflect on the care and love that God has poured out in preparing for us, his invited guests. Over and over in the Scriptures, we read of God's banquet. In today's passage from the prophet Isaiah for instance, we read: "The LORD of hosts will make for all peoples a feast of fat things, a feast of wine on the lees, of fat things full of marrow, of wine on the lees well refined. And he will . . . swallow up death for ever, and the Lord GOD will wipe away tears from all faces . . . for the LORD has spoken. It will be said on that day, 'Lo, this is our God; we have waited for him . . . let us be glad and rejoice in his salvation'" (Isaiah 25:6-9). So let us be clear that the invitation to the wedding feast for the king's son is an invitation to joy. It is an invitation to glory. It is an invitation to eternity. Who would refuse it?

Well, many, apparently. Many refused to believe in the king's son when he was standing right before them, and many refuse to believe in him today. We go off to our farms, we go off to our businesses. We go from New York to the country, and from the country to New York, and maybe we find a couple of hours a week to go to the Lord's party and maybe we don't. We are so busy! We have so many important things to think about! Church is something nice that we do when we have time, but we certainly don't rearrange our whole lives for it.

And so the king said to his servants, " 'The wedding is ready, but those invited were not worthy. Go therefore to the thoroughfares, and invite to the marriage feast as many as you find.' And those servants went out into the streets and gathered all whom they found, both bad and good; so the wedding hall was filled with guests."

This parable tells us that God is going to have his party whether you and I are there or not, and if we are going to despise his invitation he will go out and gather in all kinds of other people ("both bad and good") that nobody ever thought would get an invitation from a king. As St. Peter says in the Book of Acts, "God is no respecter of persons" (10:34). One of the main reasons that good church people don't necessarily want to go to God's party is that they might see people there that they wouldn't want to be associated with. On the other hand, the tables might be turned. I heard a true story just yesterday afternoon about a new rector and his wife in the Boston suburbs, who happened to have a certain sense of themselves as members of the upper classes. They were picked up at the airport to be driven to their new church by a member of the congregation, a man of the working class. As they drove by a country club, their driver said dismissively, "That's where the snobs play polo." Years later the congregation was still talking about how deeply offended the wife was because the driver did not show sufficient respect for her social set. "God is no respecter of persons" can cut both ways.

Lest we too quickly look down our noses at the worldly rector's wife, let me tell you a story on myself. A few years ago I was taken to the Metropolitan Opera by a rich friend. At intermission we had one of the best tables on the Grand Tier right up in the front where we were in the midst of all the action. I liked this so much that the following year when I had a little extra money I invited a fellow opera lover to go Dutch with me and I reserved a table on the Grand Tier. When we arrived, we were unceremoniously escorted to a seat in Siberia, at the very back of the room. I am ashamed to tell you that I was utterly chagrined and did not enjoy the evening as much as I would have if I had paid one-fourth the amount for hamburgers across the street. I tell this little story to illustrate the theme I have been talking about ever since I arrived at St. John's, which is that we are all members of the fellowship of human foolishness.

What is a really good party like? Well, it certainly isn't like the gala benefits where you have to shell out several thousand dollars just to get in the door. It isn't like the high school proms of today where the black students have their music in one location and the white students have their music in another. It isn't like the reception where the elderly people have to sit on the sidelines because they can't hear and can't dance and can't talk over the uproar. It isn't like the ones I've been to where there are all sorts of gorgeous flowers and a good deal of champagne but hardly anything to eat. A really good party would be one where there would be no A list and no B list and no bad tables and no one would care because they would all be having too much fun. A really good party is where everyone is having a glass of something but no one is drunk, everyone knows all the words of all the songs and has a partner for every dance, and no one is jealous of anyone else. A really good party would be full of shared affection and joyfulness and celebration, and all loss and pain and sorrow would be forgotten, and everyone we have ever loved would be there.

But there will always be people that don't want to go to a really good party. If they can't climb past someone else to get there, they won't have fun. If they can't read their own names on the select list of patrons, their noses will be out of joint. If they have to see someone they don't approve of, they won't enjoy themselves. And even if they do come, they won't dress properly. Jesus continued, "When the king came in to look at the guests, he saw there a man who had no wedding garment; and he said to him, 'Friend, how did you get in here without a wedding garment?' And he was speechless. Then the king said to the attendants, 'Bind him hand and foot, and cast him into the outer darkness; there men will weep and gnash their teeth.'"

There has been much discussion about this wedding garment. Why should a wedding guest hauled in off the street be expected to have a party outfit? Why would Jesus use such harsh language? Calvin solves the first problem nicely, to my mind, by saying in his wonderfully faithful way, "Whomsoever the Lord invites he also supplies with clothing," meaning perhaps that the guest preferred his own fashionable duds to the Lord's more egalitarian ones.[6] As for weeping and gnashing of teeth, that's an effective metaphorical way of describing what it is like to shut yourself out of the best party you've ever been invited to. The banquet hall is brilliantly lit, the music is playing, the sound of laughter is spilling out of the windows, and you are in the outer darkness for lack of a wedding garment. It's not that you weren't invited. You were. Everybody was. The invitation was sheer grace. The problem isn't the party. The problem is our unwillingness to put on the garment that God gives us. What is the garment? St. Paul tells us: "As many of you as were baptized into Christ have put on Christ" (Galatians 3:27). "Let us cast off the works of darkness and put on the Lord Jesus Christ, and make no provision for the sinful nature, to gratify its desires." (Romans 13:14).

Putting on Christ is risky, of course. It means laying oneself open to being made new. It means extending one's hand in trust to be led to places where we might not have wanted to go. It certainly means taking a new interest in God's children as far and as near as East Timor, and the rat-infested tenements of the Bronx, and the wrong side of the railroad tracks right here in Canaan, Connecticut. But most of all it means living in hope of the promise of St. John: "Beloved, we are God's children now; it does not yet appear what we shall be, but we know that when he appears we shall be like him, for we shall see him as he is" (I John 3:2).

We are going to have a party here at our church at the end of the month. It will celebrate the feast of All Saints. "The saints of God," as the hymn says, "are just folk like me," people who are fellow sinners but who have "put on the Lord Jesus Christ." Our party won't be a perfect party. Even the best human parties in this world have something wrong with them. Some people will have a better time than others. Some will feel more at home than others. Some, in spite of their best efforts to have a good time, will feel sad because they are missing a lost spouse or lost friend who won't be there.

But the promise is that those loved ones *will* be with us, as part of the chorus of "angels and archangels and all the company of heaven." No matter how imperfect our human party is, it will nevertheless be, like every Eucharist, a foretaste of the day when the

Lord will inaugurate the perfect party that will never end. Do not be fooled by the stern language of the Parable of the Rejected Invitation. For those who have ears to hear, it is your own personal invitation to joy, an unimaginable declaration of grace to every one of us, a free welcome to a royal wedding feast, the marriage of Christ the Bridegroom to the Church his Bride, and the promise of everlasting life in the kingdom of heaven. No wonder St. Paul summons us (in today's lesson) to *"rejoice in the Lord always, and again I say rejoice!"* (Philippians 4:4). *"Blessed are those who are invited to the marriage supper of the Lamb"* (Revelation 19:9).

Amen.

Endnotes

Sermon 1: The New Form of Speech

1. Maureen Dowd in *The New York Times*.
2. Edward Bulwer-Lytton, *Richelieu*, 1839.
3. John F. Kennedy.
4. Andrew Young, *An Easy Burden: The Civil Rights Movement and the Transformation of America* (New York: HarperCollins, 1996), p. 271.
5. Amos Wilder, *Early Christian Rhetoric*.
6. Louis Farrakhan's harangue at the Million Man March was assuredly not a sermon.
7. Karl Barth's phrase.
8. James F. Kay, *Christus Praesens* (Grand Rapids: Eerdmans, 1994), p. 116.

Sermon 2: What the Angel Said

1. Fra Angelico's angels are splendid renderings of beings that are humanized, yet still strange and numinous.
2. Michiko Kakutani wrote in *The New York Times Magazine*, "Consider what has happened to angels. The fierce, awe-inspiring cherubim of the Old Testament gave way to the beautiful angels of Renaissance paintings, which gave way to the somewhat-less-dignified angels of Poussin, which gave way to the bumbling angels of 1940s movies, which gave way to Michael Landon in 'Highway to Heaven.' If that were not enough, we now have cute, plump cherubs adorning everything from pillows to earrings." I would have added (on the positive front end) medieval angels with their aura of mystery and (on the negative back end) the egregious Victorian angels of Bougereau now back in fashion.

3. Hugh Kenner, "A Dutch Messiah," *Art and Antiques,* February 1987.

4. George Gordon, Lord Byron, "The Destruction of Sennacherib."

5. Front page article, *The New York Times,* September 22, 1996.

6. Negro spiritual, "Joshua Fit the Battle of Jericho."

7. Alexander MacLaren, 19th century. In the third century Origen wrote, "Who else is the captain of the Lord's host but our Lord Jesus Christ?" (Sixth Homily on Joshua).

8. Revised Standard Version. Other translations have *neither* instead of *No* or *Nay* (King James), which may be accurate enough linguistically but doesn't have the same sharp sense of negation that is so theologically interesting.

Sermon 3: Apocryphal or Real?

1. *Yankee* magazine reported that Essex was "the best small town in America."

2. They also want to call St. Valentine's Day "Special Person Day." I am not making this up.

3. The Psalms are full of this theme. Likewise Isaiah 40: "All flesh is grass. . . . Surely the people is grass. The grass withers, the flower fades, but the word of our God shall stand forever." There are only two (very late) hints of resurrection life in the entire Old Testament.

4. Prof. Alexander Nehamas, responding to the question, "What do you think is the Most Overrated Idea?"

Sermon 4: The Thankful Life

1. Reported in "Men and Ghosts of Gough Square" by A. Edward Newton. In fact, Millar was not exactly the publisher but a Strand bookseller who acted in the role.

Sermon 5: Advent Begins in the Dark

1. Christopher Dickey, "The Death of Innocents," *Newsweek,* September 2, 1996.

2. T. S. Eliot, *Murder in the Cathedral,* part II.

3. T. S. Eliot, "East Coker."

4. This phrase is borrowed from Robert Farrar Capon.

Sermon 6: A People Prepared

1. Seth Faison, *The New York Times,* November 17, 1997.

2. The emphasis should not be on the word "you." The implication is that fleeing is of no use to anyone, for the judgment of God upon all sin and wickedness will come anyway.

3. Interestingly, John the Baptist was famous in his own time. We have much more evidence of him from non-Biblical sources than we do of Jesus, whose entire history is known to us only from the New Testament.

4. Gunther Bornkamm.

5. Mark gives the full account.

6. "The One Who Is To Come" is one of Jesus' names in the Book of Revelation (*ho erchomenos* in Greek).

Sermon 7: The Master and the Best Man

1. Since 1993, when this sermon was written, the Dalai Lama has become much more famous. Two major films, *Seven Years in Tibet* and *Kundun,* have been made of his early life. He is admired around the world for his struggle on behalf of the beleaguered Tibetan people. However, the content of this sermon has not been invalidated by the new circumstances.

Sermon 8: The Bisecting Messenger

1. September 28, 1987.

2. In fairness to Mr. Updike, it should be noted that the continuation of the Finnish tale is marked by events having the character of saving grace.

3. Hymn by George Duffield, Jr., "Stand up, stand up for Jesus."

4. Thor Hall in the Advent-Christmas volume, Series B, of the *Proclamation* series (Philadelphia: Fortress Press, 1975), pp. 25-27.

5. Emily Dickinson, Poem 1411, "Of Paradise' Existence."

Sermon 9: The Magical Kingdom

1. Matthew's story of the Massacre of the Innocents teaches us never to forget the little victims.

2. Sorry, but *he* is unavoidable. The angel is sexless, so not a *she,* but personal, like God himself, and therefore not an *it.*

Sermon 10: Monsters at the Manger

1. The King's Singers, to their credit, do a blood-curdling version of it.

2. Unfortunately the journalist stopped quoting at this point and just gave a summary. One wishes for a full text.

3. I owe this insight to Christopher Morse, Professor of Systematic Theology at Union Theological Seminary.

Sermon 11: Who Are Those Magi?

1. The great Anglican Bishop Lancelot Andrewes preached a famous sermon before King James of England in Christmastide 1622: "A cold coming they had of it at this time of the year, just the worst time of the year to take a journey. . . . The ways deep, the weather sharp, the days short, the sun farthest off, *in solstitio brumali,* 'the very dead of winter. . . .'"

Sermon 12: The Bottomless Glass

1. Thomas F. Hornbein, *Everest: The West Ridge* (San Francisco: Sierra Club Books, 1966), p. 35.

2. This is still true in some Orthodox Jewish communities.

3. Hoskyns, Schnakenburg, and Bultmann all attest to this in their commentaries on John's Gospel.

4. Edwin Hoskyns, *The Fourth Gospel* (London: Faber & Faber, 1947), p. 186.

5. Reginald Fuller, *Interpreting the Miracles* (Norwich, England: Fletcher & Son, 1963), p. 117.

6. *The New York Times* obituaries, November 7, 1997. "I'm not afraid of [death]. . . . But I find death a nuisance. I object to it. I'd rather it didn't happen."

7. Some pious commentators of the past, nervous about such potential for drunkenness, tried to explain this away by suggesting that only the water that was *tasted* had been turned into wine!

Sermon 13: The Meeting of the Lord

1. In the Greek Church, the feast day is called "The Meeting of the Lord" (*Hypapante Kuriou*), because it commemorates the meeting of the infant Jesus with Simeon and Anna.

2. Anna is one of several women prophets mentioned in the Bible (Miriam, Deborah, Huldah, Isaiah's wife).

3. The Holy Spirit was poured out on "all flesh" at Pentecost, after the Resurrection. Prior to that time, the Spirit was given to specific individuals for specific purposes.

4. Indeed, Rembrandt's love of the Old Testament can be an inspiration to Christians today as we seek to place greater emphasis on our Jewish roots.

Sermon 14: The Love Olympics Go to Jerusalem

1. Alex Kuczynski, "Valentine's Day Times Three: The Horror!" January 8, 1998.

2. *The New York Times,* February 13, 1998.

3. Christ the King Sunday, next before Advent, is a close second.

4. Taylor Branch, *Pillar of Fire: America in the King Years, 1963-65* (New York: Simon & Schuster, 1998), p. 613. Emphasis added.

Sermon 15: The Ash Wednesday Privilege

1. Janet Malcolm, *In the Freud Archives* (New York: Knopf, 1984), pp. 70-71.

2. Kenneth Slack in his book about the Psalms.

Sermon 16: Noah's Ark

1. *The Epic of Gilgamesh* is a remarkable epic poem from Mesopotamia, at least two thousand years old, which was discovered in an excavation of Nineveh 1849-1855.

2. Instead of inserting numerous footnotes I will just say that much of the material here is based on, though not directly quoted from, Gerhard von Rad's *Genesis* (Old Testament Library, Philadelphia: Westminster, 1972) and Nahum M. Sarna's *Understanding Genesis* (New York: Schocken Books, 1966).

3. Kenneth Slack in his book about the Psalms.

4. The Gilgamesh Epic from Mesopotamia is very impressive. But there is a lot of difference between the gods "gathering like flies around the sacrifice" in the epic and the one God "smelling the sweet savor" of Noah's sacrifice. Sarna says that the Biblical narrative is "radically transformed" from the Mesopotamian parallels.

5. I am aware that this view is under attack in many recent books such as Jack Miles's *God: A Biography.* After many years of preaching from the Bible and comparing it with other religious texts, however, I continue to hold the view that the Bible is in a class by itself.

Sermon 17: The Strange World of Abraham

1. Ernst Käsemann makes the wonderful observation that "Sarah's laughter is faith's constant companion."

2. Gerhard von Rad, *Genesis* (Old Testament Library, Philadelphia: Westminster, 1972).

3. It is sometimes said that Abraham went along because he knew that God wouldn't go through with it. I have thought about that a lot. My first reaction is that if Abraham had known, the story would lose all its force. It wouldn't be a story of archetypal faith at all. On the other hand, though, I think we can say that Abraham did know that God was trustworthy. It was not just blind faith that took him to Mt. Moriah. It was the final stage in a forty-year journey that had brought him halfway across the known world on nothing more than a promise. Abraham lived his whole life in the belief that God was trustworthy.

4. Since this sermon was preached, I have been further edified by the observations of Professor Ellen Davis, who points out that in a late picture of the scene, Rembrandt portrays Abraham with "the disconnected stare of someone who has survived something unspeakable."

Sermon 18: Rules of the Freedom Game

1. C. FitzSimons Allison, ret. Bishop of South Carolina.

2. Walter Harrelson, *The Ten Commandments and Human Rights* (Philadelphia: Fortress Press, 1980).

3. Dietrich Bonhoeffer, *Ethics* (New York: Macmillan, 1965), p. 277.

4. Paul L. Lehmann, *The Decalogue and a Human Future* (Grand Rapids: Eerdmans, 1995), p. 85.

5. Interview with Claudia Dreifus in *Modern Maturity,* March-April 1997.

6. In one of the most profound of all Christian utterances, "O Lord!" cried St. Augustine in his *Confessions,* "Grant what you command, and then command what you will."

Sermon 19: Exiled into Babylon

1. If anyone from Las Vegas is reading this I hope they do not take it personally. I am thinking of Las Vegas more as a metaphor than an actual place. Its function in the sermon is to present the greatest possible contrast to the understated culture of rural New England.

2. This phrase is taken from John Bright's wonderful book *A History of Israel*.

3. As we have noted before, the Jewish people are in a class by themselves for a number of reasons. It can't be said often enough; as the Old Testament proves, no other group of people in the ancient world has produced a literature of such moral and theological depth while at the same time maintaining such an astonishing ability to preserve its unique identity. The Western tradition, with its Judeo-Christian roots, is under attack as never before, but I do not believe that any other tradition on the face of the earth has a comparable power of correction and revitalization from within. This is what we see happening in the Babylonian Exile. Out of the experience of the exile, Israel forged a new theological identity that far exceeded the old. It was not a departure from her ancient faith, but grew organically out of it. At the same time, however, it was larger, stronger, more spacious; and it was more radical. It was recognizably the faith of the same people of Israel in the one Creator God of heaven and earth, but from that foundation the faith of the exilic prophets made audacious connections and leapt forward into theological realms previously undreamed of.

4. Maybe we should include the Book of Revelation, but its proliferation of images makes its impact somewhat more diffuse.

5. This is a reference to a very recent event in the news.

Sermon 20: The New Covenant

1. Shel Silverstein.

2. Gerhard von Rad, *Biblical Interpretations in Preaching* (Nashville: Abingdon, 1977), p. 107.

3. "Mother Still Mourns Racial-Killing Victim," by Joseph P. Fried, *The New York Times,* December 18, 1997.

4. St. Augustine's uniquely insightful prayer in his *Confessions,* "Grant what you command, and then command what you will," is the basis of the Collect for today: "O Almighty God, who alone canst order the *unruly wills* and affections of sinful men: Grant unto thy people *that they may love the thing which thou commandest,* and desire that which thou dost promise. . . ."

5. Groups of people are typically identified in the Old Testament by the name of their ancestors. Chapters 30-31 are addressed to "Ephraim," the eponymous portion of Israel that was conquered and carried off by the Assyrians at an earlier time. The significance is exactly the same as that of the words addressed to "Jacob," under the Babylonian heel. In each case, Jeremiah is writing to people who are in a humanly hopeless situation.

Sermon 21: His Dereliction, Our Deliverance

1. John, as usual, is a special case. He summarizes Gethsemane in 12:27, and has chosen rather to emphasize Jesus' strong emotion at the grave of Lazarus, as the Lord enters upon his confrontation with the power of death (11:33, 35, 38), and at the Last Supper as he reflects upon Judas' betrayal (13:21).

2. J. B. Phillips.

3. This interpretation of the Agony in the Garden and the Cry of Dereliction is found in numerous places in the Reformed tradition. In our own day, the Roman Catholic scholar Raymond E. Brown, in his magisterial work *The Death of the Messiah,* shows that the Agony is the opening scene of the apocalyptic drama in which God initiates the final battle against the powers of darkness. I agree with this and believe that it complements, rather than contradicts, the interpretation given here. We do not have to have an either/or reading of these key texts.

4. I have recast Mr. Birgbauer's words very slightly in order to emphasize that repentance is not a *condition* of God's grace and mercy, but the *result* of it.

Sermon 22: Strange Ending, Unthinkable Beginning

1. Hymn, "Alleluia, alleluia! Hearts and voices heavenward raise" by Christopher Wordsworth.

2. This is a reference to the group that had recently committed mass suicide, believing that a spaceship was coming for them in the Hale-Bopp comet's tail.

3. The Rev. Wallace Alston at Nassau Presbyterian Church, Princeton, New Jersey.

Sermon 23: Believing Without Seeing

1. The *Newsweek* article is called "Rethinking the Resurrection" and the other two are about "the search for Jesus." All are based on the work of the Jesus Seminar and the rebuttal of Luke Timothy Johnson, *The Real Jesus.*

2. Paul Lehmann.

3. Raymond E. Brown, *The Gospel According to John* (New York: Doubleday, 1970), p. 1048.

Sermon 24: Hear! See! Touch!

1. In Greek, *psyche,* spirit or soul; *soma,* body.

2. It's true that Paul says we will inherit a *spiritual body* (I Corinthians 15:44)

but Paul's use of the word *spiritual* is very different from ours. He means that our risen bodies will be *determined by the Holy Spirit,* not by sin and death (I Corinthians 15:56). They will nevertheless be real bodies; we will not be disembodied ghosts. To the Biblical mind, disembodied life is no life at all.

3. Well . . . that's not quite right. Paul writes, "And now abide faith, hope, and love, these three; but the greatest of them is love" (I Corinthians 13). Faith and hope will fall into the background one day because we will possess (and be possessed by) what we now can only have faith in and hope for.

Sermon 25: Ascension Day in Pretoria

1. Bill Keller reporting in *The New York Times,* May 10, 1994.

2. The relationship between Mandela and de Klerk remains distant and strained — all the more reason to admire Mandela for his magnanimity.

3. *The New York Times,* May 11, 1994.

Sermon 26: Faith Overcomes the World

1. Flannery O'Connor, *The Habit of Being* (New York: Farrar, Straus, Giroux, 1979), p. 452.

2. "On Sunday" column by Francis X. Clines, Easter Day, *The New York Times,* April 3, 1994.

Sermon 27: The Apostolic Flame

1. In the month when this sermon was preached, the Hale-Bopp comet was creating quite a stir.

2. This is a difficult word to translate. The Greek is *parakletos.* Many have taken to referring to the Holy Spirit as *the Paraclete* because "Counselor" and "Advocate" and "Comforter," though they convey something of the meaning, do not do justice to the rich meaning of the Greek word.

3. This part of the Eucharistic prayer is called the *epiclesis,* and there can be no authentic Eucharist without it.

4. There were apparently quite a few apostles besides the traditional Twelve. There is Paul, of course, and in Romans 16:7 Andronicus and Junia are mentioned as being "among the apostles." It is now believed that this Junia (not Junias) was a woman. Unfortunately we know nothing more of these two.

5. There are three major New Testament lists of the gifts of the Spirit: I Corinthians 12:4-11, Romans 12:4-8, and Ephesians 4:11. There is no reason to

think that these lists are meant to be exhaustive. The gifts range from the prepossessing (apostolic teaching and evangelism) to the equally important and necessary but less flashy (works of mercy, encouragement, administration, hospitality, etc.). An important piece of background here is that a good deal of teaching about the gifts of the Spirit was going on in the Salisbury congregation.

Sermon 28: The Multicultural Good News

1. Arthur M. Schlesinger, Jr., *The Disuniting of America* (New York: Norton, 1992).

2. Quoted by Schlesinger, *The Disuniting of America*, p. 27.

3. Quirky mispronunciations and misspellings are part of the comic strip's charm.

Sermon 29: Saved!

1. Since this sermon was written, Cynthia Ozick, writing in *The New Yorker*, has forever altered the discussion of Anne's diary by showing how Anne and her fate have been drained of horror, offense, and Jewishness.

2. *Pilgrim at Tinker Creek.* Ms. Dillard would not want to be called a nature writer, but you get the point.

3. Alfred, Lord Tennyson, "In Memoriam," Part LVI, Stanza 4.

4. When the prophet Isaiah tells us that the lion will lie down with the lamb, it is the sign that the creation will be restored to its original perfection (Isaiah 11:6-9).

5. John Donne, *Devotions,* XVII.

6. "Who knows what evil lurks in the hearts of men? The Shadow knows. . . ."

7. John Bradford (1510-1555). Cited in *Bartlett's Familiar Quotations.*

8. Gerard Manley Hopkins, "I Wake and Feel the Fell of Dark."

9. Sadly, months later, it must be reported that the children were passed through five consecutive foster homes and then returned to the adoptive parents. It is another example of our fallen state. Nevertheless, the illustration of the airline passengers stands.

10. I am taking this battle imagery from Ephesians, for it is this letter that gives us the concept of *the armor of God* (Ephesians 6:10-17).

Sermon 30: Saved for What?

1. Betty Shabazz, widow of Malcolm X, and Jonathan Levin, son of the chairman of Time Warner.
2. Convicted of the Oklahoma City bombing.

Sermon 31: The Words of Eternal Life

1. My emphasis.
2. These words from Psalm 29 are inscribed around the ceiling of the seaside church where this sermon was preached.
3. "In place of us all He stands there, delivered up for us all, patently submerged in the flood" (Karl Barth, *The Epistle to the Romans,* comment on 8:31-32).

Sermon 32: Affliction, with Joy

1. *The New York Times,* October 12, 1996.
2. The Nobel Prize information is gleaned from articles in *The New York Times,* Oct. 12, 1996, and *Time* magazine, Oct. 21, 1996. According to *Time,* the two men disagree on what should be done in East Timor. The Bishop is not a supporter of Ramos-Horta's guerrilla group and its past involvement in political violence. Thus he is more Christlike, since he is not easily categorized as belonging to one faction or the other.
3. I owe this insight to the Rev. Richard Taber, pastor of the Congregational Church of Salisbury.
4. Hymn by Laurence Tuttiett, "Go Forward, Christian Soldier."

Sermon 33: Clint's Got It

1. Incarnations in Buddhism are not comparable because, among other reasons, they happen over and over.
2. A phrase of T. S. Eliot *(The Cocktail Party).*

Sermon 34: How to Dress for a Wedding

1. Chairman of African-American studies at Harvard.
2. As told in Matthew. Luke's version is less allegorical.

3. The "call" is to be interpreted as the gospel call to salvation.

4. The ellipsis indicates vv. 6-7, a Matthean interpolation too complicated to interpret in this space.

5. Edouard Schweizer, *The Good News According to Matthew* (Atlanta: John Knox Press, 1975).

6. *Calvin's Commentaries,* 22 vols. (Grand Rapids: Baker Book House, 1984), vol. 16, p. 174.